Spitfire Girls Trailblazer

Other Books by Sheila C. Serup
No Old, Bold Pilots
Found Fragments: Stories of Courage and Valour

Courage is the price that life exacts for granting peace
The soul that knows it not, knows no release
From little things;

Knows not the livid loneliness of fear
Nor mountain heights, where bitter joy can hear
The sound of wings;

How can life grant us boon of living, compensate
For dull gray ugliness and pregnant hate
Unless we dare

The soul's dominion? Each time we make a choice, we pay
With courage to behold resistless day
And count it fair.

Amelia Earhart

Spitfire Girls Trailblazer

HELEN MARCELLE HARRISON:
ATA FERRY PILOT, WARTIME INSTRUCTOR,
AND FLYING BOAT AND JET AVIATOR

SHEILA C. SERUP

AIR WORLD

SPITFIRE GIRLS TRAILBLAZER
Helen Marcelle Harrison: ATA Ferry Pilot, Wartime Instructor, and Flying Boat and Jet Aviator

First published in Great Britain in 2026 by
Air World
An imprint of
Pen & Sword Books Ltd
Yorkshire – Philadelphia

Print ISBN 978 1 03619 089 7
ePUB ISBN 978 1 03619 091 0
ePDF ISBN 978 1 03619 093 4

A CIP catalogue record for this book is available from the British Library.

Typeset by SJmagic DESIGN SERVICES, India.
Printed and bound in the UK by CPI Group (UK) Ltd.

The Publisher's authorised representative in the EU for product safety is Authorised Rep Compliance Ltd., Ground Floor, 71 Lower Baggot Street, Dublin D02 P593, Ireland. www.arccompliance.com

For a complete list of Pen & Sword titles please contact:

PEN & SWORD BOOKS LIMITED
George House, Units 12 & 13, Beevor Street, Off Pontefract Road,
Barnsley, South Yorkshire, S71 1HN, England
E-mail: enquiries@pen-and-sword.co.uk
Website: www.pen-and-sword.co.uk

or

PEN AND SWORD BOOKS
1950 Lawrence Rd, Havertown, PA 19083, USA
E-mail: uspen-and-sword@casematepublishers.com
Website: www.penandswordbooks.com

MIX
Paper | Supporting responsible forestry
FSC® C013604

Contents

Prelude vi

Part One

Chapter 1 Discovering the Golden Thirties of Aviation 2
Chapter 2 Soaring Aloft in the Wide Open Skies 12
Chapter 3 Exploring the Art of Flying Boats 24
Chapter 4 Cultivating an Aviation Career 39

Part Two

Chapter 5 Finding Freedom to Fly in South Africa 64
Chapter 6 Spreading Wings Higher, Faster and Further 88
Chapter 7 Seeking Space in the Sky 113
Chapter 8 Championing the Need for 'Atta Girls' in Great Britain 136
Chapter 9 Flying as a Ferry Pilot with the Air Transport Auxiliary 154
Chapter 10 Knowing the Sightline to the Theatre of War 175

Part Three

Chapter 11 Pursuing Flying Dreams in Post-War Canada 198
Chapter 12 Sustaining a Joy of Flying 215
Postscript Recognising Achievements Through Investitures 232

Endnotes 238
Bibliography 257
Index 260

Prelude

The *Drakensberg*, the eastern spine of the Great Escarpment, rears its angular wall of jagged spires along the verdant border of Lesotho. Known as *Maloti*, 'barrier of up-pointed spears' in Sotho, or *uKhahlamba* in Zulu, the Dragons' Mountains undulate into successive peaks and steep rift valleys.

For more than 600 miles, it curves like a sickle from the high interior northeast of Pretoria. Sweeping across the southern tip of South Africa past Cape Town, the black ramparts soar as high as 11,000 feet. At the toe of Africa, eastern winds from the Indian Ocean and western breezes from the Atlantic Ocean merge as they cascade inland. Rippling across the Cape floor, the winds funnel upwards and tumble over the steep rift walls and across the high steppe of sunbaked grasslands and tumbling brush.

Flying into Cape Town from the high savannah, pilots nose into the tumultuous torrent of winds with white-knuckled grips on their steering yokes. Like kestrels hovering in the gusts, they sideslip their small aircraft down to sea level. As they descend, the offshore crosswinds shift into updrafts that can toss a light plane against the stone-grey plateau walls or scatter it into the brush-filled natural veld.

Flying conditions in the late 1930s in South Africa were challenging as fields for refuelling were scarce and pilots relied on wireless telephone equipment that was dependent on intermittent reception and few radio stations. The ground between airfields was often unsuitable for forced landings due to thick growing brush and cement-hard clay domes. Pilot Helen Marcelle Harrison described how,

> One might approach a field that looked good from a height of a thousand feet but upon closer examination would prove useless. Ant hills caused the trouble. Not the little sandy pockmarks we call ant hills, but clay domes, three feet high, baked as hard as bricks by the hot sun. A plane landing and striking such hills would be a washout for fair. And the ants living in them can whip their weight in tigers.[1]

On many of her daily flights throughout South Africa, as she flew from flying schools in Pretoria in the far eastern interior to Jamestown, Johannesburg and Cape Town, Helen Harrison rarely had any difficulties or accidents.

Flying into Cape Town one day on a route she was familiar with, she was forced down by headwinds onto a small refuelling field covered by thick growing scrub. Taking off again, loose brush became entangled in her landing gear but she managed to lift off. Her unexpected delay meant that she would be reaching Cape Town after dark. She knew there were no lighted runways for night flying and the Great Escarpment loomed ahead of her in the deepening dusk. The airfields only turn on the runway lights when advance requests have been made.

She climbed from her cruising altitude of 7,800 feet to 11,000 feet to clear the rugged mountain range. In an unpressurised cabin, she knew she could not stay at this altitude for long. As her landing gear was snarled with brush, her small aircraft struggled to climb and clear the range before descending towards Cape Town. As she regretfully expected, the landing strip appeared darkened and deserted. Fearing that her flying career would be snuffed out in minutes, she gritted her teeth and side-slipped towards where she calculated the airfield to be.

'Then the miracle happened', she recalled. 'The lights of the field blinked on. First the runway markers, then the huge landing floodlights. Helen's heart dropped from her throat to its normal resting place – and she set her plane neatly onto the runway.'[2] Pulling up to the airport, she learned that another pilot had earlier arranged for lights to be turned on for his arrival. A few minutes after Helen had set her wheels on the ground, he phoned in from out of town to cancel his lighting request.

Sideslipping into Landing

The trick in landing successfully in crosswinds and into unknown conditions lies in the ability to sideslip one's aircraft. Sideslipping is an aerial acrobatic strategy that attests to a pilot's supreme confidence, sure knowledge, and adroit skill in landing a plane in difficult conditions. The sideslip enables a pilot to lose altitude when landing and is invaluable for launching onto any small field with obstacles all around. This technique enables an experienced pilot to make certain of neither under- nor over-shooting when it comes to landing. New pilots became thoroughly familiar with sideslipping as an objective to lose height without gaining forward speed before venturing to fly anywhere on their own.

Helen had been flying for less than five years since receiving her pilot's licence, yet her seamless manoeuvre into Cape Town on this dark, tumultuous night demonstrated her prowess and versatility as a pilot. Since arriving in South Africa in 1937 to become the country's first female military flying instructor, she had amassed hundreds of flying and instruction hours on a many different aircraft.

Her sojourn to South Africa would become one of the defining moments of her flying career. The high veld and savannah became her stage, the aging aircraft in which she taught became her tools, and the young pupil pilots whom she sent aloft with sound flying skills and cheerful confidence became the focus of a lifelong love of teaching.

The challenges of flying and instructing in South Africa stood Helen in good stead in her later career flying with the Air Transport Auxiliary in the Second World War and during the post-war years in her home province of British Columbia in Canada with its rugged Rocky Mountains, volatile winds, plunging temperatures, and wild hinterlands.

Part One

Chapter 1

Discovering the Golden Thirties of Aviation

> To have succeeded in getting into the air is today nothing of an adventure. The adventurous part of flying, however, is that part of which the earth-bound traveller knows nothing and hears nothing. No person who has ever been above an endless landscape of white, billowy clouds, the sparkling sun overhead and the mist and rain of the common world obscured by the curtain below, can ever find words to describe the exhilarating feeling which flying alone in this endless new universe can give, and for that reason what is probably the most enjoyable part of being able to fly yourself is completely lost to mankind generally.[1]
>
> *Western Daily Press and Bristol Mirror*

By the early 1930s, the golden age of flight became within reach of nearly everyone who desired to fly. Newspapers described with rich detail the exploits of flyers, including many women, who embarked on record-breaking flights and feats of endurance.

Helen Harrison's circuitous journey to her safe landing in Cape Town in the late 1930s, as one of the first female military flying instructors in South Africa, began when she soared into the air on her first joy ride.

Sitting in an open cockpit behind a pilot in an Avro 540K, as it swooped down a bumpy runway, Helen experienced the ethereal sensation of lifting off the ground and soaring into the air over farms, fields and forests. The cool wind pressed against her face. The vibrations of the aircraft shuddered through her body and up through her feet from the rattling floorboards. Below her, farm animals, people, cars and houses became miniaturised as sprawling landscape below the craft diminished.

While her first flight took only a few minutes, her first joy hop created an unexpected rush of euphoria.

In the early 1930s, as a young mother of sons, she was working as a beautician in a London salon when joy riding caught everyone's imagination. One April, while on a short vacation from a hairdressing training course, she and a girl chum travelled to Eastbourne on England's south coast.

'In search of amusement one day, their course took them by the local airport where some pilots were taking the populace up for joy hops', wrote W.A. Magill in the *Richmond Times-Dispatch*.[2]

She clambered on board and soared over the English Channel, above the long expanse of beachfront and over emerald fields. After her first flight, she was mesmerised by its unlimited possibilities. The thought of stretching her wings beyond her earthly existence began as a wisp of an idea that soon swelled into a current.

Heeding the Call of Steveston

Her capacity for curiosity, wonder and imagination was nurtured during her Canadian childhood in the village of Steveston, at the junction of mighty Fraser River and Pacific Ocean in southern British Columbia. Looming in the distance, the icy dome of Mount Baker glistened, a new world Fuji-Yama for the Japanese residents of the cannery town.

Wide open skies and the unlimited ocean enticed many people to make Steveston their home. The Fraser River, which drains the province of British Columbia, is home to the rich salmon resource that supported the multicultural population of First Nations, Japanese, Chinese and others who resided along the Fraser.

Six years after the first flight of a manned heavier-than-air powered plane by the Wright brothers, Helen Marcelle was born. She arrived on 7 December 1909 in Vancouver, British Columbia, to parents Albert and Gertrude Helen Marie Harrison Testemale, and her 6-year-old brother Percy.

Auspiciously, Helen was born in the same year of Canada's first flight. On 23 February 1909, aviation pioneer John A.D. McCurdy flew a Silver Dart approximately 2,625 feet over the icy Bras d'Or Lakes in Nova Scotia. He flew forty times further than the Wright brothers did in their first flight in 1903.

Gertrude was the only child of Margaret Helen Ayre and wine merchant Thomas Hudson Harrison, who had married on 7 April 1874 in Fulford, Yorkshire. On 30 September 1902, at the age of 24, their daughter Gertrude married a young Parisian, Albert Jules Testemale, in Eastbourne Holy Trinity Church in Sussex. A year later, on 8 November 1903, their first son Percy was born, and shortly after, the young family moved to Wales. This would be the first of many adventures as the young couple exuded a bonhomie and a zest to explore the world.

Gertrude trained as a midwife in Llantilio Crossenny, Abergavenny, in South Wales. She undertook her exam with the Central Midwives Board on 22 February 1906. While she was pursuing her midwifery practice in Wales, the young family learned that Canada was open for settlement.

Albert sailed on the steamship *City of Vienna* and arrived in Halifax, Nova Scotia, on 28 May 1906. Just a week earlier, Canadian Parliament had introduced a new 1906 Immigration Act which provided greater protection for newcomers and assured immigrants that job opportunities in Canada existed.

A year later, Gertrude and 3-year-old Percy boarded the *Empress of Britain* in Liverpool, also bound for Canada. They set foot in Quebec

City on 10 October 1907, and the pair journeyed on the transcontinental train to Vancouver, British Columbia, where they rejoined Albert.

The young family settled into the invigorating life of a new city on the West Coast. In 1908, an advertisement in the *Daily News Advertiser* noted that 'Mme. Testemale, 533 Seymour St (was) providing lessons – music, French, German, painting, $1.50 monthly.'

Their residence was a few steps away from the Clarence Hotel on the southwest corner of Seymour and Pender streets. In the opposite direction, on the corner of Dunsmuir and Seymour, stables rented horses and carriages for tours of nearby Stanley Park and the well-photographed Hollow Tree, an ancient Western red cedar. The family could walk to nearby Coal Harbour with its myriad steamers arriving daily.

Two years after welcoming their daughter Helen, Gertrude and Albert moved to Steveston in search of new horizons. This vibrant village was growing along the northern shore of the mighty Fraser where it meets the Gulf of Georgia. The origins of this gathering place for many cultures were intrinsically connected with the river. In 1911, Albert and Gertrude operated a small bakery and café in the fishing community where the sea met the sky, and where there was space and wilderness for the children to explore.[3]

In the Fraser, five species of salmon swim and spawn along with freshwater fish. For centuries, First Nations people gathered along the main estuary to harvest the resources of the area, including salmon and clams. The First Nations included the Halq'eméylem-speaking people.

At the turn of the twentieth century, a village encompassed First Nations people, farmers, fishermen and Japanese boat builders. The sockeye became the heart of its fisheries. With a view of a new-world Fuji, Mount Baker, the Japanese wove their traditions into the fabric of the community. Chinese men who immigrated earlier to build the Trans-Canada highway sought cannery jobs. Steveston became a multicultural Pacific market, providing services for farmers, canneries and fishing companies.

During the boom years of the canneries and salmon runs, Helen's parents worked long hours in the café. Percy and Helen were left on their own to entertain themselves. They were not the only children shooed outside to explore. On every corner, children ran about playing tag or games such as shooting marbles. Steveston and its riverfront fisheries provided hours of fascination and activities as it grew into a cultural mosaic of rich traditions, languages and enterprises.

At home, young Helen learned French from her father, English from her mother, and listened to Japanese and Chinese dialects being spoken in the café, shops and along the waterfront. The main street with its roofed sidewalk, shops and stores faced the canal parallel to the river. Elders watched the village life from the balconies above. Japanese shopkeepers provided endless streams of conversation and goods. Wood-frame houses with bright, gay gardens were situated on one side of the canal. The canneries were perched on the other side, balanced on stocky pilings. Further along were stilted galleries built over the water on which nets were hung. Freshly painted boats were tied up. Electric lights had arrived in 1911 which brightened the quays and boardwalks on rainy twilight evenings.

Between two canneries the main wooden wharf jutted into the river. Crowds gathered on Sunday evenings. The rules of the day stipulated that no fish could be caught between Friday evening and Sunday evenings. Before dusk on Sundays, hordes of boats entered the mouth of the mighty Fraser. Fishermen in a profusion of gas-powered boats, sail boats and row boats prepared their nets. At 6 pm, the government patrol boat fired a gun to signal the start of fishing, and nets were quickly dropped.

The children watched the frenzied fishing as boats caught an average of eight to ten sockeye a day, up to fifty[4] sometimes, before cruising to shore to deliver them to the canneries. Every four years, the sockeye salmon run reached its peak and fishing became more feverish than ever.

On 5 April 1912, the family welcomed their second son, James (Jim). Over the next few years, the life of the village ebbed and flowed with the salmon runs. For Helen and her brothers, the vast skies and river shorelines sparked play and discoveries.

Vancouver newspapers described Steveston as 'BC's most picturesque cannery town'. What was not mentioned was the undercurrent of segregation, separation and exclusion of cultural groups that was hidden but undeniable in frontier communities such as Steveston.

Shortly after their son was born, the Testemales returned to Vancouver where Albert found work with the Canadian Pacific Railway.

Tracing the Life-Changing Trajectory of Family

The trajectory of Helen's family changed abruptly when a newspaper advertisement in March 1920 caught their mother's eye. A solicitor in York, England, was seeking the whereabouts of Gertrude Testemale. Several months earlier, Gertrude's 74-year-old father had passed away.

On 11 November 1919, on the first anniversary of the Armistice, Thomas Hudson Harrison died, leaving his estate to his daughter Gertrude and his grandchildren. His sister and executor, Harriet Grace Wilburne, awarded part of his estate to Helen. The terms of his will meant her inheritance would be held in trust until she reached the age of 21, or when she married. The interest earned was intended to be used for her education.

With this turn of events, the young family decided to move to England, and sailed on 17 June 1920. Helen was 10 years old.

By autumn, Helen and her younger brother Jim began attending a series of English boarding schools. Attending St Mary's School for Girls in Calne, Wiltshire, and Down's College in Broadstairs, Helen struggled to conform to the strictures of boarding schools and strived to catch up academically. Her teen years as a boarder were stifling, and vastly different from her carefree life in Canada.

A childhood of independence and learning in a natural way in Steveston, surrounded by the expansive Fraser River, the bountiful gulf and infinite skies, had fostered in Helen an adventurous spirit.

She was sent to a finishing school in Brussels, Belgium, to complete her education, and experienced the same spirit-quenching and freedom-curtailing restrictions. Living with a family in Bruges, she became fluent in French, her father's language.[5]

When Helen was in her early twenties, she met a young soldier, Robert Walter Barnes. They married on 5 February 1927 in Steyning, Sussex, in the presence of her parents Albert and Gertrude, and his father Walter Barnes. Shortly thereafter their young family grew. Living in Bournemouth, they welcomed their sons Brian Robert on 18 May 1928, and David Brinson Albert on 31 May 1930.

Captivating Would-be Pilots with Joy Rides

In England, thousands of people took their first flights into the skies thanks to the burgeoning pastime of joy rides offered by pilots. Flying for pleasure began to emerge during the inter-war period, and private aviation was deemed advantageous for businesses and for defence. After the 1918 Armistice, civilian flying clubs stepped up to offer training for air force pilots of the future.

The exploits of stunt fliers and record breakers became more daring in the inter-war years as planes evolved. One light aircraft elevated private flying to new heights. The two-seater de Havilland Gipsy Moth brought flying within reach of many and gave civil aviation a tremendous boost.

Aviation engineer and designer Geoffrey de Havilland sought to tap into the light aircraft market and build an economical sporting aircraft. As an amateur lepidopterist, seeing his first plane's design and how the wings could be folded against its fuselage, he likened its design to that of a moth. In February 1925, he unveiled the Gipsy Moth biplane, powered by an 85-hp Cirrus engine, and revolutionised light aviation for the public.

Later, de Havilland refitted it with the reliable and remarkable Gipsy engine, and shortly afterwards it became the most popular light club aircraft. The de Havilland 60 Gipsy Moth, with its increased power of a 100 hp 'were used by nearly every British and colonial record chaser of the era'.[6]

It soon became the iconic forerunner and indisputable leader of British light aircraft. The Moths also contributed to civilian and military aviation in South Africa. Importantly, these light aircraft enabled the formation of light-plane clubs throughout the country as they had done earlier for Britain.

Thanks to the Moth light aircraft flying soon became widely accessible as pilots found it easy to fly. Simply, with seven to eight instruction hours and five hours of flying solo, a fledgling pilot could qualify for the Air Ministry's 'A' licence.

Learning to Fly and Gaining Lifelong Mentors

The Sussex Aero Club was founded at Shoreham, coinciding with the Pashley brothers moving their leisure flight business from Brooklands. Cecil L. Pashley and his brother Eric were both aviators who learned to fly in 1908, at 17 and 16 years of age respectively. Their younger brother Herbert followed in their footsteps and obtained his pilot's licence. In 1913, they founded the Pashley Brothers' Flying School at Shoreham Airport, where the Aero Club had been established. One of the many pilots they trained was Frederick George Miles who became a well-known aircraft designer. Shoreham airport was also used to train miliary pilots, as well as the base for the Southern Aero Club.

When the First World War broke out, all three brothers joined the miliary and offered their flying expertise. Cecil taught as a flying instructor at the Royal Naval Air Service training school while Eric and Herbert joined the Royal Flying Corps. Tragically, Second Lieutenant Herbert Dudley Pashley was killed in action on Christmas Day 1916 in France. His brother, Lieutenant Eric Pashley, was killed in action on 17 March 1917 near the Somme.

While Armistice brought peace and an end to war, civil flying began to decline. With partner Frederick George Miles, Cecil revived interest in aviation at Shoreham. His first commercial flying venture, the Gnat Aero Company, was successful in growing local interest in civilian flying. Under his steady direction and tutelage, the Sussex Aero Club at Shoreham airport launched many pilots into the sky.

John 'Jack' Sale, a junior instructor with the Sussex Aero Club, had introduced Helen to flying through joy rides at Eastbourne. He was an expert pilot who, when a teenager, had raced horses as a jockey at Newmarket, Wolverhampton and Lewes. The London-born jockey rode three winners. After three years of flat racing, he switched to horse jumping. When he turned 18, he earned an 'A' pilot's licence and began instructing at Shoreham in 1928. The following year he earned his 'B' licence. As an avid sportsman, dirt track riding and yachting also claimed his attention during these years.

Visiting the United States in 1929 he flew various types of demonstration aircraft before returning to England to instruct at the Southern Aero Club. While employed at Shoreham aerodrome, he helped George Miles build his first aircraft. According to the local newspaper:

> Big weekend crowds were attracted when Mr Sale gave a series of joy flights from various fields between Newhaven and Seaford in 1933. During this time, he carried thousands of passengers in the Avro 504K. The price of flights varied from five shillings to eleven shillings. He then joined the Eastbourne Flying Club as chief flying instructor but fifteen months later returned to Shoreham, mostly for charter flights over all parts of Britain and Europe, and particularly between London and Paris. Leaving Shoreham, he again connected with George Miles at Reading to demonstrate the now famous Miles Major and Miles Falcon planes.[7]

In addition to flying joyriders on short aerial circuits, Jack Sale also performed stunt flying for exhibitions. His aerial displays of haymaking and looping invariably evoked thrills and excited shouts from spectators.

The stalwart Avro Avian 504K, a First World War biplane, became a trainer of choice. It was employed to train units in the Royal Flying Corps and later the Royal Air Force. After the war, surplus Avros were used by civilian flying schools and barnstorming companies. The joy-flying business took the country by storm as pilots flew surplus warplanes with steely nerves. The Avro remained the Royal Air Force's basic trainer until the de Havilland 82 Tiger Moth was introduced in 1932 and superseded it as the 'Trainer of the Empire'. The yellow Tiger Moth, akin to a kite with a motor, kindled wonder and longing in its viewers as they gazed skyward at this delicate yet powerful biplane.

During Helen's first flight in an Avro 540K over the emerald green fields and forests of Sussex, she became enthralled with all the possibilities flying could offer. Helen enjoyed these flights immensely, especially the loops and spins. 'I used to slip away from home in my spare hours to the airfield and beg the pilots to give me a flip', she said. 'I never once dared to tell my parents what was going on.'[8]

'In fact, Helen liked it so well she went up many times while in Eastbourne, for, in her own words, she felt it almost impossible to get enough of it', a reporter described.

> One of the instructors there, noting her interest, suggested to her that she learn to fly. The idea appealed to her keenly, and so she embarked on an instruction course. As she was acquainted with the instructors at Eastbourne, she decided to do her learning at that field (Wilmington) and motored down from London whenever opportunity presented itself.[9]

After these joy rides, pilot Jack Sale became her instructor and mentor. Along with chief instructor Cecil Pashley, the pair would become her staunchest mentors as she embarked on her flying career.

Chapter 2

Soaring Aloft in the Wide Open Skies

Now we were above a bank of clouds, and even the Himalayas in the evening light could not have appeared more wonderful than these massive billows, with their summits pink and glowing under the rays of the setting sun.

It is impossible for anyone who has never flown to understand fully the significance of being away from the earth; alone, and completely independent; with the power to turn north, south, east or west at will. It is only then that one finds that sense of freedom which men have gone to the ends of the earth to seek, and which, for the most part, they have sought in vain.

And so finally one returns to earth, with a different song in one's heart – at peace with the world and oneself – and, most important of all – with a new spirit within one; for one has found time for meditation, which is the foundation of all inspiration.[1]

Gloucestershire Echo

Learning to Fly a Gipsy Moth

Helen's flying career was launched in a two-seater Gipsy Moth with dual controls. She drove from London at every opportunity to take lessons at Shoreham Aerodrome near Brighton City in West Sussex. Instructors at Shoreham included aircraft designer Frederick George Miles.

Instructors used a method of systemic flying instruction developed by Major Robert Smith-Barry at the School of Special Flying in Gosport during the First World War. His training philosophy served as the foundation for nearly all primary flying instruction provided throughout the world. His curriculum included both classroom training and dual flight instruction in what was considered the relatively high-powered Avro 504 biplane. A pupil pilot sat in the front while the instructor perched behind and issued prepared instructions through a specially designed intercom, the Gosport tube.

Rather than teaching students to avoid difficult situations, instructors taught trainees how to explore the capabilities of their training aircraft. They learned to experience the cause and effect of their movements in the air. Pupils learned how to safely extract themselves from dangerous manoeuvres such as spins. By doing so, they became confident and skilled in flying their planes to the limit.

Helen's first flying lesson began on the tarmac with a brief introduction to the mechanics of the plane.

Donning leather helmets and goggles, she slid into her seat after bending and squeezing into the cockpit. Once she was strapped in the front, she connected with her instructor through earphones attached to the speaking tube. Taxiing to the start of the runway, the instructor opened the throttle and launched the plane into the air against the wind and began climbing to gain height. In a piece for the *Evening Despatch*, a pilot wrote:

> Pilots find it difficult to realise at first that the higher they are in the air, the safer they will be. Most important of all the

> instruments is the air-speed indicator which tells the flier the speed at which the air is flowing past the plane. The importance of this is that it is the latter which keeps the plane up.[2]

Each half-hour lesson focused on a particular building block of flying. The first lesson of the scaffolded training began with the pilot learning to keep the plane flying level. The pupil pilot strived to move the aircraft in three dimensions: firstly, raising and lowering the nose by backward and forward movements of the joystick; secondly, banking the machine to the left or right by moving the joystick from side to side; and thirdly, swinging the nose of the plane from right to left by using the rudder bar.

In the second lesson, each student learned the art of taxiing. Once in the air, a learner practiced finding the correct climbing angle and the gliding angle. For the rest of the lesson, the pilot practiced gliding, climbing and flying straight.

After a review of the last two lessons, the pupil pilot was introduced to turning and banking. The instructor explained that 'in going into a turn, one should apply a little rudder and a little bank together in the direction in which the pupil wanted to turn (i.e. left turn, left rudder and stick over the left)'.[3] While learning to fly, Helen was also juggling her family and small sons with her hairdressing salon work.

The fourth lesson was a continuation of the third with the addition of practices and experimentation with the controls and its effects. Instruction on gliding turns constituted the fifth lesson. Halfway through and learning to put sequences together, Helen began to feel that she was learning to fly.

Before being permitted to fly solo, student pilots in their seventh lesson learned how to pull their plane out of a spin entirely on their own. It was necessary to teach trainees this skill as inexperienced pilots getting into difficulties most likely descended into an unintentional spin. Misuse of the controls or finding oneself in an initial stall and a slight yawing-and-rolling coupled movement were several ways of getting into a spin. Spinning was considered safe at altitudes between 2,000 and 3,000 feet but below this the pilot needed to quickly correct the spin as each turn results in a loss of altitude of 250 feet.

> Most fliers hate their first spin. They find themselves giddy and sick, and quite often mistake the ground for the sky. However, they must get used to the feeling, for the ability to take a machine out of a spin is one of the first essentials of flying, and no pilot is qualified until she has passed the exacting and dangerous test of the spin.[4]

The eighth and ninth lessons focused on learning to take off and practicing landings, respectively.

Earning a Class 'A' Pilot's Licence

Before Helen could begin to fly solo, she was required to obtain a medical certificate clearing her for solo flying as it was thought that great heights affected some people to the point of fainting.

Helen flew solo for three and a half hours. She had spent six and three quarter hours flying aloft with her instructors. Every minute in an aircraft brought her pure happiness.

With ten hours of flying time, Helen was ready to take her pilot's test. The Air Ministry had delegated to the Royal Aero Club the responsibility of conducting examinations of pilots for their licences. The Club examiner remained on the ground at the Sussex Aero Club as Helen executed the required flying and landing tasks in a 100-hp de Havilland 60 Gipsy Moth.

The test consisted of doing five figure-of-eight turns in the air and landing. She was required to lift off and soar to a height of 6,000 feet. At this height, pilots being examined were asked to cut the motor and skilfully land the plane without the help of the engine.

'It is a pretty severe test for the pupils and is designed to prevent any but the most efficient from securing a pilot's licence', observed a reporter.[5]

Having successfully passed the flying tests, on 15 February 1933 Helen Marcelle Barnes earned her Royal Aero Club aviator's certificate, No. 11711, at the Sussex Aero Club.

'During her student period, she did not tell her family of her activities but when she finally qualified to fly by herself and (was) determined to buy her own plane, she broke the news at home.'[6]

'When I got my flying papers,' she recalled, 'I rushed home and showed them to Mother and Dad. Of course, I had built them up with my stories of how safe it was to fly.'[7] With her new pilot's licence, her family embraced her newfound passion.

Earning her pilot's licence was not the only joyful news in her family. Helen was pregnant at the time of earning her licence. Her youngest son, Peter John Ratford Barnes, was born in Croydon, Surrey on 6 March 1933.

After submitting her application to the Air Ministry, she received her private pilot's licence, No. 6300, on 23 February 1934. She was licensed to fly all types of flying machines.

Her licence was renewable on an annual basis. It was estimated that her flying time, plane rental and instruction in 1932 and 1933 for her Class 'A' licence in London cost about £50.

'I learned more than flying', she recalled. 'The day I passed my test the other students and instructors took me to the local pub and gave me my first drink. It was a Pimm's No. 2.'[8]

Ascending to Higher Altitudes

After the First World War ended, women who had entered the workforce continued to work. Helen at this time was working as a hairdresser in the Surrey area. Several female pilots were already skilled and accomplished aviators while doing double-duty as parents, she had observed.

'The idea had been growing on her that the career of hairdressing would be rather prosaic compared with aviation', observed a *Richmond Times-Dispatch* reporter.[9]

Through her connections at the Eastbourne flying school, she heard about the earlier flying exploits of several women, including British pilots Lady Sophie Heath, Lady Mary Bailey and the Duchess of

Bedford. Through their record-setting flights, they had forged a flight path for other pilots who followed them.

Not only did they achieve daring long-distance flights, but they also started conversations about the inclusion of women in the skies. During the First World War and inter-war years, women aviators were becoming change-makers, breaking down institutional stereotypes and creating new attitudes and models of acceptance.

In 1925, Lady Sophie Heath, a tireless advocate for women in sport, became one of the first members of the newly formed London Aero Club to learn to fly. She was influential in attracting women to flying when she decided to make civil aviation her career. The following year, she began to set records, and garnered crowds who applauded her daring aerial exhibitions.

The year before Lady Heath earned her private licence, the International Commission on Air Navigation (ICAN) in 1924 'passed a motion that for a candidate to be eligible for the 'B' or commercial, pilot's licence he had to be of the masculine gender'. The medical sub-committee had deemed women ineligible for the licence. 'The initial "B" licence ban defined commercial airspace as masculine space by utilising existing discourses of female inferiority', wrote researcher Liz Millward.[10]

In its report, the medical sub-committee noted that the competency question referred to public transport only, and that women flying for air shows or sport was acceptable. The authors opined that women piloting commercial transport would affect public confidence, whereas in the US, women were employed as demonstration pilots to prove that flying was safe.

One author, Dr Garsaux, admitted that some of his medical arguments were 'debatable, such as the instability of the nervous system, periodic indisposition, etc'. His anecdotal report drew on current 'circulating discourses of female inferiority' and referred to 'the tropes of popular adventure stories dominated by heroic men', without recognising that women pilots also performed equally well in emergencies.[11] The report also claimed that its main findings were 'the insufficiency of female muscular power'.

The sub-commission 'decided unanimously to submit a resolution to the ICAN that "women are excluded from any employment in the navigating personnel of public transport" and that they had to pass a medical exam before obtaining a licence for private flying'.[12]

The 'B' licence bans limited women's ability to support their flying careers and their families, and it protected the commercial aviation sector, including earnings and privilege, from the aspirations of women pilots.

In a surprise announcement, Lady Bailey declared that she was leaving aviation to draw attention to the 'certain disadvantages which have been pressed upon women'.[13]

In this golden age, women could fly for themselves but were banned from carrying passengers or earning a living. She received thousands of letters from people around Britain, begging her not to give up flying.

Lady Heath, an athlete and founder of the Woman's Amateur Athletic Association, offered herself to the medical sub-commission to undergo fitness tests. The British Air Ministry tested her and found that she met the physical requirements. She lobbied ICAN signatories with the result that the Scandinavian countries, France and Czechoslovakia supported her. During England's general strike, she flew newspapers between London and Paris, and her courage persuaded the sub-commission to rescind the 'B' licence ban.

Most telling, the ban itself 'was not given any publicity', and 'women pilots continued to learn to fly under the erroneous assumption that they would be able to secure the "B" licence'.[14]

The ICAN reversed its decision in 1927, 'but with such stringent riders that even with a "B" licence women would find it exceedingly difficult to secure employment as commercial pilots'. The new regulations also required women to undergo more frequent medical examinations which affected their employment prospects. 'Despite their efforts, women pilots were ultimately unsuccessful in challenging the naturalisation of commercial airspace as masculine.'[15]

Lady Heath became one of the first women to earn a commercial licence under the new regulations.

After returning to flying as an instructor at Brooklands, she broke the world's altitude record when she reached 18,750 feet in May 1927. En route, her Avro Avian engine stopped twice, and the oil pressure failed. Her prowess as a stunt pilot and advocacy for women in flight resulted in an unexpected number of women enrolling in flying lessons at Brooklands.

Colonel Henderson, who ran the school, observed that 'flying needs no great physical strength, but rather patience, good eyesight, quick intuition and a light hand … In all of these qualifications', he summed, 'woman scores over man.'

One of her pupils was Lady Mary Bailey, a mother of five children, who achieved a long distance record. The two women engaged in a friendly competition to see which one would achieve the honour of being the first woman to fly across Africa. Lady Heath flew north from Cape Town in South Africa in her Avro Avian, while Lady Bailey flew from London in her long-range de Havilland 60 Moth south to Cape Town.

On 17 May 1928, Lady Heath 'threw' a loop over Croydon near London before gliding down and making a perfect sideslip onto the runway. Nonchalantly, she rolled up to the airport to complete her 10,000-mile flight from the Cape. Her arrival belied the difficulties she faced. Her solo journey in her Avro Avian included route planning in the absence of information about landing strips along the route, being shot at by Arabs, with bullets piercing the wings of her machine, and her fear of crossing the Mediterranean. Before crossing the sea, she wrapped a half-dozen motor inner tubes around her waist and flew at an altitude of 9,000 feet. She thought by flying high, she could glide into Africa or Europe in the event of an engine failure, but the only thing that happened at altitude was that the inner tubes popped.

Lady Bailey soared into Cape Town on 18 May 1928 after experiencing an eventful flight as well. Her blue and bronze Moth had flipped on approach to the mission hill station at Tabora which required a replacement plane. She suffered an attack of fever that forced her to recuperate at Broken Hill. She dared to fly as close as possible to the torrent of the Zambesi River as it ricochetted off the escarpment to form Victoria Falls.

Lady Heath and Lady Bailey had completed the unthinkable with sheer determination, aplomb and calmness. In doing so, they swept aside social conventions and opened the skyways for women flyers around the world.

A month after Lady Bailey completed her historic flight, another notable first was notched at Burry Cove in South Wales. American aviator Amelia Earhart landed on British shores on 18 June 1928, becoming the first woman to fly across the Atlantic. Her Fokker F.VII tri-motor seaplane, the *Friendship* had departed from Trepassy Harbour in Newfoundland. Her record-breaking flight took twenty hours and forty minutes.

Inspired by her accomplishment, Lady Heath wrote to Amelia Earhart: 'Women pilots all over the world are very proud of your magnificent achievement and the dignified way in which you've done it.'[16]

Reaching London, Amelia Earhart purchased Lady Heath's tiny Avro Avian and shipped it to the US. Explaining to the British press why she was bringing back a plane, she said that 'in America they had not developed light planes to the same extent of perfection as we had in this country'.

Lady Heath was later contracted by Royal Dutch Airlines (which later became KLM) to pilot a Fokker-Jupiter airliner from Amsterdam to London. She became the first woman in the world to act as a regular pilot for a commercial airline. Some records show that Lady Heath was considered an 'ambassador' for Royal Dutch Airlines and therefore was never paid for her work as a second pilot.

By the time Helen had earned her pilot's licence, Lady Heath had returned to Ireland where she became the first female instructor at Kildonan, near Dublin.

The records of women flyers were made possible by the advent of clubs which provided the means for women to be associated with flying, by providing pilot training. The rise of women as pilots ran parallel to the growth of women in the labour force during the inter-war years.

Employment outside the home provided women with some financial independence and the means to finance their pursuits of flying.

An emerging pilot was pioneer Amy Johnson. After earning her pilot's licence in 1929 at the London Aero Club, she began setting world records. A year later, she flew from Croydon in a Gipsy Moth on an epic journey to Darwin, and in doing so became the first woman to fly solo to Australia. In 1932, Amy set a record for a solo flight from England to Cape Town, flying a Puss Moth. Shortly after, she and her husband Jim Mollison embarked on a record-setting overseas flight to the US and flew non-stop to India during the England to Australia air race.

Racing from London to Cardiff on the 'Beastliest Afternoon'

Helen, who owned two sports cars, started to buy planes.

'The initial venture was a low-winged monoplane of ninety horsepower – a Cirrus Miles Hawk by name.'[17] This was a twin-seater light touring and training plane, possibly purchased with a view for instructing and commercial flying. She rented the second plane.

Cecil Pashley continued in his role as a flying instructor, becoming chief instructor and a flight lieutenant in the Royal Air Force Volunteer Reserves in the Second World War. Cecil Pashley became a mentor and role model for many pilots he trained. In doing so, he opened a path for Helen to become an instructor of military pilots.[18] Her instructor, Jack Sale, also became one of her most important mentors and shaped the trajectory of her flying life.

With her private licence in hand, Helen became one of 150 to 200 women air pilots in Britain. This number was expected to double by the end of 1934.

Her first job was giving 'joy rides' or pleasure flights around England. 'I didn't find people reluctant to go up with me because I was a girl', she noted.[19]

Aviation was growing more and more inclusive. This was mirrored in 1934 by the words of the British feminist Winifred Holtby when she proclaimed that:

> when an Amy Johnson breaks aviation records, when a Madame Curie discovers radium, an Ethel Smyth composes a Mass, a Frances Perkins controls perhaps the most difficult government department in the American New Deal – then it becomes a trifle harder for young girls to tell themselves: 'It doesn't matter. I'm only a woman.' The possibility of achievement has been vindicated.[20]

On 6 October 1934, Helen Barnes and her instructor Jack Sale of the Shoreham Club entered the annual London-to-Cardiff air race. The pair flew a Miles Hawk Major with a 130 hp de Havilland Gipsy engine. Advertisements promoting the annual air race included Helen Barnes as one of the fourteen famous pilots competing alongside the notable Sir Charles Rose. The most interesting entry was that of Lord Patrick Crichton-Stuart who flew a Hendy Hobo, a fast plane of unusual design. The inclusion of Helen in the promotions highlighted the growing awareness of Helen as an up and coming aviator of note.

Helen was one of three daring women who entered. The other two were Elise Battye from Reading in a de Havilland Gipsy Moth, and Paddie Naismith from London in a B2 Blackburn trainer.

Fifteen planes started at Hatfield airport in London and flew straight to a mark consisting of three bell tents at Beachley near Chepstow. The racers circled the tents at an elevation low enough for an observer to record and telephone their registration letters to Cardiff airport. Helen's colleague at the Southern Aero Club, Robin Norwood, had entered his Major Moth.

Flight Lieutenant R. Duncanson, piloting Lord Crichton-Stuart's Hendo Hobo, won the 120-mile air race. The winner completed the journey in exactly an hour, on a day that was described as 'the beastliest afternoon of the year'. Rain fell and clouds hovered as low as 400 feet near the coast.

'Elise Battye, who piloted a Moth, was the first to cross the mark at Chepstow, and her efficient, practical attitude towards aviation for women was manifest in her attire', reported the *Cardiff Western Mail*. 'She wore a black leather flying suit, the jacket of which was fastened up to the neck with a zipper and a helmet to match.' Paddy Naismith carried passenger Lord Crichton-Stuart in her Blackburn trainer.

Twenty-one-year-old Sir Charles Rose had a narrow escape when his Miles Hawk overshot the Cardiff runway and ploughed into the hedge. He climbed out of his open cockpit unhurt. Second was A.H. Cook in a Comper Swift, and third was L. Lipton in a Gipsy Moth.

Only ten pilots finished. The rest of the field was 'unplaced' due to the appalling flying conditions, including the Miles Hawk with Jack Sale and Helen on board. Also unplaced were Paddie Naismith's Blackburn trainer and Elise Battye's Gipsy Moth.[21]

Chapter 3

Exploring the Art of Flying Boats

The *ab initio* pupil on securing his 'A' licence becomes in a sense the captain of a ship navigating the currents of the air. He has learnt to control his machine under entirely favourable conditions up to the time his ticket was obtained, with someone else in his machine to fall back upon. Once solo, he finds himself, for the first time, master of his own destiny, and it is from this time onwards that his real flying training begins. From the time his licence is issued, every hour spent aloft will add to his knowledge, experience being the greatest teacher of all, and he will find the interest unending.

There can indeed be few thrills so great, in these blasé days, as that experienced by the junior pilot of the air on his first cross-country flight of two or three hundred miles, when he arrives at his intended destination closely to time and on the compass bearing he worked out for himself, proving his navigation to have been correct.[1]

Sunday Tribune
(Singapore)

With her pilot's licence in hand, Helen began in 1935 to explore how her joy of flying could shape her future. By this time, she was a single mother of three young boys: Brian, David and Peter. She and her husband Robert had divorced in early 1935. Her parents, Albert and Gertrude, became the most loyal and committed supporters of her flying dreams. The unfailing backing of her mother enabled Helen to explore and take her flying career to the skies. A family friend, Mabel Daisy Seabrook from Lowestoft, had joined the household a few years earlier as a nurse and caregiver to her young sons. Helen directed her inheritance from her grandfather Thomas to support her family while she established her flying career.

In April 1935, Helen announced she was to be known as Miss Helen Marcelle Harrison, after choosing her mother's maiden name. 'She took Harrison as a "flying name" by deed poll when she decided to make flying her career.'[2]

The unsteady years following the First World War presented new opportunities for young women. With unstinting confidence, Helen was ready to claim her space in the air. She simply wanted to fly and to earn her living as a pilot and never thought about how she was breaking ground for women pilots. Flying aligned with the adventurous independence she had discovered while growing up in British Columbia.

Helen possessed a rare ability to focus on the present, to channel all her energies and attention into the demanding details of flying. Much of this was due to the calmness she felt knowing that her mother was attending to the day-to-day details of her family.

As British aircraft design and production expanded, she began experimenting with different planes. Her first plane, a low-winged Cirrus Miles Hawk monoplane, was sold. 'This was followed by a Fox Moth, a three-seater cabin ship. After some more buying and selling and quite a few pleasant hours, she ended up purchasing a Falcon, a four-seat cabin plane rated at 130 horsepower.'[3]

Helen experienced so much joy, laughter and happiness in flying that it became obvious to all that she belonged in a cockpit soaring through the sky.

Onward to the Birthplace of Seaplane Training

An unexpected opportunity arose when her instructor Jack Sale accepted a new job in the Far East. In May 1935, he voyaged on the Dutch ocean liner, the MS *Christiaan Huygens*, to the Straits Settlement. The Royal Singapore Flying Club had appointed him chief flying instructor, a position that seemed perfectly timed for the multi-faceted aviator. The Club's former chief instructor, Mr S.H. Potter, was returning to England for a new position. During his five years in Singapore, Mr Potter had trained hundreds of pilots. Importantly, he introduced seaplane training to Singapore, a legacy that Jack Sale would build upon.

Upon arriving, he observed that civil aviation in Singapore with the new airport nearing completion, 'has a very bright future. Moreover, the club will be a unique position as the only club in the Empire having facilities for land and sea aircraft training.'[4]

Singapore was considered the birthplace of seaplane training. The swamps of Geylang basin were transformed into Kallang Airport, a potential 'Croydon of the East', which also made Singapore a centre of aviation interest. To this flying hub on the southern tip of the Malay peninsula, Jack Sale brought considerable flying experience. His six and a half years of instruction experience included work for Phillips and Powis Aircraft (Reading) and for the Brighton-Hove-Worthing Municipal airport. Importantly, he had logged many hours on Miles Hawk planes – an advantage, as the club recently acquired a new one. At the time of his posting to Singapore, Jack Sale had twenty-two types of aircraft on his licence.

'His personal keenness is naturally reflected by those he has taught to fly', noted *The Straits Times*. 'The credit for the sustained interest in civil aviation locally must go to Mr Jack Sale.'[5]

The Club's aircraft included two de Havilland Moth seaplanes, two Moth landplanes, one Hornet Moth and one convertible Moth which could be used as a seaplane and a landplane. The new Miles Hawk was one of two imported into Malaya.

'The Hawk climbs like a bird, is very easy to handle – indeed it can be flown hands-off at full throttle', enthused a reporter. 'Visibility is excellent, and it descends so smoothly as to be deceptive almost in this respect. With a cruising speed of a hundred mph and a range of nearly seven hours, it is splendidly fitted for the work it was be required to do – fast cross-country flying.'[6]

In the late 1920s, flying enthusiasts formed the Singapore Flying Club which became, not only the first flying club of Southeast Asia, but the first flying club anywhere in the world to offer training on seaplanes. The club was built at Tanjong Pagar near Keppel Harbour, east of the Singapore yacht club.

In 1928, it purchased two de Havilland Cirrus Moth seaplanes. A vital motor launch was bought for emergencies and for towing planes in bad seas. In 1929, a third Cirrus Moth seaplane was added to the fleet. The low landing speed of the Moth, around 30 to 35 mph, was suitable for training. A fourth Cirrus Moth arrived in 1930. The total of four aircraft was reduced to three when one was damaged in the Club's first accident.

The joys of light seaplane flying in Singapore was exalted by the Royal Aeronautical Society's president. Lieutenant Colonel, the Master of Sempill, William Forbes-Sempill expounded on the light seaplane, considering it to be the most pleasant of all touring vehicles. He was 'a great believer in the future of this type of aircraft for the operation of the feeder services to the trunk Empire airlines, when the route of the "feeders" lies along the coastline or follows the course of rivers.'

He explained at the time how,

> The chief advantage of seaplane travel is the elimination of aerodrome worries. The light seaplane ties up to a mooring buoy in an ordinary harbour, paying the usual comparatively small dues or may be anchored out in any convenient creek or backwater. Add to this that the owner of a small 'air yacht' of this kind may cruise without danger at a height of a very few feet above the water and the pleasures of this form of travel becomes very easy to imagine.[7]

Early in 1935, the club changed its policy of instruction. Originally, it trained *ab initio* pupils primarily on seaplanes, with advanced training to follow on landplanes when possible. The Club decided to reverse the process. After the pupils' solo flights on land planes, training would ensue on seaplanes. By switching, the club planned to lower its operation costs and increase flying hours.

The facilities offered to members of the flying club for seaplane instruction were found to be the least expensive in the world. In Singapore, instruction was provided at ten Singapore dollars an hour. (When English clubs started seaplane training, their instruction cost was £12 Sterling per hour.)

A year prior to Jack Sale's arrival, the club proudly owned a Saro A17 Cutty Sark, a glorious four-seater amphibian aircraft. Constructed of Alclad, its twin engines were mounted on pylons high above the wings to keep them clear of spray. The flying boat (registration G-AAVC) consisted of a wood frame covered with an alloy of heat-treated aluminium, copper, manganese and magnesium that provided the corrosion resistance of pure metal on the surface, and the strength of the strong alloy underneath. The Alclad hull of the Cutty Sark was suited to the corrosive environment in Singapore. High temperatures, humidity and salt spray contributed to the faster rates of corrosion.

Purchased from the Guinness family for $30,000, it was used as a touring and training amphibian aircraft by the club. The arrival of the Cutty Sark in 1931 became the precursor to an era in which seaplane instruction began earnestly in preparation for the new Empire flying boats. These large seaplanes were designed to usher in the age of international airmail and decrease the reliance on ships delivering surface mail.

When Jack Sale arrived, the Cutty Sark had been regretfully written off. It had sustained severe hull damage when taking off in heavy seas upcountry. It was then flown back to Singapore and landed safely. On inspection, it was determined that required repairs would not be economical.

By this time, the Straits Settlement stopped using British G-registrations and the Club switched all its aircraft to VR-registrations.

The seaplanes became VR-SAF, VR-SAG, VR-SAH and VR-SAQ, while the landplanes became VR-SAE, VR-SAI and VR-SAO. The seaplanes were based at Tanjong Pagar while the landplanes were at Seletar.

The window for flying long distances was dependent on sea conditions and the susceptibility of aircraft to crosswinds when landing. These winds prevail from multiple directions as Singapore is situated at the bottom tip of an island, narrowly separated from the long peninsula of Malaysia, between the Indian Ocean and the South China Sea. When the weather was bad in the harbour, planes were sometimes transferred to Changi, where they operated from its beach.

The club was cognisant of the weather-related challenges the tropics provided. The worst flying weather was usually in July and August with exceptionally rough seas and heavy rains. The months of October through to May were better suited to flying. In February, monsoons curtailed flying hours. 'The condition of the sea is always the dominating factor where seaplanes are concerned', noted the *Singapore Free Press*. 'Good seas cannot be expected before the middle of March when the monsoon begins to change.'[8]

Pilots and aircraft faced unique challenges as they learned and mastered flying with floats. The weather and sea conditions determined the time it took to obtain an 'A' licence on seaplanes. Approximately fifteen hours flying time on seaplanes was required. Flying in humid and saltwater conditions, the fuselage timbers of the Moths were renewed every nine months.

Young pilots such as Helen, who faced stiff competition in obtaining aviation jobs, considered that experience in seaplane flying would broaden her qualifications and position her for work on the large flying boats.

In mid-1935, Helen bid adieu to her family and clambered on board her plane for a journey that would become formative on many levels. Heading south, she flew over the sunlit fields of Kent and soared over the white cliffs standing sentry over the English Channel. Approaching France, the difference was discernible immediately. Helen had flown this route to Paris many times previously.

The landscape between Lyon and Marseille became varied and rugged with its twisting valleys and red-roofed towns. Following the Rhône River, she arrived at the large sprawling airport at Istres, near Marseilles. From her vantage point in the cockpit, she saw the huge capacity of the Istres air base to accommodate thousands of aircraft and flying boats in the nearby harbour. At Marseilles, she boarded a passenger steamer to the Straits Settlement. Her month-long voyage from France to Singapore ventured through the Suez Canal with a stopover in Colombo, Sri Lanka.

That Helen took a gamble to gain a seaplane rating in the Far East rather than in England was due to cost and expediency. In England, she encountered numerous barriers.

Air Services Training Ltd at Hamble, with its instruction base on Southampton Water, was known as Britian's 'university of the air'. Recognised as one of the biggest and most comprehensive flying schools in the world, it was one of the first to offer seaplane instruction. This large flying school was oriented to male pilots who were aiming to fly for air forces and or commercial airlines.

The Hamble school offered short courses on blind flying by instruments alone and seaplane pilotage. Its fleet comprised a range of aircraft from light training planes such as Avros to amphibious craft and a four-engine airliner with a 123-foot wingspan, an Armstrong Whitworth Ensign. Helen did not see an opening for her at this school and believed her chances of learning seaplane flying were better in Singapore. Fortuitously, her former instructor Jack Sale was teaching floatplane flying in Singapore and had encouraged her to broaden her skills.

Singapore, being a port of call for all ships voyaging east, was well known as 'The Gateway to the East'. The population during her visit was estimated at over a half million. The thronging metropolis on this diamond-shaped island comprised Malayan, Chinese, Indian, Eurasian and European residents.

'In connection with her stay in the Malay states, she found an opportunity to fly a seaplane which was a valuable experience.'[9] During her first flight aloft above Singapore, she became one of the few visitors to the Straits Settlement to keenly observe and experience this bustling metropolis from the air. According to the *Sunday Tribune* in 1935:

> At five thousand feet above Singapore harbour, one can observe the complete Singapore Island stretched below one like some giant contour map, the silver girdle of the Straits lying placid round its shores. To the south, as far as the eye can see, lie innumerable coral islands scattered in a sapphire sea. Each is complete with its own vivid green tuft of coconut palms, a short rim of golden sand, and then beneath the water, lie the jagged reefs of coral.[10]

Helen was able to complete a course in seaplane training, thus preparing herself for work as a pilot in flying boats.

Decoding the Challenges of Seaplanes vs Landplanes

The emergence of seaplane flying sparked debates between landplane enthusiasts and seaplane devotees. The *Sunday Tribune* captured the challenges facing seaplane pilots vs those faced by experienced landplane flyers, using the Moth as an example:

> One often hears heated discussions as to whether the landplane or the seaplane is the better machine on which to learn to fly. The true answer is, of course, that neither is the better, as each has its own particular merits and applications.
>
> It is perhaps not generally known that the 'A' licence pilot of a few hours' standing on landplanes will take as much as four to five hours dual instruction, on an average, to qualify with a fair margin of safety on a seaplane. Taking single-engine Moth land and sea craft as the basis of this comparison, the landplane pilot will require more than half of this dual instruction time to be spent on learning seamanship.

Most accidents with seaplanes do not occur in the air or even on alighting but while taxiing on the water or during take-off. An 'A' licence seaplane pilot with but a few hours solo to his credit usually requires one hour's instruction before going off solo with perfect safety on a landplane.

It is frequently held that seaplane flying is easy because, they say, there are literally square miles of ocean to land on. Nothing could be further from the truth.

The pilot who alights deliberately and without necessity, even on a calm sea, as much as a half mile from his base just because he sees a wide-open space there, is a fool, unless circumstances compel him to descend Taxiing all that unnecessary way not only seriously overheats the engine and leads to cylinder distortion, but it covers the float-seaplane and its engine with quite an unnecessary quantity of extremely corrosive salt water, which is whipped up and blown into every crevice by the airscrew.

The sensible seaplane pilot will therefore normally alight well within the usual land aerodrome distance limits of the raft or buoy which he proposes to approach.

When a landplane alights on the aerodrome, its pilot's troubles are all over. When a seaplane alights on the water, its pilot's troubles have just begun. He finds his machine, having no ground friction, immediately wants to swing on its floats into the wind. If the pilot gives a burst of engine, he probably gains far more forward speed than is either safe or desirable.

Furthermore, this speed once gained is much more difficult to lose than it would be on a landplane having a convenient tail skid on firm ground to act as a brake and possibly wheel brakes. If he does not use his engine, his machine swings into the wind but drifts with the tide.

Imagine, therefore, the embryo landplane pilot's first attempt in a seaplane and having to taxi up to a buoy anchored in the average stream of a two-knot tide flowing at right-angles to the wind. His machine faces the wind but to his consternation he discovers himself broadsiding at a rate of over three feet per second.

His approaches to the mooring have therefore to be judged in two dimensions instead of only one, and no two approaches are ever quite the same.

But this is an easy case. Imagine if, under the above usual conditions, the sea has a cross swell, and the pilot has to negotiate a tug with a string of four or five lighters in tow, and possibly the wash from a fast motor-launch or the *Kedah.*[11]

In these circumstances, with the engine running, the seaplane comes under the rules for vessels under power at sea and must obey all the rules of the road as applied to shipping. If the pilot goes across the swell, he is liable to capsize his machine.

From these few elementary cases of difficulties experienced every day by the seaplane pilot, it will perhaps become more obvious to a landplane enthusiast that a very definitely higher degree of skill and ability is required for the successful pilotage of a seaplane of a similar type.

En passant the writer of this article has had experience of landplanes, seaplanes and twin-engine flying-boats and may, therefore, lay claim to a certain impartiality in these remarks. He would like to assert that the single-engine float seaplane without water rudders is one of the most difficult and awkward craft to handle. A multi-engine flying boat is far easier to handle on the water for the simple reason that you can turn instantly and that will be a burst of port or starboard engine, as required. Moreover, slower forward speeds are possible with a boat, as a drogue may be readily put out.

The water rudderless seaplane oft 'drifteth where it liveth' and usually with the most expensive results.[12]

Discovering the Joy of Seaplane Flying

In Singapore, Helen discovered the joy of flying with floats. The seaplane channel on the Kallang River provided a safe space for trainees to experience how the Moth seaplanes handled the choppy waves and sea currents. Although she was flying more modern planes since earning her licence in a Gipsy Moth, she discovered that the Moth with its low landing speed was more forgiving than the faster planes. In mid-June, the club was using two Hermes II Moth seaplanes for instruction. (The landplanes included a Hermes II Moth, Gipsy I Moth and the Hermes Miles Hawk.)

Traditional Asian watercraft were not permitted in the seaplane channel. Singapore's harbour, the fourth largest in the world in the mid-1930s, was congested with all types of marine vessels.

The seaplane channel was marked with buoys from the inner harbour limits to the Club's aircraft slipways. Although the seaplane base was situated in an extensive and sheltered anchorage, pilots learned how to handle the variables that seaplane flying encountered beyond the anchorage. Frequently, rough sea conditions restricted flying.

The channel's strategic and potential importance to Singapore was 'all the greater in view of the experiments being carried out with flying boats on the Imperial Air routes'.[13]

The city's congested harbour presented many problems to aviation authorities who were confronted with the task of providing a safe landing place for seaplanes. British law was well defined, as reported in the *Singapore Free Press*:

> When a flying-boat is in the air, it comes within the control of the Air Ministry and is under an obligation to avoid collision with shipping. Once on the water, the flying-boat becomes subject to ordinary maritime regulations. Being a mechanically propelled vessel, it has to yield right of way to sailing craft.[14]

Before each training session, Helen and her instructor obtained tide, wind and other weather information to plan for the conditions of the day. She experimented with the plane's response to her controls on the throttle and flaps for steering during each lesson. The floats on the Moth seaplanes were rudderless at the time which added a degree of complexity to taxiing, take-offs and landings. The timing of each became critically important.

With each take-off, she experienced the rush of adrenaline mixed with fear and commitment as the throttle was pushed forward. As the seaplane surged faster across the sapphire sea, she observed how the floats below her released themselves from the water's grip. The plane's fuselage and wings rattled and shook as the floats gradually rose above the water's surface. As a pilot, she learned to closely watch for any sudden obstructions such as boats or debris. As the nose of the plane tilted higher and higher with the wing flaps down, the commitment to flight was confirmed.

Within seconds, the plane had freed itself from the sea's grasp and was quietly aloft. Easing the throttle and settling into a steady climb, the plane began to purr. Aloft in the silent air, Helen experienced the extraordinary feeling of weightlessness and the timeless world of the strait beckoning before her.

Landing in the channel across the vast and busy Keppel Harbour in a small floatplane became an art. On the slow descent, somewhere between a steady speed and a stall, the pilot rapidly sensed and calculated all the three-dimensional factors that go into a successful touchdown in the seaplane channel. Wind, current, speed, and the timing and location of landing were the rapidly changing coordinates that needed to be mentally computed while managing the controls. The pilot learned to anticipate any responses of the aircraft to its environment.

Helen kept a careful watch on the airspace and sea laneway in front of her for any wayward boaters and was prepared for an instantaneous change of plans. Aborting a landing and nosing up into an immediate climb required throwing the throttle open and pulling back on the steering – all at the same time. The pilot learned to keep a light hold on the controls to prevent any freezing on the controls.

When landing a seaplane, the nose of the plane is kept upturned to prevent the tip of the floats from digging into the water and catapulting the plane upon first contact. After much practice, she learned to land her plane concisely and smoothly on the water, waves and currents permitting.

In seven hours of seaplane flying, Helen learned the art of take-offs and landings on choppy seas, taxiing in clear channels, and the rules of marine navigation. She learned the tricks for landing on glassy water.

The chief instructor conducted tests for seaplane licences and ratings. At this time, the Singapore Flying Club was affiliated with the Royal Aero Club, the official aviation body in London which issued licences to pilots who passed their tests to the satisfaction of the chief instructor.

With her newfound experience flying floatplanes in Singapore, Helen qualified for her seaplane rating.[15] The single-engine seaplane rating was placed on her flying certificate.

To earn a seaplane rating, pilots needed to demonstrate complete proficiency and mastery of planes over the sea. Helen's acquisition of a seaplane rating in the mid-1930s illustrated her ability to comprehend and put into practice key seaplane aeronautic principles, marine navigation rules and adapt to different flying conditions. She quickly learned how aircraft such as Moths responded with cumbersome floats on seas, and without rudders!

Around the time Helen was learning to fly seaplanes, there were two weather-related incidents which resulted from the convergence of wind and seas on small vulnerable aircraft. In April 1935, one of the Club's Moth seaplanes capsized soon after alighting on the sea. The bottom of the port wing required repairs.[16]

Less than a month later, threatening weather forced the cancellation of a flying lesson and necessitated a tow back to the seaplane base.

While being towed, a sudden squall lifted the seaplane's wing and threw the machine over. It was a common practice for seaplane instructors and pupils not to fasten their seat harnesses due to the higher risk of being flipped into the sea and in this case, the club instructor and trainee were quickly rescued. Fortunately, the machine floated and the only damage was to a wing, which was repaired.[17]

Helen's fortuitous opportunity to learn floatplane flying in the mid-1930s came just as the era of flying boats and seaplanes was taking off in far flung places, including northern Canada.

During Helen's time in Singapore, *The Straits Times* aviation correspondent wrote of Canada:

> One glance at the map of Canada reveals the immense scope afforded by the great Dominion for the use of seaplanes. In the summer, the thousands of lakes and the larger rivers afford excellent natural aerodromes for water-borne machines. In the winter, when lakes and rivers are frozen over, much flying can still be done by the same aircraft fitted with ski-undercarriages instead of floats.

The reporter noted that the Canadian subsidiary of the de Havilland company had produced a seaplane version of the Dragon twin-engine landplanes. This version was planned 'to meet Canadian conditions which demand that a seaplane shall be exceptionally robust, able to withstand strains imposed by constant beaching on lake shores and to carry, without suffering damage, the kitchen stoves, bags of bullion, lumps of machinery and other rough and heavy gear' that was flown to and from mining areas.

'From the surface of glassy water and with no helping wind – most difficult of all conditions for seaplane take-off – the fully-laden Dragon rose easily after a forward run lasting thirty seconds', the reporter continued. 'Its initial rate of climb with full load on board was recorded as 600 feet a minute.'

The versatility and range of seaplanes in Canada's Arctic was demonstrated by a flying Bishop in 1935. Dr William A. Geddes flew 2,000 miles to outlying regions in the Yukon, as far north as Old Crow on the Porcupine River, 80 miles above the Arctic Circle.

The freedom and adventures promised by seaplanes and flying boats began to whet the appetites of many would-be pilots. Helen departed from Singapore with a new love in her heart of floatplane flying, and a seaplane rating.

She 'possibly became the first woman in the British Empire to do so, and certainly the first Canadian woman'.[18]

Chapter 4

Cultivating an Aviation Career

The day breaks upon a dull world below the clouds, but our pilot has had his weather report and takes off undaunted. He climbs steadily up through a gap in the clouds until at three thousand feet the last chill mists eddy past his machine and he emerges into bright morning sunshine. Below him now the clouds lie, dazzling white like some lonely snowbound land of the Arctic, flat and interminable as far as the eye can see. The earth is lost and there are no landmarks here, unless perchance the head of some lofty mountain peak lying on his course juts proudly through the clouds.

The pilot's navigation must now be accurate, as the absence of landmarks allows him no correction. If, after the calculated time has elapsed, he goes down to find his destination aerodrome beneath him, he may consider he has done his first real navigation test with success. He will next want to fly 'blind', that is, to learn to fly in clouds or fog for long periods with safety.[1]

Sunday Tribune (Singapore)

By the summer of 1935 it was widely advertised in Great Britain that fifty commercial pilots were needed urgently. Even though there were 530 commercial pilots engaged, more aviators were needed as airline operators. Flying clubs and joy-riding firms besieged the Guild of Air Pilots and Air Navigators for assistance in filling job vacancies. Through the Guild, one joy-riding firm offered £12 to £15 a week to any pilot they could find.

The opportunities for women were not figured in the needs for commercial pilots, as reported in the *Evening Standard*:

> While there may not be opportunities for English girls in military aviation, what are their chances in 1935 of establishing careers in civil flying?[2]
>
> If we look at some outstanding personalities among women flyers today, it will be seen that although there is a prejudice, yet if there is a will, there is a way. Amy Johnson carved her way to fame. The air girls who have made the best commercial success are Pauline Gower and Dorothy Spicer. These two worked with determination to take all the certificates and licences they could win. It meant study, practical engineering and workshop experience and examinations.[3]

After her whirlwind journey to Singapore, Helen was home in England contemplating her next steps to launch her new career in aviation. Having examined 'possibilities in flying, [she] decided that a fair future was to be met within South Africa, so she and her family made the long trip to Cape Town', a reporter wrote.[4]

On 2 August 1935, 25-year-old Helen and her family boarded the Scottish-built steamer *Balmoral Castle* for Port Elizabeth. Her sons were 7, 5 and 2 years of age. Moving with them to South Africa were her parents Albert (60) and Gertrude (56), and the children's caregiver Mabel Daisy Seabrook (41). The *Balmoral Castle* docked in Port Elizabeth, one of the world's windiest towns, where its trees grew almost horizontal from south-east winds sweeping off the Algoa coastline. They arrived just as the South African winter was warming into spring.

The family travelled along the glorious stretch of coastline to Cape Town, a 190-mile journey flanking expansive golden beaches and rocky peninsulas. The rail journey traversed through tropical forests and the famous Montague Pass en route to the town of George, the most picturesque village in the country. Wildflowers bloomed alongside the tracks, and sea birds circled overhead.

Arriving at the tip of South Africa, they were greeted by a burgeoning town which wrapped itself around turquoise-hued False Bay. The massive basaltic Table Mountain loomed low and broad along the Cape of Good Hope, where it meets the Atlantic and Indian oceans. The balmy tropical temperatures were welcomed after the long ocean voyage.

Her family settled in Somerset West where Helen purchased a home, and the family eagerly looked forward to the South African summer. The grey chill winters of England would soon be forgotten. The bay in front of Cape Town lay as aquamarine blue as a South Pacific lagoon. The vast bulk of the Table Mountains reared up, often shrouded by enveloping mist, shielding the mysteries of the vast South African interior with its high plateaus and stark mountains.

In the tough city of Cape Town it was soon observed that tensions from the Boer War lingered on. In South Africa, there were 'many mixed elements', noted Helen's mother Gertrude in a media interview. She observed that the Boers who were still fighting the war resented the British and their language.

To get along in Cape Town and other South African cities, Helen and her family began to learn Afrikaans, one of the local languages. Cape Town was as much colonial Dutch as it was colonial British. Snatches of conversations in the streets reflected the multicultural population of Cape Town which also included citizens of Malay and Bantu descent.

Helen joined a flying club and continued to build her flying hours.[5]

Employment as a pilot was easily obtainable in South Africa and Helen began to take courses to qualify for her 'B' ticket. She realised that,

> more flying hours were required for a commercial pilot's licence than in England. Her total flying time to date would qualify her to take the examination in England, but almost 100 more hours were needed to earn the same certificate in South Africa. It was for this reason she decided to return to England, if but for a short time. Her return trip was by airline to Port Said, thence by boat to England.[6]

With her family settled and two sons enrolled in school, Helen set her compass for Johannesburg, the hub of South African air travel and the vast interior to the north. Leaving the white carpet of low Cape Town bungalows fringing the shimmering sea, she nosed her plane northeast and embarked on an adventurous traverse of South Africa.

Circling upwards, she battled the clashing crosswinds from the converging oceans. The conditions were similar to what she had experienced in Singapore. Both cities lay on the bottom tips of peninsulas and were exposed to ocean and air currents. Reaching an altitude of 8,200 feet over verdant farmland, she faced the first of many challenging mountain crossings.

The Cape Fold Belt ranges form an almost impenetrable barrier to the vast African interior. The rugged Hex River mountains are the second highest range jutting upwards in the Western Cape.

She followed a course midway between the Swartberg Mountains, the Black Mountains, to the south and the Great Escarpment to the north. The railway wound below through the semi-arid desert of the Great Karoo, !'Aukarob. The Great Karoo lies in the rainfall-shadow of the Cape Fold mountains. Early explorers and hunters journeying into the High Veld deplored the area as a frightening place of great heat, severe frosts, extensive droughts and devastating floods.

With the Hex River mountains behind her, Helen's flight followed the railway line to her first refuelling stop at Beaufort West. This small town nestles at the foot of the Great Escarpment which runs from the border of Zimbabwe and Mozambique in the east through South Africa, and northwest to Angola and Namibia. Her plane rose high to crest the escarpment and cross the Upper Karoo. The Orange River, which originates in the Drakensberg mountains in Lesotho, forms the unofficial border between the Great Karoo and High Veld.

She refuelled at Victoria West which lay 1,312 feet above sea level in the Northern Cape province. In Bloemfontein, the 'city of roses', she replenished her plane's tanks. Bloem, also known from Afrikaans as the 'fountain of flowers', lies 4,500 feet in elevation along the Highveld's southern edge in Central South Africa.

The interior wild grassland of South Africa gradually rises in elevation. Reaching Johannesburg, she landed in the rarefied air at Rand Airport and completed her first leg of her flight, nearly 800 miles from Cape Town.

In his book *Swinging the Equator*, William Makin wrote about flying the length of Africa in 1935:

> As a city, Johannesburg had less than fifty years of history. Before that, the place was a wilderness of veld. Johannesburgers lived fast and furiously. At an elevation of nearly 6,000 feet and standing on the greatest treasure house of the world, it is impossible to exist otherwise. Life bubbles, champagne-wise. Hospitality is generous and even overwhelming. Millions are made and lost and won again within a few months. Youth, wealth, excitement and optimism. That is the spirit of Johannesburg.[7]

At Rand airport, Helen stepped out of her single light plane and boarded an Imperial Airways flight to Cairo, Egypt, on a combined air-and-ocean ticket.[8] Over five days in late October, she flew northward along the eastern spine of the continent. The flight saved her considerable time, as she was intent on reaching England in a timely manner to complete her hours and training.

'The trip northward across the length of this vast continent proved a wonderful experience', reported W.A. Magill of the *Richmond Times-Dispatch* after interviewing Helen. The journey offered an insight into flying conditions in Africa. Magill continued:

> Most of the country flown over would have proven dangerous for landings, and the fields for refuelling were few and far between. The plane carried wireless telephone equipment, but the radio stations contacted were not that many and the reception of signals difficult due to constant heavy static.
>
> There were no lighted airways for night flying, no well-equipped landing fields operated by government and municipalities every few hundred miles. The pilots were dependent on their own ability for navigation as the radio range beacons is an absent quantity in Africa.[9]

Flying the Length of Africa

After the First World War, air travel was considered a speculative venture. Egypt was positioned as a junction for air routes to India, Singapore, Australia and Africa.[10] By 1920, surveyors had established a flying route along the length of Africa with forty-three airfields which were 125 miles apart. Twenty-four served as oil stations for refuelling.

On 20 January 1932, Imperial Airways launched its inaugural London-to-Cape Town commercial flight at Croydon airport. Passengers boarded the Handley Page HP42 *Helena* for the first leg to Paris. This was the first segment of an eleven day, 8,000-mile journey across Europe and Africa that included five aircraft and two train trips. This introductory flight represented a monumental achievement that overcame myriad difficulties and challenges.

The *Times* marked this as an 'Imperial event of outstanding importance'. The rail journeys included the Paris-Brindisi and Alexandria-Cairo sections.

Passenger flights over Africa in the early years consisted of 225-mile segments on average, with flying time of four to four-and-a-half hours long. Air travel commenced at daybreak as pilots flew by visual flight rules during daylight hours. Planes were unequipped for navigation at night. Overnight rests provided superb wildlife sightings and diverse cultural experiences for the passengers.

The performance of their planes, with their limited geographical range and need for refuelling stops, transformed air travel into sightseeing adventures. But overall, trans-Africa flights were significantly faster than five-week voyages by steamer. By the early 1930s, commercial aviation transformed sightseeing as passengers became incidental air tourists.

'The slow, low altitude, daylight flights that stopped frequently for refuelling' combined with 'infant aeronautical technology and air travel economics created tourism of sorts along new routes.'

'Aircraft size, aircraft construction materials, aircraft payloads, engine power and fuel efficiency affected how far aircraft could fly before landing to refuel.'[11]

The airline's timetable listed twenty-two stops between Cairo and Cape Town. In her five-day trip north, Helen's flight stopped at up to twenty different places en route. At each stop, passengers experienced the scenery, people, cultural traditions, spoken language, local climate and local architecture. At isolated inland outposts, Helen observed how the airline managed its ground operations, including its station buildings, crew and facilities for refuelling.

Some stops were unplanned. 'Storms, flooded airfields, hard landings, damaged undercarriages, empty fuel tanks and technical failures delayed service on several occasions. Passengers awaiting replacement aircraft, parts or fuel could spend time sightseeing at airline expense.'[12]

On the northern half of the African air-route, Imperial operated two fleets: the Eastern, or 'Hannibal', class, which carried twenty-four passengers, and the Western, or 'Hercules', class, which carried thirty-four. These were known as the Eight Big Sisters of the Air.

These aircraft were capable of handling dramatic altitude changes. From Cairo to Juba, the desert rises to 1,500 feet. Continuing southward, the plateau climbs to 3,726 feet to Port Bell and Kisumu on Lake Victoria. The 8,000-foot high Rift Valley mountains lead to Nairobi, Kenya.

On the southern half of the route, between Kisumu and Cape Town, Imperial Airways switched their de Havilland 66 Hercules planes with the faster Armstrong Whitworth Atalanta aircraft. The Hercules was a seven-passenger, tri-motor biplane which would fly at altitudes of 5,000 to 6,000 feet over the long, high plateau stretching thousands of miles to the edge of the Karoo in the Cape. The geographical challenges required planes that could adapt to all the changing variables of the journey.

With its four engines, the Atalanta provided Imperial Airways with relative immunity from the forced landings that plagued single-engine aircraft. The Atalanta could carry an increased number of passengers – between nine and seventeen. Interestingly, the Atalanta was designed expressly for Imperial Airways' Africa route. It was built as a monoplane to lower its drag and become more aerodynamically efficient. Constructed with a streamlined fuselage and a clean square-section body with rounded corners to reduce friction, the Atalanta's sleek look was advanced for its time.

Imperial Airways purchased eight Atalantas, and each received an ethereal name rooted in Greek mythology: *Arethusa*, *Andromeda*, *Atalanta*, *Artemis*, *Athena*, *Astraea*, *Amalthea* and *Aurora*.

Before each flight left the ground, crews weighed every gallon of petrol, oil and water, as well as every passenger, luggage and all mail. The weight budget for each passenger was 221 pounds, including luggage. Passengers booked on round-trip flights were informed of any allowances upon check in. For example, if a passenger was under their allowance, one was tasked to remember this for the return flight. It was crucial for flight crew to know their plane's loaded weight for fuel consumption, speed and navigation calculations, given the rudimentary controls and flight limitations.

An important navigational aid was a chain of wireless stations of approximately 3-kilowatt strength along the flight path. Shortwave instruments were established at certain points in an attempt to address gaps in radio service. Wireless services were built in Cape Town, Victoria West, Johannesburg, Bulawayo, Broken Hill, Nairobi, Mbeya, Kampala, Juba, Malakal, Khartoum, Wadi Halfa and Cairo. Later stations were added at Mpika, Dodoma and Moshi. Weather observation stations provided pilots with vital forecasts and information about flying conditions. These stations kept pilots in touch with either of two adjacent stations up to two-thirds of the distance between them.[13]

Passengers looked forward to seeing Africa from a rare vantage point that had never been widely accessible prior to commercial aviation. 'The drama of wildlife in Africa as one sees it enacted from the air was a marvellous experience', a passenger from Pretoria, Mrs James Leisk, described to a reporter.[14]

Journeying on the First Leg from Johannesburg to Khartoum

From Johannesburg, Helen's journey on an Atalanta bore straight north to Harare, formerly Salisbury. Through the mica windows on the right side, the wild, jagged heights of the Drakensberg mountains pierced the rarefied air.

'These tornado-swept heights are feared by the aviator, more than the lonely drivers of ox wagons led by the *voorloopers*', wrote W. Makin.

> It was while flying over these mountains that the plane piloted by Glen Kidston was literally blown to pieces. Bathed in the sunshine, the Drakensberg Mountains look ordinary enough. It is only when one is riding them that the howling wind and dust storms strike terror into the hearts of even the boldest aviators.[15]

Nearing Bulawayo, south of the Zambezi River, Helen's plane flew over a spreading expanse of sand. From the air, a growing desert seemed to be consuming South Africa. The aircraft flew over Lusaka in Zambia and stopped at Kabwe, also known as Broken Hill, for refuelling. Kabwe served as the junction for the Congo and the Radium Mines of Katanga.

The journey between Kabwe and Mpika was bumpy and uncomfortable due to turbulence caused by the intense heat.

'A strange, lost landscape, the veld', observed W. Makin. 'The coffin-shaped kopjes, the dry sandy channels where rivers once flowed, the clumps of thorn bush and the eternal smear of khaki before the eyes. At high noon, the sun has a tropical fierceness; at night it is as cold as the steppes of Siberia.'[16]

At Mpika, the airstrip was known to be haunted by lions and according to W. Makin, in the evenings the locals signalled approaching planes with landing flares. 'In the darkness, the roaring of lions is terrifying. They (the locals) tremble with fright so much that they rattle the buckets containing the landing flares.'

The powerful almost stupefying heat on the ground airstrips contrasted with the intense cold at 10,000 feet. Pilots had to contend with the effects of fluctuating temperatures on aircraft.

Passengers were treated to rare close-up views of herds of wild animals when pilots were able to bring their planes down safely to lower altitudes. Herds of elephants, sometimes up to 500 in number, could be observed, along with hippopotami, antelopes, giraffes and zebras. Seeing multitudes of wildlife from the air imparted a magical experience for passengers.

From northern Zimbabwe (formerly Rhodesia) to Lake Victoria, the plane flew over dense forests, an area described as 'a difficult piece of country'. Another stop en route was Dodoma, where cavalcades of lions were not unknown on the airfield.

East of Victoria Lake lay the vast sun-drenched Serengeti plains where hundreds of wildlife roamed. Helen's flight may have stopped for refuelling at Moshi, close to Mount Kilimanjaro with its eternal snow draping its peak. As the plane headed towards Nairobi on its high plateau, the captain weaved the plane to enable passengers to see the moving wildlife below. The passengers would have gazed upon rhinos, warthogs, tawny lions, and herds of eland, hartebeest, capering wildebeest and leaping impalas.

Grace Crile, a passenger who flew the same route as Helen in 1935, observed:

> We flew so low and could see so clearly that it seemed as if we could hear not only the patterings of the hoofs but the excited panting of hundreds of antelopes as they leaped from under our plane and scattered to both sides of us as we winged our way.[17]

Imperial's planes crossing Africa in the 1930s cruised at very low altitudes, not more than 10,000 feet high. Planes flew with limited fuel reserves and could not afford to expend fuel on climbing. 'Another reason for low flying was that prominent ground features and markings (hills, rivers, towns, railways) were crucial for navigation before the advent of navigation charts and radio beacons.'[18]

Helen's flight sailed over the high plateau of the velvety teal escarpment before reaching Nairobi in Kenya, where they overnighted. The accommodation provided comforts of England with African touches, such as mosquito netting over the beds and local produce served in traditional English meals.

Nairobi's high altitude of 5,889 feet provided an insight into how planes, weather and geography intersected at elevation. The East African Plateau loomed in the north with Mount Kenya piercing the sky at 17,057 feet and Mount Kilimanjaro in the south rearing to 19,341 feet. On the airfield, graceful Grant's and Thomson's gazelles, zebras and hartebeests were grazing peacefully.

Leaving the city at daybreak, Helen and her passengers flew over rose-rimmed lakes. Hundreds of thousands of Lesser and Greater flamingos were feeding in the semi-saline and saline lakes of the Great Rift valley. The whirring mass of flamingos rushing aloft was an unforgettable sight from aloft.

Helen's flight skipped along Kavirondo Bay and across the tip of the northeastern shore of Lake Victoria in the shimmering haze to reach Kisumu. Lying on the equator, Kisumu's port in the heart of Africa at 3,759 feet high served both a shipping and an aviation industry. In this Central African airport, passengers changed planes as it was the terminus for Imperial's northern Cairo section and its southern or Cape section. Kisumu also served as a key station for the Uganda railway to Nairobi and Mombasa.

From Kisumu, her flight veered west to Entebbe over the northern end of Lake Victoria. Lake Victoria Nyanza, the second largest lake in the world, evoked in passengers the same terrifying feeling of flying over a lost sea. Grace Crile recorded how, on the edge of this inland sea, 'one glimpsed green swamps with trees rotting and tumbling into the slime. Papyrus grass and every form of swamp vegetation grappled in a green inferno. The sudden slither of crocodiles as they plunged into the lapping lake water.'[19]

Above Jinja, passengers observed the cascading water from Victoria Nyanza careening over Ripon Falls. The Victoria or White Nile begins here, winding northwards to the Nile's source at Lake Albert.

Helen's plane banked and came round the chartreuse coast where the well-laid out town of Entebbe slipped beneath its wings. North of Entebbe, the airliner passed a small monoplane, its wings flashing silver, slowly sinking into a marsh. It reposed like a giant dragonfly, sprawled across the glistening water.

On the next leg, Helen's plane flew 350 miles north above the White Nile, named for the light grey sediments from its equatorial source at Lake Victoria, and landed to refuel in Juba. Grace Crile recalled:

> Over the fertile fields of Uganda, we soared, over dense forests and waving swamps filled with hippos. We crossed, then re-crossed, the Victoria Nile, flying over Masindi Port and picking up the White Nile near Nimule. Birds of every description and hue rose as we passed. Just before swooping into Juba, we passed over Rejaf, which is about 3,000 miles from the mouth of the Nile. At Juba, the swamp ended, and the Nile boats started their downward trek to the great Delta.

Leaving Juba, the five-hour and twenty-five minute flight to Malakal crossed the vast, deadly wetlands known as 'The Sudd'. Here the floating vegetation almost obliterates the channel of the Nile.

> Hundreds of white egrets were floating on the pools of water, and from the air the white water lilies looked like pearls embosomed on the green leaves. We soon reached the Nile, a level stream winding in and out through the plain, like a great serpent, its banks so nearly spilling over. Across it, over and over, we flew, the marabou storks and herons whirling in circles under our wings until we came to the high grass, the swamp.
>
> Higher and higher we flew, undoubtedly, to avoid the bumpy hot-air currents, until, with a swoop, we crossed the chocolate-coloured Nile, right over the native fishermen, then rolled along on the riverbank into Malakal.[20]

Between Malakal and Kosti, the flight lasted three hours and thirty minutes, and passengers could observe the famous Bor herd of between 300 and 400 elephants. Between Kosti and Khartoum, the journey was two hours and twenty minutes. In contrast, a paddle steamer took twelve days to travel from Khartoum to Juba.

On the final stages of the flight to Khartoum, the aircraft bumped its way up to 7,000 feet or more with the brown, unlimited plain stretching in all directions. 'Like an eagle in its flight, a solitary wanderer we seemed, in this apparent emptiness of space. As the hot sun poured down its rays, the world became hazy and uncertain in the shimmering and iridescent sunlight of a tropical noon', noted Grace Crile.[21]

The plane descended into Khartoum, where the Blue Nile, catching the sun at the right angle showed its bluish hue, flowed into the White Nile. During the layover in Khartoum, passengers stretched their legs along the promenade by the Nile.

Experiencing the Second Leg from Khartoum to Cairo

The Sudanese capital of Khartoum flourishes where the White and Blue Nile rivers meld together. The Blue Nile originates in the highlands of Eritrea and Ethiopia where sediments give it its bright blue colour. As it passes through Sudan, it picks up darker sediment that deepens the hue of the Blue Nile.

Very early the next morning, Helen and her fellow travellers departed from their comfortable quarters overlooking the wide-flowing Nile. Taking off before dawn and soaring into the desert sky, passengers watched the pale silvery night fade away. The vast Nubian desert glistened in the far east. Grace Crile again:

> Slowly the world came into colour and being in the rising sun; the big red sun, like a ball of fire out of the sea, reached higher and higher, until even the last strands of moonlight turned to rose in the morning's glow.
>
> …
>
> Early flying is cool and smooth. Midday flying is rough and bumpy. In the early dawn, the light is clear and restful. At midday, the whole atmosphere twinkles: it is even difficult to see steadily through one's field glasses.[22]

From the air, the ribbon of the Nile could be seen, winding like a water snake through the desert sand. South of Kareima, the plane flew over the fourth cataract of the Nile. Nearing Wadi Halfa, the Nile River valley gradually appeared jade green and fertile with small fields under cultivation. 'The river was dotted with islands, and near the banks we could see patient camels turning the age-old water wheels.'

After a refuelling and breakfast stop in Wadi Halfa, the passengers had barely settled into their seats when the rock-hewn temples of Abu Simbel loomed into view. 'It seemed as if every ray of the great Egyptian sun illuminated the imperturbable countenances of those colossal images of Rameses II.'

When Helen's aircraft reached the irrigation works, the landscape changed dramatically. The Aswan Low Dam had been constructed three decades earlier at the first cataract of the Nile. This stonework dam stored floodwater in Lake Nasser behind it and controlled the dry season flows.

Downriver of the dam, the passengers could discern a sharp dividing line between the wheat fields, swirling cotton fields and tawny sand. The cultivated fields extended outwards for at least a mile on either side of the river before ending abruptly.

The Temple of Isis, originally built on Philae Island just downstream of the Aswan low dam and Lake Nasser, stood by the Nile. From the air, it was noticeable how the Temple stood like a sentry, surrounded by water. Airliners flew at an altitude of 2,000 feet and at a speed of 120 miles per hour which afforded clear views of ancient structures. Viewing Luxor at close range, passengers could discern the gradient colours on the pillars of the mighty old Karnak. The Karnak Temple Complex could be seen on the east bank amid the black basaltic hills and the Valley of Kings on the west bank.

At Assiut, the plane coasted over the Great Barrage, another flood-control infrastructure on the Nile.

Historian Gordon Pirie in *Incidental Tourism: British Imperial Air Travel in the 1930s*, described 'the notion of flying as touring through history'.

As an example, he wrote of how a week's journey to Zimbabwe (formerly Rhodesia) 'traced the history of civilization via Rome, Greece, Crete and Egypt to the spot where humans may have first emerged.'[23]

On the final 250 miles along the Nile to Cairo, Helen and her companions viewed the temples at Thebes and Horus, the Colossi of Memnon, and the Pyramids of Giza. In Cairo, the white mosques with their walled enclosures and graceful minarets glistened as her plane descended towards Heliopolis airport.

In Cairo, she bid adieu to her fellow passengers and travelled to Port Said where she boarded the RMS *Durham Castle*, a Union-Castle mail steamer. She arrived in London on 8 December 1935 and immediately started to earn her commercial 'B' licence.

Helen's journey along Eastern Africa opened her eyes to the sheer scale and size of the continent. Through the passenger mica windows, she observed its vast sunbaked plains, desolate mountains, and life-giving rivers. The aircraft, soaring at lower altitudes and at slower velocity, offered closeups of Africa's myriad wildlife. The reduced speeds and low altitude of airliners enabled pilots to show passengers the natural and built environments being revealed to them as they flew onwards.

On this flight, Helen witnessed the power of commercial aviation. She observed how pilots sparked awe and curiosity in their passengers by enabling clear views of the landscape and ancient sites, as well as local flora and fauna. Sightseeing became an integral part of the flight itself.

The thrill of flying, Helen discovered, was enhanced by the pilot's expertise and knowledge of the land, wildlife and local cultures.

Most importantly, this flight reaffirmed how commercial aviation would reshape travel and tourism worldwide in the decades to come. Her experience as a passenger on this wondrous crossing of a magnificent country kindled an unquenchable fire to become an airline pilot. She wanted to be among the vanguard.

Bearing Witness to Cutting-Edge Innovation

In the 'B' licence program at Hatfield airfield, Helen began training on de Havilland aircraft. Commercial study included ground training in aeronautics, navigation, and meteorology, among other subjects.

'The pilot who wants a "B" licence must swot up on her mathematics, for she is required to pass a strict navigation test, must answer questions in meteorology and give technical details about plane engines', noted *Evening Despatch* reporter Yvonne Gordon.[24] In addition, the Air Ministry of Great Britain required each aspiring commercial pilot to have at least 100 hours of solo flying experience.

Pursuing a career in commercial aviation was not an easy path for women in the mid-1930s, particularly as the commercial industry accepted few women flyers. Helen's sights were set on earning a position in the left seat in the cockpit of a commercial airliner.

On 12 February 1936, as Helen was building her flying hours, the Air Service Training school announced that 180 pilots would be trained for Imperial Airways over the next 3 years. The training program at its Hamble facilities, near Southampton, was aimed towards the ongoing substitution of flying boats for landplanes on most sections of the main Empire air routes. The program was designed to equip successful pilots with a commercial pilot's licence, a second-class navigator's licence, and the appropriate ground engineer's licence. The pupils would train on thirty-seven aircraft, including flying boats.

The school had predicted that the growth of air services in the following two years would create a demand for commercial pilots. This served as an additional impetus and validation for Helen to pursue her 'B' licence. Her path going forward was clear with the program she had chosen at Hatfield, and the aviation jobs she had lined up in South Africa.

About 20 miles from London, Hatfield airfield had become the home of the de Havilland manufacturing plant and the London Aeroplane Club. Hatfield inadvertently became a centre of aerospace innovation and Helen witnessed the rapid, cutting-edge developments in aviation.

The de Havilland factory began production of the de Havilland 85 Leopard Moth and the DH 82 Tiger Moths along with their successful DH 84 Dragons and DH 89 Dragon Rapides. The latter two were being sold to national and international airline operators. The Leopard Moth was similar to the Puss Moth in physical look and feel, but the Leopard was constructed entirely of wood. The Puss Moth had a metal frame. Both aircraft could carry two passengers behind the pilot. In the Leopard Moth, the passengers sat side-by-side, but in the Puss Moth the passengers sat slightly staggered behind the pilot. The Leopard Moth cruised at speeds of between 155 to 120 mph, while the Puss flew at 100 to 110 mph.

Elementary Flying Training Schools were established around England, and the Tiger Moth became the Empire's standard trainer.

The two-seater biplane with a 130-hp Gipsy motor included a hooded rear cockpit for blind flying instruction. Departing from Hatfield, bright yellow Tiger Moths dotted the skies above cities, towns and country as they were delivered to civil schools around the country.

The training syllabus at No. 1 Elementary Flying Training School at Hatfield included aerobatics, advanced navigation, instrument flying and aerial photography. The two-month program included five hours of blind flying instruction and a total of fifty-five hours of flying time logged by each student. An additional forty-five hours were needed to meet the minimum number of hours required by the Air Ministry.

Mastering the Art of Flying Blind

The blind flying test was one of the most important tests that an individual who dreams of becoming a first class pilot was required to undergo. The blind flying component was a very exacting test. It required the pilot to 'demonstrate his ability to steer a straight course and execute ordinary manoeuvres without an exterior view and guided solely by blind flying instruments'.[25]

In this test, the pilot was enclosed in a hood in the cockpit and focused on the instruments to control the plane. Using a compass and watch alongside a map, flight plan and instruments, a pilot learned to fly an aircraft in blind conditions.

'The natural conditions which make instrument flying essential are those of cloud or mist, when neither the ground nor sky are visible at the height at which the airplane is flying. A thorough knowledge of the art will give a pilot additional confidence under all conditions as well as aiding him to check his flying and keep his course accurately. This is particularly valuable at night.'

A blind-flying instrument on board was an essential safety feature. It became invaluable when pilots found themselves flying in adverse weather.

'If you are very unlucky, you might fly without warning into heavy rain, very thick weather or even into snow if you are flying in the winter', observed a columnist. 'You may decide to turn back, to carry on with the knowledge that the trouble is purely local, or to climb up through it in the hope that a gap will appear on the horizon.'

'Practically every club and school in the country now runs a standard instrument-flying course. I have learnt to believe implicitly in the instruments – and that is ninety per cent of the battle. There must be few feelings of sheer triumph equal to that experienced by a pupil who, after making a tedious triangular flight, lifts up the hood and sees the home aerodrome within easy gliding distance.'[26]

'The triple check of compass, map and watch can relieve one's mind to no small extent when the weather is closing in or darkness falling a little earlier than was originally expected.'[27]

Gaining a Commercial 'B' Licence

After earning 100 hours of solo flying experience, Helen undertook her commercial pilot's examination which included a 3-hour solo flight and a practical test in blind flying. Prior to undertaking her flying tests, she passed her medical assessment and a technical examination. To qualify for her 'B' licence, she needed to pass a series of practical flying tests, 'including several cross-country flights, each of 200 miles, a flight for one hour at a height of not less than 6,500 feet, and a night flight of thirty minutes duration.'

Helen earned her 'B' licence in April 1936. This qualified her to fly commercially and generate revenue while studying for her instructor's rating. The days were becoming longer and the evenings lighter, which boosted flying opportunities.

W.A Magill reported that 'having sold the Falcon [Helen] bought another ship, a Spartan, for the joy ride trade, operating near Portsmouth for several months. By this time, her flying time had reached credible proportions.' She set up her business in a farmer's field and laughed as she recalled:

> I almost put myself out of business before I began. Hoping to entice the locals to take a flight, I planned to do a few flips around town to attract their attention. When the engine did not start on the first few swings of the propeller, I advanced the throttle. It caught on the next swing and as I started to climb in, the darn thing began to move. I had forgotten to chock it!

Shouting for help, which never materialised although an interested audience soon gathered, Helen tore after the plane. 'Fortunately, it did not pick up enough speed to take off, but it did nose over and break the prop … I don't think I impressed anyone that day.'[28]

Meanwhile, Magill noted that 'it was during this period that Miss Harrison experienced her first forced landing, due to a broken cylinder. She landed without mishap on a military field.'

In the early stages of their flying careers, pilots were always on the lookout for suitable landing places in the event of having to make a forced landing. As aircraft design evolved and undercarriage construction improved, forced landings were gradually becoming a thing of the past.

Women Pilots Creating Record-Setting Flights

Women pilots continued creating record-setting flights. Kenyan pilot Beryl Markham, a mother of a 7-year-old son, launched *The Messenger* on 4 September 1936 from the Royal Air Force airfield in Abingdon, England. Battling rain and stormy skies, she soared across Ireland towards North America.

Over the grey Atlantic, she flew her Percival Vega Gull, Kenyan registration VP-KCC, onwards to New York City. The de Havilland Gipsy 6 I engine maintained a cruising speed of 170 mph, but in the headwinds she estimated her speed at 90 mph. Her turquoise, blue and silver plane mirrored the undulating surface of the ocean:

> At twenty-five minutes to eleven (pm), my motor coughs and dies, and the Gull is powerless above the sea. I realise the heavy drone of the plane has been, until this moment, complete and comforting silence. It is the actual silence following the last splutter of the engine that stuns me.
>
> I can't feel any fear; I can't feel anything. I can only observe with a kind of stupid disinterest that my hands are violently active and know that, while they move, I am being hypnotised by the needle of my altimeter. If it is night and you are sitting in an airplane with a stalled motor and there are two thousand feet between you and the sea, nothing can be more reasonable than the impulse to pull back your stick in the hope of adding to that two thousand.
>
> I sit there and watch my hands push forward on the stick and feel the Gull respond and begin its dive to the sea. At three hundred feet the motor is still dead, and I am conscious that the needle of my altimeter seems to whirl like the spoke of a spindle winding up the remaining distance between the plane and the water. I do not know how close to the waves I am, when the motor explodes to life again. But the sound is almost meaningless. I see my hand easing back on the stick, and I feel the Gull climb up into the storm, and I see the altimeter whirl like a spindle again, paying out the distance between myself and the sea.
>
> I ought to thank God – and I do, though indirectly. I thank Geoffrey de Havilland who designed the indomitable Gipsy, and who, after all, must be designed by God in the first place.[29]

The relentless winds meant that her fuel consumption rate was increasing, and fuel reserves were difficult to calculate. On 5 September, her Percival

Vega Gull landed, ignominiously, nose down in a bog at Baleine Cove on Cape Breton, Nova Scotia.

She landed far short of her intended destination of New York, 750 miles to be exact. Receiving a cut to her forehead and scrapes to her hands, Beryl Markham had landed in North America and survived. Her journey became the first solo flight across the Atlantic, from east to west, by a woman. Her lonely flight was completed in twenty-one hours and twenty-five minutes.

Becoming England's Second Woman Instructor in England

Helen earned her commercial pilot's licence at a time when there were more than thirty different aircraft active in British aviation. These varied from the forty- to forty-two-seater planes used by Imperial Airways on the Empire routes, to the three-seaters best suited for charter and taxi work.

An aviation reporter observed that the rapid development of aviation created 'vacancies in all branches covering commercial pilots and instructors, engineers, wireless operators, navigators, draftsmen, etc.' Salaries ranged from £250 to £800 a year for engineers, and £450 to £1,400 a year for instructors and commercial pilots.[30]

As she was hunting for flying jobs, she found that no one wanted to hire a woman. After much searching, she found an employer who was willing to hire her to fly passengers if she provided her own aircraft. Helen's three-seater Spartan biplane fit the bill. Ferrying passengers granted her the hours needed to qualify for her instructor's rating.[31]

In October 1936, Helen earned her instructor's certificate, along with her multi-engine and instrument rating. She was qualified to instruct in both night and instrument flying.

'Upon qualifying, (Helen) became the second woman instructor in England at the time', reporter W.A. Magill announced.[32]

Gabrielle Patterson of Castle Donington had qualified earlier in May 1936. At Walsall aerodrome, she began teaching as an instructor at the South Staffordshire Aero Club.

As England's first female flying instructor, Gabrielle took a practical approach to teaching flying. 'The air instructor has, of course, to make it perfectly clear from the outset that he, or she, is boss and must instil a suitable kind of respect into the student – having done which, all usually goes well.'[33]

Helen 'pointed out that there were no women pilots on the main commercial airlines in Great Britain, but she considered that there were distinct opportunities for women in aviation overseas'.[34]

Helen sold her three-seater Spartan and launched her aviation career. On 27 November 1936, she bid adieu to British shores at Southampton and stepped on board the RMMV *Athlone Castle*, bound for Natal in South Africa. The passenger manifest listed her as 'Miss Harrison, aged 26, aviatrix.' She had proudly listed her profession. The month-long voyage along the Atlantic coasts of Europe and Africa brought Helen home to her family in time for a sunny Cape Town Christmas.

Part Two

Chapter 5

Finding Freedom to Fly in South Africa

> Initially, there was that indescribable, glorious feeling of freedom: of having successfully defied the laws of nature and 'slipped the surly bonds of earth'. What had so often in the past formed a living part of my dreams was actually happening – this time in reality. I was above the earth, in the air, free as a bird!
>
> First there was the bumping of the wheels on the hard veld, lessening as the machine gathered speed and gradually lifted; the strong wind against my goggle less face, making my eyes stream; then the earth falling away, like watching a scene drop, and the sharp unfolding of the landscape viewed from a new angle as though seen through the wrong end of a telescope; the bush country, trees, out hangar, the white road and tramline to Kimberley.[1]
>
> Major General K.R. van der Spuy

At its start in 1920, the South African Air Force had been dependent on private companies, flying schools and South African Airways to provide a reserve of pilots as the growth of civil aviation took off.

Major General Kenneth van der Spuy noted that the First World War had proved conclusively that an army or navy without air power was about as useful as a blind tiger: 'It had taken a war, and millions of lives to convert the generals and admirals to this truth.'[2]

In the early years, civilian and military aviation was intertwined in South Africa. Light aircraft such as the Gipsy Moth became a catalyst, inspiring interest in civilian flying and small clubs, and opening the skies for air mail service.

The hard-scrabble mining town of Kimberley became the site of the first flying school in South Africa. It was chosen for its flat terrain and infrequent winds of moderate velocity. The conditions at Kimberley, in a barren area of South Africa, proved to be a testing ground for future aviation and the development of airfields. The runway consisted of a large circular track cleared from the scrub and with a diameter of about a mile. The surface was 100 feet wide. On this circular track, pilots could choose which direction to land, nose into the wind, no matter which direction the wind was blowing.

The fauna of the area included *dubbeldorintjies*, devil's thorns with three prongs, which grew rampantly. To prevent tires from being punctured, the rubber wheels were covered with thick leather.

The new air force was given a huge boost when Great Britain delivered a most munificent gift, worth millions of pounds. The UK government offered the four self-governing dominions – South Africa, Canada, New Zealand and Australia – an imperial gift of aircraft and equipment to establish their own air forces. South African Prime Minister Jan Smuts, from his past military experience, realised that 'control of the air' was just as important as 'command of the high seas'.

Not only was the South African Air Force given a hundred aircraft complete with engines and spare engines, it was also supplied with workshops, motor cars, motorcycles and trailers; hangars for housing aircraft and stores; wireless and photographic equipment for two squadrons; tools to completely equip its air force mechanics; and enough spares to run its operations for a year. As well, the air force received complete workshop materials to complete any type of engine, aircraft and transport repairs and overhauls.

'Had it not been for such a gift, our start and growth would indeed have been slow and difficult', recalled Major General van der Spuy.[3]

Major General van der Spuy and Pierre van Ryneveld, two exceptional South African officers, championed the successful establishment of the air force. Major General van der Spuy served in the German Southwest African campaign and then in the East African campaign during the First World War. In 1918, he formed and commanded an air arm to operate with the British, French and White Russian forces in the Russian north, based at Archangel. A year later, his Sopwith Camel aircraft crash landed and he was captured by Bolshevik troops and imprisoned until 1920.

The South African Air Force, as an arm of the Union Defence Force, came into being in 1920. Robert Heights became South Africa's military centre, 5 miles outside the capital city of Pretoria. Its military pilots continued to train aloft and test out new types of aircraft. They went on cross-country flights, early morning hedgehopping, cloud flying and 'wool mountaineering', chasing up and down the steep valleys formed by towering masses of cumulus clouds.[4]

The post-First World War depression, as well as the world depression between 1929 and 1934, slowed the development of the South African Air Force. The early 1930s saw the emergence of the small aircraft industry in South Africa, beginning with the local production of thirty licence-built Westland Wapiti aircraft in April 1931. After the South African economy recovered in 1934, the air force expanded to seven squadrons and new bases. Flight schools were established at Waterkloof, outside Pretoria, Bloemfontein, Durban, and Youngsfield near Cape Town. In that year, the air force acquired three de Havilland 66 Hercules transport planes, a single Gloster A.S.31 survey aircraft and seven Hawker Furies.

Giving Wings to a New 1,000-Pilot Training Plan

While Helen was en route to South Africa by steamer, details of a new 1,000-pilot training scheme in South Africa were unveiled.

Earlier in 1935, amid Italy's invasion of Ethiopia, the South African Minister of Defence Oswald Pirow announced exciting expansion plans for South Africa's military. This included a scheme to train 1,000 air force reservist pilots by 1942 through the aegis of approved civilian flying clubs and training schools. They would be trained at government expense on the understanding that they would form part of the special reserves.

Minister Pirow inaugurated a five-year plan to train young men to strengthen the air force. By the end of 1936, letters had been sent to ten flying clubs and companies across three provinces inviting them to join the scheme. The *Rand Daily Mail* reported that:

> It was explained by Defence Headquarters, that the personnel to undergo training will be drawn from universities and other walks of civilian life, and that all selected applicants will be required to enrol in Air Training Squadrons of the Active Citizen Force. After passing as pilots, they will be required to serve in the Special Reserve of the South African Air Force for a specified period.

In late 1936, the program was modified to provide training for 630 university students and 450 civilian and railway employees. It was believed that university students had more time for training than employees. Students would be trained over a 21-month period, accruing 110 flying hours. Civilian trainees would receive instruction over a period of 3 years and 3 months, and earn 215 flying hours. The training program began in 1937 with 125 pupil pilots. By the end of 1941, 1,000 pilots would have earned their wings.

The beneficiaries of the state-subsidised training plan were the civilian flying schools and flying clubs. Aviation was sufficiently new in South Africa, and the number of aircraft so small that as a result the industry enjoyed a certain allure. A few clubs ceased to operate during the Depression, but the two which survived on the Reef had a combined membership of 560, of whom only a few were pilots. The social status of flying and the freedom of the skies played a role in attracting trainees.[5]

Various civil light plane clubs and schools provided initial flying and other ground training. 'Other intensive training courses were held from time to time at the South African Air Force Central Flying School at Roberts Heights near Pretoria', wrote the *Rand Daily Mail*. It was initially planned that branches of the Central Flying School would be established at Cape Town, Durban and Bloemfontein and would cater for the intensive training of pupil pilots drawn from the surrounding districts.

Pupils would be provided with free rations and pay, along with a messing allowance, uniforms and access to free flying equipment. According to the *Rand Daily Mail*:

> During the first three months of a pupil pilot's service, he will be required to put in fifty hours' flying, consisting of approximately twenty-five hours dual instruction and twenty-five hours sole flying, together with fifty-four hours of ground instruction. Immediately thereafter, he will attend a month's course of intensive training at the Central Flying School.[6]

Students under the age of 25 from universities and colleges were eligible for training. The government proposed to pay a subsidy to the flying clubs for each man trained by them. The cost was estimated to be between £4 and £5 per flying hour for each man. Civil flying clubs were expected to get a big boost from this proposal. The scheme would provide stability and a source of revenue to maintain a roster of instructors and training aircraft.

Six months after the announcement of the scheme, the Department of Defence had received 2,010 applications. All applicants indicated they could complete the training within twenty-two months. Although not stated explicitly, the outline of the scheme implied that it would be limited to 'white male applicants'. Pupil trainees were predominately English-speaking. Importantly, 'there was still no specific exclusion based on gender. It was presumably being taken as a given that women simply did not fly for the Air Force.'[7]

Applicants were required to volunteer for four years or for the duration of hostilities, whichever would become the shorter. They were required to be medically fit for flying duties and able to satisfy a selection board of their suitability for an appointment.

The 1,000-pilot scheme began in April 1937 and consisted of 13 flights which were divided into subsets of 4 squadrons across the country, each being operated by a civilian company. It also spurred the creation of South African Air Force training schools in the four provinces of Cape Province, the Orange Free State, the Transvaal and Natal. This spectacular scheme was referred to as the Pupil Pilot Training Scheme.

The African Air Transport originally had training schools in three cities: Cape Town, Port Elizabeth and Kimberley. Due to the high winds present at Port Elizabeth, this school was moved to Grahamstown. Kimberley's school was moved to Bloemfontein. The government settled on an hourly rate of £4 7s 6d for the coastal areas, and £4 15s for the inland areas. The higher rate for the inland areas was set due to the longer time it took pilots to gain altitude during training flights in the rarefied high veld air of South Africa's interior.

Helen's arrival in Cape Town in early 1937 was fortuitous as South African airmindedness was growing. She started instructing civilian pilots with Air Taxi Co. Ltd in January. During her four-month contract, she also trained South African Air Force reserve pupil pilots and quickly earned a reputation as a hard-working instructor. She also taught at the Cape Town Flying Club.

Helen had arrived at the right time as the Pretoria Flying Club was seeking an instructor to train reserve pilots for the South African Air Force. Helen possessed all the desired qualifications, including instructor, multi-engine and instrument ratings, and the latest instructor's 'patter'. The club hired her on the spot as she was 'too good a bargain to ignore'.

'Although she was advised that as a woman, she would not have a chance for a position as instructor, Miss Harrison applied for such duty and was taken on.'[8]

Helen recalled, 'All the instructors wanted to fly with me before taking their check rides. Even the chief flying instructor flew with me.

He wasn't too pleased when I failed him though – he attempted to turn back on a simulated engine failure on take-off.'[9]

To Helen's surprise, the air force check pilot allowed Helen to take the military instructor check ride.

'I was amazed that he would test me', she recalled, 'and even more amazed when he told me I could take the refresher course at the Air Force in Pretoria and be checked out as one of the civilian instructors for the Air Force.'[10]

The South African Air Force offered her an instructor's refresher course on military aircraft at the Roberts Heights military base in Pretoria. The newly acquired Hawker Harts, equipped with dual controls, had been used as advanced trainers by the Royal Air Force. Now the South African Air Force followed suit. During her training, she welcomed an acrobatic course on the two-seater Hawker Hart fighter planes. Each Hawker Hart was furnished with a Rolls-Royce Kestrel twelve-cylinder engine. With two strong men turning the prop, it fired up in a fury of smoke and noise, and its take-off was lively.

After training at Robert Heights, Helen became the first woman pilot in South Africa to fly military aircraft. She qualified for a South African commercial pilot's certificate and earned her instructor and instrument ratings for South Africa.

Although her friends were unsure of her chances of being hired in one of the instructor positions, she was undeterred. After demonstrating her flying abilities to the military brass, she was awarded a position to train reserve pilot candidates in the flying and ground school at Robert Heights. In her new role, she notched another first: she became the first woman military instructor in South Africa.

'Her job then was to train civilians in actual flying, ground school and dual instruction. The government inspectors on their rounds covered her work and it was considered satisfactory.'[11]

'I was the only woman on the base and the first woman in the British Empire to fly and instruct on military aircraft', she said.[12]

She also taught pilots on Moths, a Ryan 'ST', Bücker Bü 131 Jungmanns, and Bücker Bü 133 Jungmeisters, among other training planes.

Notably, she mastered a Hawker Fury among other types. The South African government had purchased seven Furies which became the first single-seater fighters for the air force. Equipped with a Rolls-Royce Kestrel IIS piston engine, the biplane raced at a speed of 223 mph.

In Pretoria, she was also employed by the Pretoria Flying Club as an assistant instructor, and she also filled in as a charter pilot for Air Taxi Limited. 'She was quite a character and got along well with everybody', recalled K. Weinstein, an Air Taxi pilot.[13]

The British media quickly caught on to the significance of her achievements in South Africa: 'A woman – the first to do so in South Africa – has joined the small band of flying instructors at Cape Town', reported a Yorkshire newspaper.[14]

In an article in the *Huddersfield Daily Examiner* headlined 'Her Imperial Airway', a Reuters reporter introduced her:

> She is Miss Helen Harrison, a Canadian girl, who received her education in England. Miss Harrison holds a commercial 'B' licence endorsed for instructing and blind flying. She has been engaged by the African Air Transport.
>
> 'I had some trips to begin with and liked them,' the tall, fair, pretty airwoman explained to Reuters in a special interview. 'Then I wanted to fly myself. That was three and a half years ago. I took the course, went solo after six and three-quarter hours, and eventually got my "A" licence. Then I trained at Hatfield as a commercial pilot.'[15]

In South Africa, Helen received instruction work in civil aviation and 'was engaged in such a capacity at Grahamstown, Johannesburg and eventually her best job at Pretoria, the capital of the Union'.

'A few days each week, she flew into the Orange Free State from Johannesburg, a distance of about 150 miles, to conduct a flying school. … Helen was now a regular flying school marm.'[16]

Flying conditions in South Africa were different in many ways, noted writer Sally Knapp. 'In addition to the lack of extensive weather reporting agencies, radio service, etc., the weather conditions were rather variable, and much trouble was experienced with headwinds. In addition, the ground presented problems for forced landings.'

Living and flying in South Africa, pilots heard the stories of flights over the rugged mountains gone awry.

Several years earlier, a Puss Moth was dragged up into violent air turbulence over a jagged escarpment of the Free State-Natal border. Lieutenant Commander Glen Kidston, a wealthy British sportsman, and Captain T.A. Gladstone, a pioneer of the Empire Flying Services, were on a flight from Johannesburg to Pietermaritz. Their aircraft broke under the strain over the Tandjiesberg mountains. The airmen were hurled to an untimely death in the deep valleys of the Drakensberg foothills.

This tragic accident was followed several months later by a fatal air mail disaster in the jumbled mountains only 30 miles from Cape Town. A Puss Moth piloted by Captain William Frost Davenport encountered a heavy gale over Sir Lowry's Pass mountains.

'Plunging through the storm, Captain Davenport held his buffeted machine into the gale. Suddenly, without warning, the port wing collapsed under the pressure of a severe down draft. Hurtling out of the control, the Puss Moth crashed to destruction on the rocky mountain slopes.'[17]

Helen was all too aware of the risks when flying into Cape Town during a howling southeaster and having one's machine blown into the sea off Milnerton beach in the Cape.

It was sobering to hear of past tragedies. These terrible accidents, in the teeth of jagged ramparts, served to keep pilots humble and keenly aware of their environments and weather conditions as they flew into the high interior of South Africa.

However, cross country flights were continued by pilots infused with enthusiasm and absolute confidence. 'Thus were the records broken and rebroken as the gallant air adventurers spun the sky trails over South Africa.'[18]

Absorbing the Shock Waves over Disappearance of Flyers

In May 1937, the small flying community in South Africa learned that the Duchess of Bedford had soared aloft on a solo flight over southern England and had not been seen since.

The 71-year-old flying Duchess left Woburn in Bedfordshire on 22 March. She was in her usual cheerful spirits and in excellent health. On a bright sunny afternoon at 3.30 pm she had clambered into her green Moth for a quick spin. Her course was set in the direction of Cambridge, a short distance away. She was on a flight path that would have taken only three-quarters of an hour as she did not propose to land anywhere. Her aircraft had fuel for only a few hours. It carried no lights.

Unbeknownst to many, a blinding snowstorm erupted over her flight path between 4 and 5 pm.

Flying came late into the life of the duchess. At the age of 60, she took her first flight from Croydon to Woburn and discovered it to be 'most exhilarating of all sports'. Flying offered her a new freedom and vocation to pursue as she feared her deafness from typhoid fever earlier in her life would cut her off from her hospital work.

The duchess was born Mary du Caurroy Tribe, the second daughter of the Ven. Archdeacon Tribe. After completing her college education at Cheltenham Ladies' College in Zurich, she joined her parents in Lahore (in India at the time) where her father's ministry had been established. Here she was affected by typhoid fever, an illness which she attributed to the deafness that afflicted her later in life. She met her husband, Lord Herbrand Russell in Simla, India, and they married at Barrackpore, India, on 31 January 1888. His dukedom included Woburn Abbey. In London, the family owned Russell Square, Bedford Square, a large part of Bloomsbury and the whole of Covent Gardens.

Not a person to sit still, she built a cottage hospital in 1898 at Woburn. Mary worked in every department and subsequently became a radiologist in charge of X-rays. The Woburn hospital was converted into one of twelve military orthopeadic hospitals for the aftercare of soldiers wounded in the First World War.

Living life to the full, she spent holidays birdwatching in the Scottish Hebridean Islands and at Seahouses in Northumberland.[19]

When she took her final flight, the Duchess had 199 hours of solo flying under her belt. She felt the urgency to reach 200 hours as she feared her pilot's licence would not be renewed due to her hearing loss. Two pieces of an aircraft that washed up in the Yarmouth River were identified as parts of her plane. Her body was never recovered.

Several months later, shockwaves reverberated around the world with the news that American aviator Amelia Earhart and navigator Fred Noonan had disappeared over the Pacific Ocean en route to Howland Island in the Pacific Ocean. The date of 2 July 1937 would remain forever etched in the minds of the aviation community.

In her flying career, Amelia became the first woman to fly solo eastward across the Atlantic when she flew in 1932 from Harbour Grace, Newfoundland, and alighted in Culmore, Londonderry, Ireland. Her trans-Atlantic flight took fourteen hours and fifty-six minutes.

On 17 March 1937, Amelia Earhart and Fred Noonan took off from Oakland, California, on an attempt to circumnavigate the world. Reaching Miami on the US east coast, they flew their Lockheed Electra, registration NR16020, to Puerto Rico, Venezuela, and across the Pacific to Dakar in Senegal. Several stops across the central African Sahara brought them to Assab in Eritrea. From the far eastern shores of Africa, they flew to Karachi, which was part of India at the time. Continuing eastward, they refuelled in Calcutta in India, Rangoon in Myanmar, Bangkok in Thailand, Singapore, Bandung in Indonesia, and Darwin in Australia. On 29 June 1937, they landed in the small port town of Lae in Papua New Guinea. In this tropical rainforest, Amelia and Fred rested while their Electra underwent a thorough mechanical check-up.

On 2 July 1937, Amelia Earhart and Fred Noonan launched their Electra over the Pacific Ocean towards tiny Howland Island. The pilot, navigator and their plane never arrived at their destination. Their disappearance over the Pacific became shrouded in mystery and launched many massive searches over the decades.

Growing in Demand as an Instructor

When the Pretoria Flying Club named Helen Harrison as a pilot instructor, the *Rand Daily Mail* heralded the appointment: 'It is a feather in the cap of the pilots and clubs concerned that South Africa is following in England's example in giving responsible posts to women.'[20]

At the Durban Air Pageant in late July 1937, Helen, along with fellow pilot Doreen Hooper, did not take part in the big air race but entered other events. Helen was instructing at the Pretoria Flying Club at the time.

By October 1937, Helen had settled into her role as a flying instructor and started working for a new flying club at Midrand. The *Rand Daily Mail* offered a tantalising glimpse into Helen's life when it published an interview with her, headlined 'First Woman Instructor':

> On Saturday morning, at the Grand Central Aerodrome, half-way between Pretoria and Johannesburg, I met a dog whose name maligns him. He is a small Irish terrier pup called Demon and as dogs go his manners are exemplary. However, he was named after the aircraft, Demon Hart and he is owned by South Africa's first woman flying instructor, Miss Helen Harrison.[21]
>
> Miss Harrison, who was born in Canada and educated in England, likes her job and wouldn't change it for another. Instructing she finds strenuous but it is interesting watching how her thirty pupils take to flying.
>
> 'One thing about women being appointed instructors,' said Miss Harrison with a smile, 'it disproves the old tradition that you cannot teach a pupil to fly without swearing at him.'
>
> She came out to South Africa ten months ago and for five months worked for a Cape Town flying company. She then had the distinction of being the first woman to go through a training course at Roberts Heights where she took

> a three-week instructor's refresher course and since then, she has been an instructor at the Pretoria Flying Club.
>
> Now Miss Harrison has joined a new flying firm. In spite of her qualifications and 700 flying hours, there is no grim airwoman pose about Miss Harrison. In fact, Demon seems to find it pretty easy to manage her when it comes to an extra saucer of tea, or a free flip in a Waco.[22]

By the beginning of 1938, Helen was employed as pilot instructor and charter pilot for African Flying Services in Johannesburg, and at Grand Central Aerodrome in Midrand. She oversaw the flying school in Kroonstad, Orange Free State. On 16 February, her engagement to Colonel Louis Botha de Waal was announced in the *Rand Daily Mail* with the additional note that Helen, after her marriage, would continue her work with African Flying Services.

Helen had learned that in late December 1937 her fiancé's brother Danie de Waal, a flying instructor, had been forced to land on the African veld in a storm. After leaving Senekal, he realised that his plane was being driven off course by buffeting winds. He was tempted to go on to Bloemfontein but decided to turn and make for Kroonstad.

Unbeknownst to him, when officials at Kroonstad determined he had not arrived as expected, twenty cars proceeded to the aerodrome. They remained until 11 pm with their lights switched on to illuminate the airfield should he arrive. The same thing occurred at Bloemfontein airstrip, where residents' cars lit up the landing strip, in case he should arrive there.

After flying a few miles, he had realised he was running out of fuel and executed a perfect landing in a ploughed field. His landing spot was not far from the main road, and after hailing a car, he was taken to Eensgevonden, a siding 20 miles from Brantfort (now renamed as Winnie Mandela). He then took the train to Kroonstad and returned to his plane as the weather had cleared.[23]

In Pretoria, visitors from Johannesburg and Pretoria were expected to gather on Saturday evening at the Fountain Kiosk following the wedding ceremony. The cocktail party was to be hosted by Mrs Annie Emmett Hingeston, the groom's sister, and her husband Captain Peter Hingeston of the South African Air Force.[24]

The day before their wedding at Pretoria City Hall, the *Rand Daily Mail* announced that the ceremony would take place quietly and the cocktail party was cancelled due to the serious illness of Colonel Louis Botha de Waal's father, The Honourable Mr Justice de Waal.

The Honourable Daniel de Waal, Judge-President of the Transvaal division of the Supreme Court, had been suffering from a long illness. After earning a degree from Cambridge University, he served as a practicing barrister in Transvaal before the Boer War and was appointed to the Bench in 1920. Earlier, he had married Christina MacMillan and together they had two children, Pieter and Kathleen. After her death in 1906, he married Helena Letitia, the eldest daughter of General Botha and Annie Emmett. The couple's four children included sons Louis and Danie, and daughters Annie and Magdalena (Madeleine). The couple divided their time between his home in Pretoria and their farm.

Unexpectedly, Mr de Waal passed away on Saturday, 19 February 1938, on the morning of the wedding. The couple's ceremony proceeded as planned but was muted in respect of the family's loss.

In the Union government building at the top of Meintjieskop, Pretoria's highest point, Helen Marcelle Harrison, 28, married Colonel Louis Botha de Waal, 29. The colonel was a grandson of General Louis Botha, Commander of South Africa and the first prime minister of the Union of South Africa.

Following their wedding, a funeral was held for The Honourable Daniel de Waal. The principal mourners were Mr and Mrs Louis de Waal, reported the *Rand Daily Mail*. Five judges of the Supreme Court, the Administrator of the Transvaal and leading members of the Pretoria Bar were among the distinguished gathering at New Cemetery, Pretoria.[25]

Helen's services as an instructor grew in demand among several flying clubs. A local pilot from Greytown, George Raisbeck Haller, grandson and namesake of a Hull shipbuilder, saw a growing need for flying lessons. George, who was the same age as Helen, started Haller

Aviation in Port Elizabeth in 1937. He extended his flying school activities to East London and Grahamstown where the Grahamstown Flying Club was formed in 1937. Haller Aviation provided both aircraft and instructors, hiring Helen, Jack Dalrymple and John Meiring. George Haller also served as the representative for Aeronca Aircraft corporation in South Africa.

In the spring of 1938, the *Rand Daily Mail* reported that a similar pilot training plan was underway in Canada with civilian flying clubs training pupils. More than 200 pilots who trained with flying clubs were enrolled in the Royal Air Force. 'The flying club movement was established some ten years ago for the threefold purpose of creating interest in aviation, training pilots for commercial and military flying, and developing airports', the *Mail* reported.[26]

Helen was employed by Haller Aviation as a flying instructor and chief administrator for the government training schools in Port Elizabeth and Grahamstown for six months in 1938.

'She stated that she had had three forced landings while she was training the air force, but on all occasions her engine had failed either over or near a flying field', observed the *Hamilton Spectator*.[27]

One of the first pupil pilots at Haller Aviation was a young South African Air Force trainee, Tom Cockbain from Port Alfred. He started flying lessons in early June 1938 at Grahamstown en route to a storied military career which culminated with the rank of major general. In his book *Sweeping Circles in the Sky*, he wrote that his interest in aviation grew, 'encouraged by the opening of a flying club at our small Grahamstown airfield'.

'The renowned Mrs Helen de Waal (née Harrison) was my first flying instructor', he exclaimed. She possessed 'a surprisingly vivid and sometimes quite appropriate vocabulary which was a source of envy among her pupils', wrote Major General T.G.E. Cockbain, SSA, SM.[28]

In his book, he shared that 'in any event, she was an excellent instructor and got me off solo in quick time on our Ryan ST low-wing monoplane. It was quite a remarkable aircraft in those days.' After starting his lessons in early June, he flew his first solo flight a few weeks later on 8 July 1938. Flying lessons propelled him forward into an illustrious career with the South African Air Force.

In addition to giving instruction, Helen occasionally took part in flying exhibitions too, the *South Africa Airnews* relayed:

> Miss Harrison is one of the most skilful stunt pilots in this country. Only a few weeks ago, her turn at Baragwanath during a show arranged in honour of the film stars Bebe Daniels and Ben Lyons was one of the highlights of the program. Her inverted flying was one of the most polished features of the exhibition.

In addition to exhibition flying, Helen often piloted passengers to remote destinations across the hot dry African hinterland.

Once, flying a military doctor over the African veld, she found herself way off course. Later she found that the physician's electrical equipment in his instrument case had thrown the compass off:

> Out of gas and lost, she picked out a relatively smooth stretch of ground near a native village and gingerly set the ship down. It rolled to a bumpy stop and immediately natives ran out, chattering and making wild motions with their arms, obviously very excited. Neither Helen nor the doctor could make the natives understand that they just wanted to know where they were. Finally, one native was found who understood a little English. Helen showed him the map and explained their predicament. He nodded, snatched the map from her and ran off as hard as he could go. The natives stood around, grinning, obviously waiting for his return. Before long an ancient car was seen bumping along the ground toward them. Out stepped the local missionary who showed them their position on the map. He provided gasoline which had to be strained through a silk handkerchief into a can.

> Then Helen lugged the eight-gallon can up to the opening on top of the ship and poured the fuel in.[29]
>
> …
>
> She was told by the missionaries that any child born within the next few months would be given the name of her airplane and their ages in future would be counted as from the day the airplane came.[30]

Well known in Pretoria as an instructor, Helen's disappearance prompted widespread concern and an SOS was issued. The *Rand Daily Mail* noted that Helen flew from Grahamstown on Monday, 1 August 1938, with a passenger and 'some hours afterwards, discovered she had lost her bearings'.

Founding a New South African Women's Aviation Association

In 1938, a groundswell of women interested in aviation began to grow.

'I climbed into the cockpit of my machine and eventually taxied out on to the runway and flew away into the blue', enthused new pilot Marjorie Bird, shortly after earning an 'A' licence in 1937. 'It was very beautiful, and a thought came to me – I wished that more women could have the opportunity of seeing such beauty as this.'

Thanks to a small legacy left by an aunt, Marjorie Bird fulfilled her wish to become a pilot. It cost her £70, and she obtained her licence three hours after her first solo flight. She recalled that an hour later, she competed with twenty-two men in the Aero Club's Round the Reef Flying race. To her surprise, she placed fourth.

> As I banked to turn towards Germiston, I saw another plane piloted by a man, a pupil under the Government's scheme and another thought flashed across my mind: By Jove, there is something very wrong here. I am flying at a cost

> of three pounds per hour and this man is flying for nothing! Being completely overcome by this observation, I decided that something must be done to aid women and some way provide cheaper flying for them.
>
> I flew, with wide-open throttle, to Germiston, circled round the aerodrome, made a terrific landing, and taxied back to the Rand Flying Club, jumped out of my machine, sought out my instructor and told him I was going to try and get cheaper flying for women.[31]

In the autumn of 1938, two airwomen petitioned the Minister of Defence Oswald Pirow for the formation of a women's section of the Civil Air Guard. Joan Blake and Marjorie Bird had gathered the signatures of 150 women in a petition for the inclusion of a full complement of women in the Guard.

Joan Blake told a *Rand Daily Mail* reporter that:

> it was possible for South Africa to have a similar organisation to the Civil Air Guard in England where all men and women were taught on equal terms – to fly at two pounds and six pence an hour, on condition that if their country should need their services, they would be at their country's disposal in all national emergencies.'[32]

The two women pointed out how the 1,000-pilot program discriminated against women. 'The cost of learning to fly in South Africa made it impossible except for the privileged few, as an "A" licence cost a minimum of £100 and a 'B' licence nearly £600 to acquire.'[33]

'There are numbers of women as keen as we are to fly', said Joan Blake to the reporter. 'But at three pounds an hour, it becomes prohibitive. Not only are we prepared to fly, but we will serve our country when called upon.'

Oswald Pirow acknowledged receipt of the petition. The *Rand Daily Mail* noted that 'Mr Pirow replied that he could not do anything until he had 1,000 thoroughly trained men and then he would think about the question.'[34]

'We feel, however,' said Joan Blake, 'that we should take the initiative in this matter as we know scores of women, who are keen to learn to fly. But without government assistance, it is out of the question.'[35]

The women pointed out that pilots received twenty to twenty-five hours of training, of which ten to fifteen hours comprised dual instruction to qualify for an 'A' licence. The minimum cost, excluding the flying kit, was £70. Furthermore, 'B' licence qualification required a minimum of 200 solo hours, apart from the technical examinations, and cost approximately £570.[36]

Mr Pirow's response was most discouraging, wrote Marjorie Bird. She connected with her instructor Doreen Hooper 'who had proved that women were capable of functions outside their traditional roles, and she promised to give us every atom of help she could'.[37]

Doreen Hooper had cut her flying teeth in a Tiger Moth in 1935 under the tutelage of Captain Stan Halse. In October 1936, she obtained her 'B' licence and by January 1938, her instructor's rating. She then rejoined the African Flying Services, for which she had earlier flown commercial flights, based at Grand Central Airport.

Visiting Britain, Marjorie Bird noted that the Civil Air Guard in Britain allowed for subsidised flying instruction for men and women who were willing to serve as reservists. Her view was that 'in time of war there would be many roles in aviation (as in other industries) that could be taken over by women so as to release men for combat'.[38]

Together, Marjorie Bird and Joan Blake made it clear that their aims were sincere and that they would 'not encourage any woman to fly merely for fun or glamour'.[39]

A few enthusiastic women who formed a committee asked Leila Deneys Reitz, a Johannesburg Member of Parliament, to chair a public meeting at the Wanderer's Club. Leila Reitz was viewed as the airwomen's best representative as she had contested the 1933 South African general election on the heels of the 1930 Women's Enfranchisement Act.

> When the meeting was held on the evening of 5 December 1939, we found the hall packed to overflowing: 110 women

> having enrolled for the evening. Everybody was most enthusiastic, and it was decided that we would call ourselves the South African Women's Aviation Association.[40]

Leila Reitz shared with the audience that while she believed in conscription to a certain extent,

> every man and woman should have a post allotted to him or her in defence of the country. We women cannot expect to have equal rights and franchise if we only let the men fight and are not prepared to defend ourselves.
>
> If you sign on to this Civil Air Guard movement now, you may bring to the notice of the government that you are willing, and it will realise your use as have the governments in Great Britain and other countries.[41]

The Association became popularly known as the Women's Civil Air Guard, with multiple objectives. The organisation was formed to release men from civil aviation in time of a national emergency, to ferry and transport aircraft, provide ambulance services, and flying mail and dispatches. The women also offered to provide charter flights, instruction and technical aviation services.

By January 1939, the South African Women's Aviation Association was viewed as responsible for the enthusiasm of women flyers in the Transvaal. 'The ranks of women flying pupils are growing', reported the *Rand Daily Mail*.[42]

At this time, South Africa had only three women 'B' pilots: Helen Harrison, Doreen Hooper and Rosamund King Everard. Helen was a popular flying instructor who had taught at many of the flying clubs around South Africa as well as for the South African Air Force.

Rosamund King Everard, a landscape painter and a brilliant violinist, took up flying with her brother Sebastian in 1935. The sprawling family ranch at Mpumalanga, with its panoramic views of the unlimited Transvaal, was best viewed by plane. Here she excelled in cattle ranching, became an expert judge of Ayrshire cattle, a superb wool classer, and spoke French and siSwati. She had qualified for a 'B' licence in England and flew several international solo flights. By 1939, she had obtained the South African 'B' licence and instructor's licence. In addition to her instructor's endorsement and second-class navigator's certificate, she considered taking her ambulance certification for aerial ambulance work.

Rosamund advocated the importance of women pilots undertaking steady work and becoming successful, to break down barriers. To illustrate her point, she quoted women who had done this, and included Pauline Gower, Dorothy Spicer, Margery Spiller, Winifred Crossley, Grace Brown and Sabiha Gökçen, the adopted daughter of the late Turkish founding president Kemel Atatürk, who instructed at the Military College in Angora, Turkey. For South Africa, she added Doreen Hooper, an instructor at the Grand Central Aerodrome and Helen Harrison, an instructor at both Grand Central and Grahamstown.[43]

'When women branch into anything new, they receive scant encouragement', reporter Jane Vibart shrewdly observed in the *Rand Daily Mail*.[44] 'In flying, [women] have often been met with a raw deal. It is a strange fact that while flying, veterans are well known and respected as Captain Stan Halse and Mr Rod Douglas hold out great hopes to women in aviation.'

The *Rand Daily Mail* continued, 'There are 600 pilots with civil air licences in South Africa. Of these, twenty-one are women. On the list of lapsed licences there are twenty-six women. That means forty-seven have held flying licences.'[45]

The tenacity and enterprise of a few airwomen resulted in the formation of the South African Women's Aviation Association, and their persistence contributed to the strength and depth of the air force in South Africa.

A reporter mused:

> I don't know whether the recent formation of the South African Women's Aviation Association is responsible for

> the enthusiasm of women flyers in the Transvaal, or if it is just a sign of the times, but the ranks of women flying pupils is growing daily. Grand Central Aerodrome alone can now claim seven women pupils.[46]

The flying students included Marjorie Egerton Bird and Murial Shires, South Africa's youngest woman flier who aimed to get her 'B' licence.

Venturing Towards New Horizons

By mid-1938, the international tension in Europe was rippling out to far-flung countries such as South Africa. The news from continental Europe reported on the rise and expansion of Fascist Italy and Nazi Germany which concerned residents of South Africa.

At home in the Cape, Helen's three sons were living with her parents and caregiver Mabel Daisy Seabrook. Her father, Albert, was the manager of the Albion Hotel in Muizenberg in the Western Cape. The long sandy beach had attracted vacationers for decades and was a popular seaside locale. Helen was frequently away instructing at Grand Central airport in Midrand, in Pretoria, Grahamstown and other locations in the Transvaal.

Primarily, she was instructing future military pilots through flying clubs and instructing was strenuous work. Not only was it physically demanding but it also required a high mental alertness and acuity in the air and on the ground to ensure the safety of her pupils, herself, other pilots, and ground crew.

As a mother and flying instructor she was being pulled in different directions by her work, family and her new marriage. Her husband, an army colonel, was also facing unprecedented change as South Africa prepared to gird and defend itself. Colonel Louis de Waal was deeply rooted in South Africa through his family and the military service to which he was committed.

With Europe in a state of unease, and many countries continuing to experience the economic crisis of the 1930s, Helen knew that should a war break out, all civilian flying would cease. In addition, the real likelihood that private aircraft would be commissioned for military purposes would certainly put a halt to all flying instruction by clubs.

By early 1939, the 1,000-pilot scheme had created a positive impact in the aviation industry as the number of flying clubs had grown as a result, with a dozen active flying clubs around South Africa.

The concept of using civilian flying clubs and schools to undertake pilot training instead of the air force reduced state expenditures as clubs already had the infrastructure, aircraft and instructors in place. This program meant that the air force reserve of pilots could grow without introducing conscription. Under the plan, flying schools provided 10,250 hours of flying instruction in 1937, which increased to 20,035 in 1938 and 28,645 in 1939.[47]

Helen faced stark choices. The 1,000-pilot training plan was nearing its conclusion. The outbreak of war would certainly force the cessation of civil flying in many countries. Despite the formation of the South African Women's Aviation Association, women pilots still faced considerable difficulties obtaining flying roles in the South African Air Force. However, Helen was optimistic that with her extensive experience training military pilots and superb flying skills, she would find a challenging and rewarding role.

Her family set their sights on the United States where she could train for a US commercial flying licence and pursue work. Before Christmas, her 60-year-old mother Gertrude departed from South Africa on the MS *Dunnottar Castle*. Sailing past the Statue of Liberty, she arrived in New York on 16 January 1939. Immediately, she found a house for the family in the city of Richmond, Virginia.

After Christmas on 28 December 1938, Helen, her three sons and their caregiver Mabel Daisy boarded the SS *Themistocles* for London. Helen Harrison was listed as flying instructress on the passenger manifest. By this time, she had separated from Louis Botha de Waal and was ready for a new adventure with her boys, who were now 10, 8 and 5 years old.

News had spread in the small tight-knit community of South Africa that she was leaving for America. 'We will probably soon be having flying news of her', reported a *Rand Daily Mail* columnist.[48] During her two years in South Africa as a military and civilian flying instructor and stunt pilot, Helen Harrison had become recognised nationally. Her public stature and contribution to South Africa was so significant that she was included in a 1941 book titled *Personalities in South African Motoring and Aviation,* written by C.F. Clarkson.

Sailing from tropical South Africa and the community of pilots she trained and worked with for new adventures, she would come to realise a wonderful truth.

'South Africa was the only country,' she mused, 'where I didn't have to battle to get ahead. I was accepted as a pilot.'[49]

Chapter 6

Spreading Wings Higher, Faster and Further

The plane went into a tight spin. The reporter playing student in the Royal Canadian Air Force for fifteen minutes felt as if his stomach was being driven back against his backbone, and then it was all over. He was flying blind. A white hood had been pulled back over the cockpit, enclosing him a little world of his own.

The newsman, following instructions that came barrelling through the headphones at 3,000 feet, pulled the hood back. What had been happening when he was under the white hood? He asked the instructor to start all over again from scratch. This time all sensations were heightened. Now able to look around, he sighted the Kitchener-Waterloo airport and kept it in his range of vision. Now the plane went into a flick roll, a show roll, spin, stall turn barrel roll and inverted flying. One minute the earth was gliding by below, then it had rolled around until one had to strain the head back to look straight down and locate the airport.

Back on the ground, the reporter wobbled, gulped for air and then tried an ineffective grin. But in a few minutes,

> the reporter realised this business of flying had something. It was definitely attractive. It gave one ideas. It made me want to climb back in and do it all over again.
>
> It showed definitely why young Canada is clamouring at the portals of the Royal Canadian Air Force just begging to be taken on.[1]
>
> *Waterloo Region Record*

Seeking New Possibilities in England

Helen and her sons arrived in England on 8 February 1939 after a peaceful voyage along the west coast of Africa and Europe. After their two-year sojourn in glorious South Africa, her family looked forward to new adventures.

Her sons, along with their caregiver Mabel Daisy, sailed west across the Atlantic on the SS *Aquitania* from Southampton. Helen stayed behind in England to seek additional paid flying and instruction experience for a few months. She tried to enlist in the Royal Air Force but was rejected.

The creation of the Civil Air Guard, growth of civilian flying clubs and the demand for Royal Air Force reserve pilots led to a serious shortage of civil flying instructors. In *No Place for a Lady*, author Shirley Render wrote that Helen 'next attempted to get on as a civilian instructor for the military. Turned down again, she accepted the position of Chief Flying Instructor with the Sheffield Aero Club.'[2] According to Joyce Spring in *Daring Lady Flyers: Canadian Women in the Early Years of Aviation*, 'It was quite unusual for a woman to be a flying instructor, and to become chief flying instructor was a tribute to Helen's expertise.'[3]

This was a temporary role in South Yorkshire, albeit a more senior position, but at the same time she astutely recognised that barriers for women pilots in Great Britain remained relatively high.

She and her compatriots understood that commercial flying operators were not ready for them. Women pilots who had completed all the aviation and medical requirements to hold commercial licences were stymied in their efforts. Nonetheless, determined airwomen continued diligently to keep their flying hours current, to stay fit and ensure their own mental acuity to pass the frequent examinations required to keep their licences. As well, they strived to gain flying experience on the evolving new aircraft and technology which were emerging from factories.

At this time, newspapers reported on the increasing staffing needs in the commercial aviation sector. 'The rapid expansion of commercial air routes has produced a demand for young men with previous flying experience to become airline pilots', noted *The Daily Telegraph*.

In addition, women pilots were barred from undertaking flying duties in war. A committee of the London Forum Club's aviation section held a conference discussing how women pilots could be trained for national emergencies. The committee comprised airwomen Pauline Gower, Amy Johnson and Dorothy Spicer, who had previously organised a series of lectures for women pilots. The conference included discussions on women's duties and the ferrying of planes from one point to another.[4]

The *Birmingham Evening Mail* noted:

> Women were coming forward to join the Civil Air Guard and qualify themselves as pilots. The volume of recruits would probably be larger still but for a certain degree of parental opposition. An instructor has said that women aviators are very like women motorists. When they are good, they are extraordinarily good, and many seem to have that instinctive touch which has made the English pilot supreme among the flying men of the world.[5]

A news debate on the subject so captivated the public that it soon spread to the top levels of government.

At the beginning of January 1939, just prior to Helen's arrival in England, the *Daily Herald* asked for debate on a motion proposed by the Women's Federation League. The motion being 'that women should be allowed to join the Royal Air Force and according to their ability fight side by side in the event of war.' The League wrote a letter to the Prime Minister and the heads of government departments, urging that the 'womanpower of this country should be used to the full'.

League Secretary Miss F.A. Underwood opined:

> There is no reason why women pilots should not be utilised by the Royal Air Force. If their flying ability is the same as that of men, if they can pass the same medical and technical tests, they should be used in all branches of Service flying.
>
> There are exceptional women pilots, just as there are exceptional men, and we argue that their ability should decide their usefulness, not their sex.

In opposition to the motion, the Air Minister, Sir Howard Kingsley Wood, advised that the Civil Air Guard scheme would be divided into three groups:

> Groups A and B will consist of men capable of serving as pilots, air gunners, observers or instructors. Class C will consist of men not fitted for the first two classes, and *all women members*. They will not be engaged in active service but will carry out ferry work and observation duties.

Dorothy Selder, a 25-year-old Ealing member of the Civil Air Guard, thought that the Women's Federation League was right: 'Women should have equal opportunities of going into active flying service. In wartime, no woman would shirk the dangers of actual service flying, and many would feel more content and do better work than they would if relegated to ground activities.'

The debate on women air pilots in wartime reached the UK House of Commons when Member of Parliament Lieutenant Commander P.G. Agnew asked what the position of women air pilots would be in time of war. Captain H.H. Balfour, undersecretary for air, confirmed, 'there would be cases in which women pilots would be of value on ferry work and instructional work'. He did not wish 'to lay down any hard and fast rule as to the degree of utility of women pilots in the event of war'.[6]

Rising to Greater Heights in North America

Helen served as the chief instructor at the Sheffield Flying Club in England from February to April 1939. By this time, she had taught 150 pilots in South Africa and accumulated 600 to 700 hours of instruction.

According to Joyce Spring, instructing had never paid well and by the time Helen decided to leave for the United States, she was short of money. Boarding the SS *Laconia,* she departed from Liverpool on 28 April 1939. The passenger list recorded 29-year-old Helen Marcelle Harrison as a flying instructor. Helen was described as 5 foot and 10 inches in height with fair complexion, fair hair and blue eyes.

Stepping on shore in New York on 9 May 1939, she strode forth confidently with a clear vision. Helen was a career pilot with commercial pilot's licences from Great Britain and South Africa. She brought 5 years of experience as an instructor and a record of 1,100 flying hours, all detailed in her logbook. Through hard work and sheer determination, she had contributed significantly to the training of 1,000 pilots for the South African Air Force reserves. The South African pupil pilots hadn't resented being taught by a woman, and this knowledge gave Helen the assurance that she was on the right track.

She immediately set to work to complete the Federal Bureau of Aeronautics requirements for a US commercial pilot's licence, successfully passing her physical and medical exams.

While undertaking her studies, the aviation community heard that on 9 May, well-known female aviator Lady Sophie Heath, 43, had died. She had succumbed to injuries sustained from a fall on the steps of a London tramcar. 'She rose from poverty to wealth, and from obscurity to fame, but she was unable to find contentment.'[7]

Her passing was a shock to the aviation community on both sides of the Atlantic. Her life illustrated the difficulties that women pilots faced in finding long-term roles in aviation, and being able to sustain their flying careers.

Shortly afterwards, the *Richmond News Leader* reported that 'Miss Helen Harrison was granted a US commercial pilot's licence after completing a written examination and required flying tests at College Park, MD.' The test was conducted by Tom Gates, an inspector for the US Civil Aeronautics authority.

Commenting on the test in the *Hamilton Spectator*, she noted that 'it was pretty stiff, I can tell you, and the written exam was the hardest I have ever tried'.[8]

Subsequent newspaper articles followed, including a Victoria *Times-Colonist* article with the headline, 'Former BC Girl is Now Expert Pilot':

> Twenty-nine-year-old Helen Harrison, native of Vancouver, who claims the distinction of being the second woman in England to obtain an aviation instructor's licence and the first to hold such a permit in South Africa, would like to see women aviation enthusiasts step up and demand more recognition in commercial aeronautics.
>
> For two and a half years, Miss Harrison earned $250 to $350 a month as an instructor in South Africa and England, and has flown, since 1934, more than 1,000 hours over three continents.

The *Times-Colonist* noted that Helen declared that 'the lack of opportunity for women fliers in the US probably will result in her transferring her aviation prospecting to Canada'. She observed that she would like to see more women aviation enthusiasts step up and demand more recognition in commercial aeronautics.

> My opinion is that it is up to women to make their own way in aviation. I've been earning my living for several years and haven't had any trouble.

> If women would go ahead and qualify themselves for commercial flying positions, Miss Harrison believes they would get them – in time. But there are not enough going after them now, she says, thus restricting women's orbit in the air.[9]

By July 1939, Helen and her family were living in Ottawa, the capital of Canada. She contacted Wing Commander A.T. Cowley as she sought her Canadian commercial licence.

Of her meeting with the top brass, the *Ottawa Citizen* commented: 'A British Columbia girl Helen Harrison walked into the offices of the civil aviation division of the Department of Transport on Monday and in the course of her conversation with seasoned fliers it developed that she had been places.'[10]

Commander Cowley referred her to Colonel D.G. Joy, inspector of civil aviation, who in turn told her to come to Hamilton so that 'she might be put over the aeronautic jumps' by Ernest Taylor, flying instructor of the Hamilton Aero Club.

The Hamilton Spectator reported that 'Mr Taylor found her flying highly advanced due to her knowledge of blind and night flying and has recommended that she be given a commercial licence in this country.'[11]

Landing a job in Hamilton, her arrival in Canada caused a stir among the national media. From coast to coast, reporters wrote about her thrilling aviation career. The *Expositor* newspaper in Brantford, Ontario, noted that most of her time during the past six years had been spent in the air. Landing in North America, she found that Canada and the US were far from being as air-minded as Europe or even South Africa. The *Edmonton Journal* reported that 'she said she found flying cost money, so she turned instructor at the Pretoria and other flying schools throughout South Africa'.

Of her brief stay in the US, the *Star Weekly* reported that Helen,

> believed that flying was more advanced there than any other country. I found that was true – in one direction. There is

> no doubt that the United States is tops in airline flying, but they don't seem to have any fixed methods of training their military pilots. Anyway, there didn't seem to be much place for a woman flier there, so I decided to try the old native land for a change.

Helen insisted that,

> being a woman is no drawback to a career as a professional pilot. Only you have to make people understand that you are serious about it – that it's not just a gag. In South Africa, one man, 65 and set in his ways, positively refused to take flying lessons from a woman – until he found that my pupils were advancing faster than he was. From then on, he wouldn't have any other instructor![12]

On 18 July, she earned a Limited Commercial Air Pilot's Certificate, C-1610, that was valid only in Canada. The certificate listed the Hamilton Flying Club and qualified her for day flying only.

The conditions printed on the certificate stated that the holder was 'not to carry passengers for hire unless he has completed at least 100 hours as first pilot. Certificate subject to the holder passing a satisfactory medical examination and being certified as fit to fly, at least every four months.'

The text had not yet been amended for a woman pilot, nor for a pilot with Helen's flying hours.

With her class two instructor's rating, she was endorsed to provide dual flying instruction. The types of aircraft for which this certificate was valid included: de Havilland 60, 82, 87 and 89 Moth; Aeronca, Fleet, Cubs, Rearwin, Fairchild 24, Stinson-Reliant, Waco, Stinson 108, Taylorcraft, Percival Proctor, Anson V, Globe Swift, Fairchild M62A3, Cessna 120-140, Luscombe 8E, Stinson 108-216 and Cessna 195.

With her Canadian ticket, Helen now held five aviation licences including the English 'A' and 'B' and commercial, a South African 'B' and both United States and Canadian commercial certificates.

Despite her qualifications, she still found it difficult to obtain work. She planned to leave Hamilton for Northern Ontario, where she hoped to be employed as an instructor and as a commercial pilot flying mail into isolated camps. 'I couldn't find anything in Toronto or Ottawa, so I hung around the Cub factory in Hamilton until I was hired as a test pilot', she recalled.[13]

As it turned out, the Hamilton Flying Club hired Helen to train thirty pilots with the Royal Canadian Air Force. At the time, civilian women flying instructors could train air force pilots but were not permitted to join the service. In 1939, Canadian aviation was still in its infancy and only a few instructors were available to train pilots.

The aviation community had noticed that Helen brought to Canada experience of flying more than twenty types of aircraft, from tiny aircraft to the twin-engine de Havilland 60 Dragonfly.

R.L. Gibson, the president of Cub Aircraft of Canada which maintained a flying school at the Hamilton airport, had just announced that the company was busy constructing a new Cub plane which Helen Harrison would fly. She was pleased to take citizens up for a trip over Hamilton and the surrounding countryside.[14] 'The test flying wasn't much', she said. 'All I did was put the aircraft into a spin and do a few other checks on it.'[15]

She was 'very matter of fact about her job and would like to organise in Canada a corps of reserve women pilots', noted the *Star Weekly*.

The first step towards this corps, she said, would be to get women into the air and interested in aircraft. 'Both England and South Africa have reserve corps, and there is no reason why Canada shouldn't have them too.'

Helen noted that there was,

> no end to the jobs women pilots could do in time of war. They could deliver military planes, fly mail and transport and instruct war pilots in flying. Really, they could do all the behind the lines jobs and release the men for the actual business of fighting.

> Women fight? There's no reason why they shouldn't, if it were absolutely necessary. Some of the bigger flying ships, of course, may need a man's strength to handle them. But temperamentally, women would probably make as good fighters as men, if it were a case of 'I get you or you get me' in aerial combat. Women, you know, can be as ruthless as men – perhaps more so. I wouldn't like it myself, though.

Of her career goals, Helen shared that her dream was to fly transport and passenger planes in Canada and become the first woman pilot of Trans-Canada Air Lines. Just two years prior, the Trans Canada Air Lines Act was given royal assent, and an airline was formed to provide air transportation, freight and mail service from coast to coast. It became a subsidiary of the Canadian National Railway Company. 'But I'm afraid they wouldn't have me', she said regretfully. 'That's one branch women don't seem to be able to crash.'[16]

Of the aviatrix extraordinaire, the *Hamilton Spectator* observed that it was 'indeed hard to believe that such a delightful person could have accomplished so much in so short a time in a sphere where men have generally ruled'.

In addition to being a military flying instructor and the only woman ever to hold such a position in South Africa, the *Spectator* reported that she was the 'only woman ever to fly a military airplane in that country'.

The *Spectator* noted there is 'nothing of the braggart' in Helen. 'She stated that she had had three forced landings while she was training the air force, but on all occasions her engine had failed either over or near a flying field'.

Wing Commander T.A. Cowley advised the *Ottawa Citizen* that 'very few women make good flyers, but when they are good, they are very, very good.' He was on a national tour of inspection as the Canadian superintendent of air regulations.

He mentioned Helen in his interview: 'So far,' he informed, 'that very attractive young lady is the only woman instructor we have.'

Notwithstanding his remarks that 'women will never make transport or army pilots' as 'they haven't the physical strength', he figured that 'there is a future for them as flying instructors, not only in time of national emergency, but right now'.

'I'd like to see one or two women instructors in all of bigger clubs', he expanded. 'Women are naturally good teachers, and in Canada, we have several women commercial pilots who would make excellent instructors, Vancouver's Rolie Moore, for instance.' Rolie Moore was the president of the Flying Seven, Canada's only flying club for women.[17]

Thundering Air Drama at Canadian National Exhibition

By mid-1939, excitement for the Canadian National Exhibition in Toronto, particularly the Big Air Show, was reaching a feverish pitch.

The news media announced that six Fairey Battles, the most potent air fighting unit Canada had ever received, had rolled into Barrie and Camp Borden on eight railway cars. There they would be assembled and prepared for the exhibition's show over Lake Ontario. Only the Hurricane Fighters were the fastest machines used by the Royal Canadian Air Force at 300 mph. But the new Fairey Battles promised to deliver a sizzling show of aerial prowess.

As well, the Royal Canadian Air Force planned to display modern air-fighting planes including a Hawker Hurricane, Lysander and a Harvard low-wing training plane. With the theme of transportation and communication, the exhibition organisers believed that Royal Canadian Air Force's flying demonstrations would boost attendance.

In addition to the Royal Canadian Air Force's demonstration of its planes and aircraft, several aerial performers featured in the build-up to the Big Air Show including Helen Harrison. On several days leading up to the major air spectacle, Helen performed aerial acrobatics in her yellow Tiger Moth plane.

'Exhibition crowds of Labour Day viewed a Canadian women's display of stunt flying in a wind of high velocity', reported the *Toronto*

Star. 'With hours of night and blind flying to her credit, Miss Harrison went through rolls, loops and dives.'[18]

In an interview afterwards, with the spectre of war on people's minds, Helen stated that she was willing to train pilots to serve in the war. By this time, she had 1,200 hours of flying time to her credit. 'She said she may possibly be used to help train men for the Royal Canadian Air Force but there is nothing definite yet', reported the *Gazette*. 'Miss Harrison said she would serve as a pilot for war duties if called upon.'[19]

The next day, on 5 September, the Federal Defence Department announced the withdrawal of all Royal Canadian Air Force planes at the exhibition in response to the UK's declaration of war on Germany.

Training Provisional Pilots with the Kitchener-Waterloo Flying Club

The close of the Canadian National Exhibition marked the end of summer and the start of a sombre autumn as Europe intensified its involvement in war. On 1 September, all civil aviation throughout Great Britain was curtailed. The Air Ministry had issued a notice that the whole of the eastern half of England and Scotland had become a prohibited area for flights by civil aircraft. The curtailment of civil flights affected pilots, pupil trainees, flying instructors and civilian plane clubs.

In other Allied countries, similar bans were issued. In South Africa, from 1 December onwards, instructional facilities in the Johannesburg Light Plane Club were completely utilised for the training of South African Air Force cadets.

By early November, Helen had been appointed second instructor at the Kitchener-Waterloo Flying Club. This opportunity arose when the club's first instructor James Nash joined Trans-Canada Air Lines. With 2,000 flying hours, he was appointed first officer and the co-pilot position on Trans-Canada Air Lines' flights. The Club's second instructor, Harvey MacPherson, was promoted to the position of first instructor.

On his departure, James Nash noted that Great Britain was offering $4,000 to US aviators to fly American-built Lockheed Hudson bombers to England. He thought Canadian pilots may be employed to deliver planes as well. He then presented a farewell exhibition of barrel rolling, cut-off loops, spins and other aerobatics.

Her new role instructing with the Kitchener-Waterloo Flying Club may have viewed hopefully by Helen as a path towards an eventual career with Trans-Canada Air Lines. Helen recalled that the men she trained at the Club were a 'great group', as they were college educated and were excellent flying students.

'The Royal Canadian Air Force officers who gave them their check flights said they were very impressed with these pilot officers' progress and gave Helen the credit', notes Joyce Spring. 'Helen's response was that she trained these young men the same way she trained all her students, and it was the calibre of the students that made the difference.'[20]

Former students fondly remembered Helen Harrison's time as an instructor at Kitchener-Waterloo, recalled club secretary Florence Elliott: 'We used to sit outside the hangar while she glided a student in and we could hear her yelling, "Keep your bloody nose on the horizon!"'

Said Helen, 'Those Royal Canadian Air Force officers kept me on their pins with all their questions, I'd be rough and tough with them. Once in the air, I wasn't male or female; I was an instructor. We got along fine.'

As she was very successful with her pupil pilots, she asked to be considered as a civilian instructor for the British Commonwealth Air Training Plan.

When the Second World War broke out in 1939, Canada was far removed from the armed conflict in Europe. With its wide open spaces and airports safe from active fighting, this northern country was considered by the Commonwealth to be ideal training grounds for the thousands of pilots and aviation crew needed. Believing that the power of the aeroplane would win the war, the Commonwealth devised a multinational training plan.

In an agreement reached in 1939 between Canadian Prime Minster William Lyon Mackenzie King and the British government, Canada provided facilities and training for pilots, navigators, gunners, flight engineers, and wireless operators from around the Commonwealth. Canada had access to fuel, an aviation industry and plentiful airspace.

Canada built 151 schools and facilities in 231 locations throughout the country. The plan included building twenty-five service flying training schools, fifteen air observer schools, fifteen bombing and gunnery schools, three air navigation schools and one wireless training school. The plan would cost the Canadian government 40 per cent of the total cost of $88.5 million over three years.[21]

The Canadian government built 7,000 hangars, barracks and drill halls. Most training schools had three runways, each 100 feet wide and 2,500 feet long. During its operations, it employed 3,540 aircraft, 33,000 air force personnel and 6,000 civilian employees.

Canada was, in US President Franklin D. Roosevelt's words, 'the aerodrome of democracy'.[22]

Doors Opening in Europe for Women Pilots

Canadian women flyers stepped forward to assist as instructors and with ground services. There were sixty-five licensed women pilots in Canada and of these, half were estimated to be actively flying. Helen was Canada's only active women instructor. Daphne Shelfoon of Toronto was the only woman transport pilot. In addition to Helen and Daphne, four women held commercial licences. In Ottawa, five women fliers signified their intention to offer their services in the event that Canada became involved in the war. In Vancouver, the Flying Seven group offered their services. And across Canada, there were several women who had specialised in ground services for the aviation sector.[23]

Overseas in Britain and France, doors were opening for women pilots behind the war front.

The French Red Cross had announced that a women's volunteer air ambulance corps would be used to bring wounded soldiers back from the front lines. Five hundred women joined the corps.

According to the *Manchester Evening News*, 'Each entrant must have at least ten hours flying time to her credit and must pass an examination in nursing.' As well as evacuating the wounded, the corps would fly transport planes bringing parcels to the front.[24]

In England, one brief news item, headlined *Women Pilots Not Needed in RAF*, raised eyebrows. An official had tersely informed the *Birmingham Gazette* that 'we have all the young men we require at present undergoing training and there will be a plentiful supply to make up for casualties. The standard of personnel joining the Air Force is higher than ever.'[25]

With this breaking news, The *Daily Mirror* in London expanded on this with a more forceful headline: 'RAF Will Have No Women Pilots'.[26]

The Air Transport Auxiliary is Born

With the potential demands of a looming war, plans were underway in the UK to ensure a sufficient supply of new aircraft. In early 1939, the task of ferrying planes from factories to airbases became the responsibility of the Royal Air Force to prevent aircraft from becoming sitting ducks in the event of enemy bombing. The Royal Air Force was also responsible for additional behind-the-scenes services including maintenance units which detracted from its primary *raison d'etre* of providing frontline air fighting squadrons.

Sir Francis Shelmerdine, director general of civil aviation at the Air Ministry, prepared a plan in which experienced pilots who were ineligible for the Royal Air Force would be used to fly a fleet of light communications aircraft in the event of war. The director general had received approval to form a civil reserve of pilots for the new British Overseas Airways Corporation. It was planned that the Royal Air Force would be supplemented by thirty-two pilots from its Royal Air Force volunteer reserve which operated two ferry pools at Derby and Bristol. From this reserve, the Air Transport Auxiliary was born.

In August 1939, British Airways director Gerard d'Erlanger began selecting pilots from a list of 'A' licence holders and formed a pool for wartime aviation tasks. Initially, it was proposed that the Auxiliary would transport dispatches, mail and news, medical supplies, civil authorities and medical officers. The Auxiliary would also work cooperatively with the police and fire brigades.

At the outbreak of war, all civil aircraft flights over the UK were prohibited. On the day war was declared, 3 September, Commodore Gerard d'Erlanger received approval from the Air Ministry and a week later twenty-three pilots were accepted. The male pilots selected for the Auxiliary were experienced ex-airline and civilian flyers who were unable to pass the strict medical examinations required by the Royal Air Force. Pilots were between 28 and 50 years of age with 250 flying hours. Pilots who were accustomed to flying light single-engine aircraft were given conversion courses at the Royal Air Force's Central Flying School at Upavon on more sophisticated planes.

By Autumn 1939, Air Transport Auxiliary pilots, outfitted in their dark blue uniforms, began ferrying aircraft from factories to Royal Air Force training stations and maintenance units at home and abroad.

While the official motto of the Air Transport Auxiliary was '*Aetheris Avidi*' or 'eager for the air', the male civilian pilots called themselves the 'Ancient and Tattered Aviators'.

Their humorous, self-depreciating moniker belied their ceaseless work. 'It is a title that bears no relation to their untiring efficiency week after week, month after month, against all hazards and in all weathers', reported the *Herts and Essex Observer*.[27]

Pilots came from around the world, including Canada, Australia, Poland, Holland and the US.

As new war planes were designed and rolled out of factories, the need grew to train pilots on specific aircraft. Flying schools were formed, particularly an elementary training facility at Barton-in-the-Clay, an initial flying school at Thame, and an advanced flying school at White Waltham.

There were no illusions about the hazards that Air Transport Auxiliary pilots faced. Ferry pilots continued to deliver machines even on low-visibility days and in weather conditions that would ground most pilots.

Flying in wartime with imposed conditions and tight timelines was not easy. If they got lost, which happened to the best of pilots, there was the possibility of encountering a balloon barrage in the mist. 'They have no wireless, there are no guiding beacons, and camouflage has altered the whole aspect of the country. It is difficult to recognise even their own aerodrome when they are right above it on their return just before darkness falls', reported *The Guardian*.[28]

As the number of ferry pilots grew, the decision was made to separate the Auxiliary from the Royal Air Force. In May 1940, the civilian Air Transport Auxiliary assumed responsibility for the transport of aircraft from the Royal Air Force, thus freeing up their pilots for combat. From this point on, the Auxiliary moved most of the new, repaired, and damaged aircraft. From factories, planes were ferried to maintenance units where they were outfitted with radios and guns. The initial air taxis of Tiger Moths were supplemented by Ansons which could transport up to eight pilots at a time.

As ferrying work rapidly increased, the need for pilots intensified. Anticipating the need for more pilots, this requirement brought up the question of employing women pilots.

A new scheme was developed by the Air Ministry to integrate a women's squadron of the Air Transport Auxiliary. The new section, from the moment it was formed, was destined to make history. The Air Transport Auxiliary 'was a glorious experiment that came off', observed a flight captain who was responsible for arranging the ferry schedules in the Operations Division.[29]

It was an experiment that had never been tried before and was based on an innovative operating structure that was designed to expedite the delivery of planes in the most efficient manner. The *Medway News* beamed:

> For the first time in the great story of British aviation, women will pilot Royal Air Force planes from the manufacturers to the flying schools and reserve centres, will pilot light machines at first, but later, they may be called on to handle

> bombers and 350 mph fighters. No woman has ever been allowed to fly Air Force machines.[30]

Pauline Mary de Peauly Gower, 27, a strong pilot in her own right, was appointed as the lead administrator. The daughter of Sir Robert Gower, MP for Gillingham, Pauline held 'A' and 'B' flying licences, a second navigator's ticket, a blind-flying certificate, a wireless licence and a parachute licence. The only licence she had yet to earn was the first-class navigator's licence.

Experiencing poor health in her youth, Pauline chose flying and was so enamoured that she gave violin lessons to finance her flying lessons. She moved to Stag Lane flying school and became friends with renown aviator Amy Johnson. Her father gave up his resistance and bought her a Spartan plane for her 21st birthday. With her friend Dorothy Spicer, she launched a taxi service in Kent. In their jointly owned Gipsy Moth, they flew 20,000 customers on joy rides from 185 airfields around England between 1930 and 1939.

At the war's start, Gerard d'Erlanger and Sir Francis Shelmerdine met with Pauline to discuss how the original twenty-seven male Air Transport Auxiliary pilots could be supported by twelve women pilots.

In her recruitment, Pauline requested that women pilot applicants have 1,000 or more flying hours of solo flying to their credit. They were advised that they would 'face some "sticky" journeys in the air' as there would be no wireless in their planes and they would have to fly aircraft in all weathers.[31]

Underneath the excitement, the requirements for women pilots were markedly different:

> Shelmerdine had managed to soothe the worried brow of the Royal Air Force by assuring them that their male pilots would not have to fly with the women pilots of the Air Transport Auxiliary. Moreover, the women would all need at least 500 hours flying experience before being given

> access to the Royal Air Force's precious planes, and anyway there were only going to be eight of them after he decided to reduce the initial number from twelve.[32]

Additionally, Pauline Gower had received her 'women's section on the condition that their pay would be twenty per cent less than those in the equivalent men's rank and the women, unlike the men, were required to pay for their own lodgings and living expenses'.[33]

Helen applied immediately. Having accumulated 1,500 hours flying time, as well as instructor and commercial licences for four countries, she brought a wealth of flying experiences that most male pilots could only dream of. In addition, she had flown over twenty different aircraft types, including a military fighter, the Hawker Fury.

The day before Christmas Eve, eight British women had been selected for the Air Transport Auxiliary. Most of the eight pilots brought records of over 1,000 flying hours each. Dorothy Spicer, who had been Pauline Gower's partner in their aviation ventures, was not initially selected as her daughter had been born the previous month.

The first team of women included: Winnifred Crossley who had learned to fly five years earlier and gave aerobatic displays at air circuses; Margaret Cunnison, 25, chief flying instructor with the Strathtay Aero Club in Perth; Margaret Fairweather, a Scottish Flying Club instructor with 1,050 flying hours and experience piloting over eleven different aircraft types; Mona Friedlander, 25, who was the first woman to perform army cooperation flying by piloting planes for training searchlight crews; Joan Hughes, 22, who was Britain's youngest girl flier when she was 17-years-old; Gabrielle Patterson, one of the first instructors in the Civil Air Guard and the leader of the National Women's Air Reserve; Rosemary Rees who had flown to Czechoslovakia the previous Christmas to distribute food and gifts; and Marion Wilberforce, a flying instructor and charter pilot for the Southend Flying Club.

While the male pilots were contracted via British Airways Ltd on three-month terms, women were contracted monthly.

Rosemary Rees recalled how:

> the storm of publicity burst and with quite a bit of fury. People wrote angrily to the papers to ask, 'Why should women do this emphatically masculine job while there are many men still available and looking for work?' Quite forgetting that, although these men existed, they possibly did not know as much about flying as we did.[34]

The National Men's Defence League wrote that 'the appointment of eight women ferry pilots marks another stage in the advance of the feminine invasion of men's jobs'. Through the British Broadcasting Corporation, Pauline Gower responded, 'we are a small group of women pilots with a job to do. We are just helping, along with others, to win the war. Our job will be unobtrusive, but it is going to be well and efficiently done.'[35]

The team was slated to begin work on New Year's Day. Quarters were provided at an airfield near London from where they would begin ferrying aircraft. The women's squadron donned the Air Transport Auxiliary dark blue uniform of a tunic, skirt or trousers, flying boots, a great coat and a forage cap. Over the gold wings on the jacket, the letters ATA were embroidered. The women supplied their own black shoes, black ties, stockings and the Royal Air Force blue shirts.

'Even when they had passed the initial assessments and begun ferrying aircraft, women were not regarded as full members of the Air Transport Auxiliary until they had passed the "Official Acceptance Test" with Mr A.R.O. MacMillan at Whitechurch', noted pilot Lettice Curtis, who joined the ATA in 1940.[36]

Throughout the first winter, the women ferried Tiger Moths, bright yellow biplanes with open cockpits, to northern England and Scotland. The Moths were cold and drafty as they flew through the bitter winter. The women fliers made their own way back, sometimes overnighting on crowded trains and sleeping in the luggage racks.

Sometimes they flew their Tiger Moths in gaggles or small groups to assist the Observer Corps who were on the ground. Rosemary Rees recalled:

> Gaggle flying was exceedingly irritating for seasoned cross-country fliers, accustomed as we were to getting ourselves around in our own way. It was impossible, except in perfect weather, to keep an eye on another airplane and at the same time on the map and on the ground to know exactly where we were. But in 1940, we were told to do it and we felt obliged to do it in this strange new world … with people on the ground likely to shoot, and ships almost certain to shoot. They were very trigger happy and we were told to give them all a very wide berth.

And they flew with the glare of publicity and hostility shining on them, lest they make a mistake:

> If one of the men broke an airplane it was a black, of course, and much to be deplored. But if one of us had broken one it would immediately have been, 'There, you see, we always said they couldn't do it and they can't.' … At each step forward we made, this terrible bogey was with us breathing down our necks.[37]

She recalled how their leader, Pauline Gower, met each prejudiced remark with calmness and aplomb. A common refrain was that 'women can't fly fast, complicated, heavy, fighting aircraft', and that they were not 'built or conditioned for it'. Her standard response was: 'Of course they can, just try them and see.' And then it was up to the ferry pilots to prove it. Rosemary Rees noted that this was 'a very massive weight to bear in chancy things like airplanes and English weather'.[38]

As the ferrying commenced, an MP in the House of Commons raised the question of their salaries compared to the pay of Royal Air Force pilots.

'In some quarters, the view has been expressed that they are overpaid for their admittedly important duties, having regard to the rate of pay of Royal Air Force pilots who face the hazards of war over enemy territory', reported the *Manchester Evening News*. Shortly afterwards, the news noted that women pilots employed to fly aircraft from factories to airports on delivery in 1940 were paid £250 a year, plus an £8 a month flying allowance.

The media had a field day on this subject. According to Rosemary Rees, Lord Haw Haw, William Joyce, in his broadcast from Hamburg, Germany, said something like this:

> The rich men in Britain who are being ruined by the war, have found a new way to get some of their money back. They are putting their wives and daughters into the Air Transport Auxiliary, at enormous salaries, to fly vicious fighting airplanes, which these unnatural and decadent women will doubtless enjoy.

Rosemary remembered her salary being modest – and becoming far less as the hostilities escalated and the challenging work increased.

She observed that

> there were many, many movements of different types of aircraft for which we did not know the reason, nor did we want to know. Once we had deposited an airplane at the place where it wanted to be, we immediately forgot it and went on to the next job. All these duties would have had to be done by operational Royal Air Force pilots, adding a lot of fatigue, travelling and organisation to their already heavy load of fighting the enemy in the air. It was to relieve them of this lesser load that the Ferry Service was inaugurated.

During her training, she recalled what a test pilot once said to her: 'The principle of flying is the same in all of them. Flying a lot of different types is just a state of mind.' The women ferry pilots had to acquire the state of mind which really boiled down 'to a justified confidence in your own ability'. The Air Transport Auxiliary technical department 'undertook the formidable task of giving us the state of mind and ability and they carried it out with remarkable success'.[39]

From the public's viewpoint, looking upwards in the sky, the work of the ferry pilots seemed blissfully serene and joyous. The reality was quite the opposite.

Rosemary's commander Pauline Gower had asked her one day:

> 'Here Rose, you've got some brains, would you like to come and help in the Office?' I said I was very sorry, but I really wanted to keep my brains for my own use. Pauline thought this amusing, but it was true. The stress and strain of those early days was such that I felt I needed all my faculties to deal with them.

One night in early January 1940, she remembered walking with Joan Hughes, 'or rather slithering on ice from Hatfield Railway to the Stonehouse Hotel' where they were staying. 'It was one o'clock in the morning, everything was icy and freezing, we were carrying our parachutes and our night bags, and we said, "If this is what it is going to be like the whole time, we really don't believe we can take it."'[40]

Training Military Pilots on the Homefront for the War Effort

At home in Canada, Helen continued to instruct provisional pilot officers who were aiming to join the Royal Canadian Air Force. At the Kitchener-Waterloo Flying Club, she expressed her determination to show the Royal Canadian Air Force that women could play a role in the air during the war. Media across Canada picked up the story that she had not been selected despite her stellar record. 'But she can point to a record as instructor of military pilots for South Africa, test pilot for a Canadian aircraft company and a total of 1,500 hours in the air', noted the *Victoria Daily Times*.[41]

The *Calgary Herald* reported that she is the only woman instructor of military pilots in the world. She was 'putting five men through their preliminary training', including provisional pilots Paul Henderson, David Knox and Donald Lowery.[42]

'If they didn't like a woman instructor, they didn't show it', Helen grinned. 'I was the first one those military pilots had ever had. I got on well with my men students, but of course, they were under military discipline and couldn't very well object.'[43]

She suggested that her presence in the officers' mess in Kitchener may have prompted the young Canadian pilots to learn a different language. 'When I was associated with the officers in South Africa, the Colonel one day asked how it came about that so many of the young officers were displaying an interest in Afrikaans, the Boer language', she recalled. 'No one seemed to know, until at last one officer admitted that they couldn't very well swear in English in front of a woman.'[44]

The *Windsor Star* observed that even though she couldn't land a role with the Royal Canadian Air Force, she continued to train fliers for war service. She taught the preliminary course for the Provisional Officer Pilots, she said, teaching blind flying, ground school aeronautics and aerobatics, including elementary types such as loops and inverted flying slow rolls. 'I think a woman instructor can be as every bit as good as a man, and perhaps better sometimes', she noted.[45]

The *Ottawa Citizen* recalled an earlier interview when she was studying for her instructor's licence in Ottawa:

> At the time, she told *The Citizen* that she believed women could play an important part in civil and wartime aviation.
>
> In the office of Group Captain A.T. Cowley, superintendent of air regulation for Canada, Miss Harrison bubbled over with enthusiasm for the future of aviation.

> At that time, there was no declaration of war, but she said she would be prepared to teach men to fly in the event of war.[46]

In Johannesburg, the *Daily Rand Mail* captured the positive support of the aviation community when they learned of Helen's success instructing.

> Flying people in the Transvaal, in fact throughout the Union, are saying, 'Well done, Helen', as the news has come through that Miss Helen Harrison, formerly an instructor at the Grand Central Aerodrome, Johannesburg, and later at Grahamstown, is the first British woman to instruct military pilots in this war.
>
> Even in England, where women have been employed as ferry pilots, not one of them possessing an instructor's licence has been called on for service instructional work. Miss Harrison is busy in Canada, the land of her birth, teaching young Canadian Air Force pilots to fly.[47]

Chapter 7

Seeking Space in the Sky

> Women with wings are soaring towards the sun. Flinging off the shackles of the earth, they swoop where once only their dreams dared venture. And Vancouver women have been among the first to try their wings and make records for themselves. Vancouver can boast the first woman in the world to receive a master's degree in aeronautical engineering (Dr Elizabeth MacGill) and the only woman on the continent to act as army instructor for training men pilots (Helen Harrison).
>
> The drone of the wings of a new generation, following their sisters' air lanes, can be heard on the horizon. Symbolic of these, who too lifts eyes skyward, is Beryl Armstrong, whose morning hours since April have been spent in the air.
>
> 'Flying is the most wonderful sensation in the world,' says Beryl. 'It's something I've always wanted. After all, the future of transportation is in the air. I want to be ready.[1]
>
> Margaret Ecker Francis, *The Province*

By the beginning of 1940, twenty-two clubs across Canada were offering elementary flight training in coordination with the British

Commonwealth Air Training Plan. It was originally intended that the Kitchener-Waterloo Club, for which Helen was instructing, would train twenty-four pilots a month. Then it was determined that training would be more effective if the group sizes were smaller, with classes limited to five men. Helen taught the first group of provisional pilots at the club.

On 5 January 1940, three of her pupils – David Knox, Romney Lowry and E.C. Kenrick – passed the stringent fifty-hour test. They departed for Trenton Air Base in Ontario for additional training.

The remaining two, Don Lowry and Paul Henderson, were unable to take their exams due to inclement weather. Passionate about flying, Paul had applied to the Royal Canadian Air Force upon high school graduation and had been accepted just prior to Great Britain declaring war on Germany. On 8 January 1940, Don and Paul passed their flying exams at Toronto airport. Fight Lieutenant Peter West and Flying Officer Robert Byers conducted the flight exams.

Instructors Helen Harrison and Harvey MacPherson were complimented by Flight Lieutenant West 'on the general high standing of the students'.

'Particularly noteworthy was the proficiency of the students in aerobatics', he said. 'Generally, students coming up for their fifty-hour test show little ability in aerobatics.' He informed the pair that they did comparatively well in their earlier written tests. The standing of Helen's pupils at the Kitchener-Waterloo Flying Club was third out of six such groups in his jurisdiction.

Immediately, Helen began training a second class of provisional pilot officers. Flight Lieutenant West explained that 'the training to be given was different than anything they may have received in the past', as the course was difficult.[2]

Becoming Involved in Growth of Airmindedness

Interest in aviation was fast growing among women across the Canadian provinces. *Canadian Aviation* magazine in February 1940 featured women's involvement in the growth of airmindedness and flying throughout the country. The article noted that women were designing aircraft and instructing future pilots. Women in increasing numbers were becoming employed in aircraft factories and air transportation companies, including Trans-Canada Air Lines.

Canadian Aviation noted that the women making a difference in aviation included Dr 'Elsie' Elizabeth Gregory MacGill, chief aeronautical engineer for the Canadian Car and Foundry Company, and Helen Harrison, the first licensed woman flying instructor to teach in Canada.[3]

By May, 306 pilots were being trained at 22 flying clubs which had offered their facilities to the Royal Canadian Air Force. The majority of the clubs had secured contracts, including the Hamilton Aero Club which was contracted to train seven student pilots. Helen returned to the Hamilton Club to which she had brought her Royal Canadian Air Force provisional pilot instructional knowledge and skills. Instructor James Davidson was hired to fill her shoes at the Kitchener-Waterloo club.

On Canada's west coast, pride began to grow that women trailblazers in Canadian aviation were all born in British Columbia. In addition to Helen and 'Elsie' MacGill, who were born in Vancouver, the Flying Seven had become Canada's largest women's flying club. It was also the only organised group of licensed women pilots which, in the early days of the war, offered its services to the government.

According to *The Province*, 'As yet they have not been accepted and Tosca Trasolini, Elianne Roberge, Margaret 'Margo' Fane, Mrs S. Barratt 'Rolie Moore', Betsey Flaherty, Mrs Jeanne Gilbert and Jean Pike go about earthbound tasks with their thoughts racing skyward.' The trailblazer of the sky was Jeanne Gilbert who, in 1929, was the first BC woman to earn a pilot's licence.

The paper emphasised that 'Helen Harrison, whose plane has throbbed above England, South Africa, United States as she became one of the outstanding flyers of the world, is Vancouver-born.' Elsie MacGill had become 'the first woman to fly on the maiden flight of a plane she designed herself.'[4] The Maple Leaf Trainer, a biplane, was designed in 1938 and manufactured by Canadian Car and Foundry. Though not a pilot herself, Elsie MacGill opened many doors and opportunities for women in aviation.

Across the nation, a groundswell of support for Canada at war began to grow. The National Film Board focused the third film in its series on women's efforts on the home front. The ten-minute, fast-moving film featured women working in war offices, factories, hospitals and in their homes, both in towns and on farms, and in unique roles. The film's narrator described 'Elizabeth MacGill of Port William designs aircraft for the Royal Canadian Air Force and Helen Harrison of Kitchener takes off in her plane to instruct a recruit in the first principles of flying'.

The film also showed women training in skills, such as driving and repairing trucks, which 'will enable them to take the place of the men who are called on to fight'.

'They work in munitions and aircraft factories, as well as in textile mills. And in their leisure hours, there are the many things they do in canteens and in the social services to help the man on active service and their families.'[5]

Seeking Recruitment in the Royal Canadian Air Force

'We want every man for the Air Force we can get', broadcasted Royal Canadian Air Force recruitment officers during the summer of 1940. Recruiters outlined 'the tremendous training program ahead for Canadian airmen, wherein 30,000 flyers will be turned out each year by the assistance of another 40,000 in ground schools'. Men were being 'called up fairly quickly now', explained recruiter Flying Officer William S. Lighthall.

The greatest need, he iterated, will be for airmen, particularly pilots, observers, gunners, and wireless operators. Also needed were applicants for instruments, engine mechanics and metal airframe mechanics. The Dominion-Provincial Youth Training Program was expected to keep a 'steady flow into the ranks'. A large increase in applications had been received since 'the government announced its intention to conscript men'.[6]

While men were being recruited for the Royal Canadian Air Force, flying clubs across Canada were stepping up. The first elementary flying training school in the British Commonwealth Air Training Program opened at Malton airport near Toronto, which had opened the previous year. Twenty-four students arrived from all corners of Canada to complete the second stage in their training. Malton was home to wartime industries including Victory Aircraft.

The eight-week program was designed to provide each Royal Canadian Air Force student with fifty hours of flying time and 150 hours of ground instruction. Students were trained in instrument flying, aerobatics, machine-gun firing on the range, wireless telegraphy and parachuting in addition to many other aviation skills.

The school, operated by the Toronto Flying Club, used twenty-seven Fleet trainers (Finches) and employed fourteen instructors. Every four weeks, twenty-four pilots were expected to graduate and progress to their secondary training phase.

The Royal Canadian Air Force's expansion drive continued to deny Canadian women pilots the opportunity to directly contribute to Canada's war efforts.

In the *Toronto Star*'s weekly column 'With Canada's Airmen', Daphne Shelfoon raised her ire about the exclusion of qualified pilots based on gender. Daphne was the only female transport pilot, and the first woman instructor to be trained in Canada. With Helen Harrison, both women anxiously sought 'an opportunity to give the country the benefit of their flying ability'.

Daphne wrote:

> The way I feel about it is that I am a pilot and I want to do something to help our country at war. However, when I ask to take the four-week Royal Canadian Air Force instructor's course at Trenton, they throw up their hands in horror at the thought of a woman at an air training school.

By this time, Helen had about 2,000 flying hours in her logbook and vented her frustration to the *Toronto Star*'s columnist: 'For goodness sakes, If I can't do as good instructing as these lads with 100 or 200 hours, I'll go out and shoot myself.'[7]

Turning a Focus Towards Ferrying Planes

By mid-summer of 1940, the Second World War in Europe showed no signs of abating nor reaching any peace negotiations. Aerial warfare was reaching catastrophic heights with countless numbers of lives lost, families devastated, aircraft destroyed, cities bombed and ships sunk. Factories were working round the clock to manufacture bombers and fighter aircraft for the Allies. The need for pilots to ferry planes from assembly lines to military airports was growing rapidly. Additionally, plans were underway to start ferrying American-built fighter craft across the Atlantic. Multi-engine bombers would soon be flying a great circle route across the North Atlantic between Newfoundland and Ireland.

The British government recognised that assistance was needed immediately from North America to meet the demands for aviation personnel.

Experienced civilian pilots were needed in three fields: as instructors in the air corps, as pilots for transporting planes from English factories to air bases, and as pilots to ferry North American-made bombers across the Atlantic.

The British and Canadian governments collaborated on a program in which experienced American aviators would be invited to apply for a position with either the Royal Air Force or Royal Canadian Air Force. The Canadian government would be the conduit through which American pilots, co-pilots and navigators would be recruited, hired and given flying assignments.

Top fliers were brought on board to promote the recruitment processes, including Canadian trans-Atlantic pilot Captain J. Errol Boyd, round-the-world flier Clyde Pangborn, and First World War veteran and ace illustrator Clayton Knight.

As recruitment for male American civilian aviators had captured the public interest, female pilots were questioning why there was no space for them to contribute.

'There is no question that for every woman pilot who can be used, more able men will be released for combat and other military phases of aviation', wrote the *Chattanooga Daily Times*. It noted that of a potential air reserve of 18,500 American civilian pilots, 600 were women 'who could give a good accounting of themselves if utilised in proper places'.[8]

At the beginning of August, Clyde Pangborn galvanised women pilots when he commented that 'there was a possibility women pilots might be hired to fly planes for the British in Canada and England'.

'If the British approved the idea', he noted, 'women fliers would be used as ferry pilots or other civilian tasks.'[9]

Helen reasoned that if experienced Canadian women pilots could not get into the Royal Canadian Air Force instructor's program at Trenton, this plan might open doors for women pilots, including herself.

In a New York City recruiting office, Captain Boyd served as the chief hiring manager and advisor for the Canadian government. In addition to checking the applicants' skills and licences, Captain Boyd tested their qualifications in multi-engine planes.

'Our aim is to get the finest material possible without jeopardising the airlines here', he said. 'Only those who do not have jobs on commercial airlines and who have had considerable training in flying large ships have been accepted.'[10]

Pilots were required to have both transport licences and instrument ratings. After passing the exams, and being recommended for service, they travelled to Canada for further tests. Successful recruits entered the employment of the British or Canadian governments when they signed contracts. Aviation personnel flew to Montreal in Quebec on expedited passages. From Eastern Canada, they travelled to England on British-owned commercial flying boats, or they waited for their assignments to ferry planes across the Atlantic.

Assisting Captain Boyd in New York with the momentous administrative work was his 20-year-old daughter, Kathleen. She noted that her father was receiving 'in the neighbourhood of 150 inquiries a day', and 'had received an application from a woman in Toronto who wanted a position for ferrying aircraft duty in England. This was Helen Harrison, who has the training of some 50 Canadian pilots to her credit.'

Helen expressed her opinion to the *Star Weekly* that there was 'no reason why women shouldn't be playing a greater part in the air in this war …. There is too much prejudice regarding women in the air. I have tried to get a job ferrying military aircraft. They wouldn't have me before, but there is no reason why I couldn't do a job like that as well as a man.'[11]

The *Star Weekly* agreed and wrote: 'There is no doubt Helen Harrison is well-qualified for the ferrying job, but the decision to admit women pilots has not yet been reached.'[12]

Captain Boyd explained that pilots ferrying planes from factories to airfields in England would be, in effect, relief pilots for the Royal Air Force. They would have civilian jobs but not wear uniforms and not belong to the British military. They could not be over the age of 35 and were required to have experience in piloting pursuit and bomber-type planes.[13]

Thousands of young men were prepared for training in Canada, reported the *Kansas City Star*, but the instructor situation created a severe bottleneck.[14] 'Pilots engaged to shuttle warplanes from factories in the British Isles to military centres are being sent abroad by boat at a rate of twenty-five to thirty a week', reported the *New York Daily News*.[15]

In the autumn, crews began ferrying bombers along the aerial highway to Great Britain. The plan to ferry Douglas, Martin and Lockheed bombers was made possible by the resumption of Atlantic flights by Imperial Airways. Imperial's flights had restarted on a longer circuitous route, with

Helen Harrison, Air Transport Auxiliary, 1942.

New pilot Helen in the centre of a group of Southern Aero Club pilots and friends with an Avro Avian plane, G-AAWA. Standing from left to right: Robin Norwood, Flight Lieutenant Roy L. Brown, Mr Adams, Mr Siffleet, Mr Dawson, Cecil Lawrence Pashley (chief instructor), John 'Jack' Sale (junior instructor), Mrs Helen Barnes, Mrs Pashley and George H. Miles. Sitting, from left to right: Mr Buchan (head), Nowi Pashley (Cecil Pashley's daughter), Mr Stevens and Fraulein Manpell. Photo taken 19 August 1934. (*Canadian Aviation Hall of Fame*)

Left: Helen Harrison, Air Transport Auxiliary, 1942.

Below: Royal Singapore Flying Club. (*Canadian Aviation Hall of Fame*)

Helen Harrison as chief flying instructor at Sheffield Flying Club, England with an unidentified pilot, 1939. (*Canadian Aviation Hall of Fame*)

Helen Harrison in a Cub Aircraft, Hamilton, Canada 1939. (*Canadian Aviation Hall of Fame*)

Helen Harrison (fourth from left) with RCAF provisional pilot officers at the Kitchener-Waterloo Flying Club, Canada. Standing in front of a training Tiger Moth aircraft, registration DH82C, 1939. (*Canadian Aviation Hall of Fame*)

Above and below: New ATA pilots Polly Potter, Ann Wood, Helen Harrison, and brothers Captain Tom Smith and Captain Harry Smith, Montreal, Canada 1942. (*Canadian Aviation Hall of Fame*)

Right: Helen Harrison in an aircraft cockpit with Air Transport and Training Ltd at Toronto Island Airport, 1941. (*Canadian Aviation Hall of Fame*)

Below left: First Officer Helen Marcelle Harrison, Air Transport Auxiliary, 1942. (*Canadian Aviation Hall of Fame*)

Below right: First Officer Helen Harrison, Air Transport Auxiliary, Spitfire Mark IX.

Left: First Officer Helen Harrison with Third Officer Helen Richey, March 1943. (*Illustrated London News*)

Below: Pilot Helen Harrison in the cockpit of a Percival aircraft with two unidentified males, Toronto, 1946. (*Canadian Aviation Hall of Fame*)

Right: Pilot Helen Harrison in the cockpit of a Percival aircraft, 1946. (*Canadian Aviation Hall of Fame*)

Below: Second Air Industry and Transport Association instructor refresher course for Royal Canadian Flying Clubs' Association pilots in Lethbridge, Alberta. Women pilots completing the course, from left to right: Elizabeth Kerr, Dawn Dawson, Mary Willcox, Vera Strodl, Helen Harrison and Phyllis Drysdale, 1953. (*Canadian Aviation Hall of Fame*)

Helen Harrison with pupil pilot Svend Serup at the Prince George airport in northern British Columbia with a Luscombe Silvaire, CF-GYM, 1954. (*Sheila Serup*)

Helen Harrison Bristol with students in front of one of the planes she used for instruction. Taken at Quesnel Flying Services in northern British Columbia, 1968. (*Canadian Aviation Hall of Fame*)

Air Transport Auxiliary pilots Polly Potter, Ann Wood, check pilot and Helen Harrison at Dorval airport, Montreal, Canada. April 1942. (*Toronto Star*)

armed escorts along the British coast. The route between New York and Europe commenced via Newfoundland in Canada, and Ireland.

'It will be these experienced Imperial Airways pilots who will lead the way for the groups of twenty-five planes or more with American fliers at the controls', reported the *Kansas City Star*, 'while the veteran trans-oceanic pilots will lead the way.'

Clyde Pangborn explained that 'each pilot of the other bombers must have sufficient training in navigation to be on his own'.

The formations of bombers would be guided by surface aids on the 2,000-mile, 10-hour flight. Fighter aircraft would meet the squadrons near the coast of Ireland and serve as escorts. 'None of the bombers will be armed and the radio operator's quarters probably will be in the bomb racks.' Each bomber would be equipped with a crew comprising of a pilot, co-pilot and radio operator.

In mid-September, the Canadian Minister of Defence for the Air, The Honourable Charles G. Power, reported that by 1 October there would be 26,500 officers and men enlisted in connection with air training. Of these, 1,600 officers and 15,000 men were included in the British Commonwealth Air Training Plan. Additionally, there were 3,500 civilians serving in connection with the plan.

Within a two month period, 107 trained US pilots had been recruited, with an additional 65 in the process of being enlisted in the Royal Canadian Air Force. Most were pilots and a few were technical specialists. Some were destined to become fighter pilots, while others would be used for ferrying planes.

By the beginning of December 1940, warplanes were streaming out of factories in such large numbers that hundreds of ferry pilots in England were making three or four deliveries a day. The Air Transport Auxiliary had recently added 200 pilots to their ranks and plans were underway to enlist 250 pilots as soon as they could be recruited and trained. So keen was the Auxiliary to bring on board more pilots that they were willing to consider pilots from the Civil Air Guard who had progressed a few hours beyond the 'A' licence stage. Applicants were required to be between 20 to 45 years of age.

'We'll be Ready!' Preparing Women Pilots to Aid in War Effort

After finishing her term at the Kitchener-Waterloo Flying Club, Helen met with the Royal Canadian Air Force in Toronto and offered to assist in a more active role.

According to Sally Knapp in *New Wings for Women*, 'Months of interviews with Ottawa officials followed, and, like many other frustrated patriots, Helen arrived exactly nowhere. The Air Force refused to recognise her status, evidently because she wore skirts when she said she wanted to instruct army pilots or ferry military planes in Canada.'

Although disillusioned, she did not let this slow her down. 'She decided that if she couldn't get her idea through the front door she'd try the back. Her idea to form a women's flying club was snapped up by Bob Redmayne's flying school.' As an instructor, she concentrated on attracting women to the school.

Forgoing the purchase of new autumn hats, twenty-five women enrolled in ground school and flying lessons at Air Transport and Training on Toronto Island. It only took two months for the school to boost interest. Inquiries flooded in from several hundred more women who were interested, but not financially able to take the course.[16]

> 'You can't buy new hats and stockings and fly too,' grinned Mabel Maxwell, as she wiped smudges of oil off her hands. She had just crawled under the nose of a small training plane to fasten the cowling pins. 'But it's worth it.' A teacher at Port Credit, Mabel Maxwell was typical of the flying students in the class. Pupil pilots were stenographers, clerks, teachers, factory workers and one was a housewife.
>
> 'I always wanted to fly,' she said. 'This class provided the opportunity. None of us expect the Royal Canadian Air Force will ever accept girls, but the time might come when there will be a shortage of male commercial fliers and then we'll be ready.'[17]

The pupils took flying lessons as their income permitted. It was recognised that 'at this rate, they wouldn't be qualified for any practical air job in less than two years'.

But what Helen hoped to do was to form a Women's Auxiliary Airforce, like those operating in Australia, England and South Africa. She envisioned that influential women in Canada who were war service workers would boost the movement, firms and sponsors would provide the aircraft, equipment, uniforms and other necessities, and she hoped to train women specifically for ferrying work.[18]

Despite her passion and efforts, Helen realised there weren't enough qualified women pilots yet to 'make any sort of impression on the military or government'.[19]

Speaking to a reporter from the *Toronto Star*, Helen shared that this was the reason why she started the class. She pointed out that women were already 'doing a fine job ferrying military planes' from factories to air bases.

'We're going to be ready for any eventuality', she added. The course consisted of lectures on Mondays and Wednesdays on flight theory, navigation, mechanics and meteorology. Flying lessons on dual-control planes were on Saturdays.[20]

Word had reached the West Coast that the Commonwealth would soon have a group of twenty-five women 'schooled in aeronautics and ready to aid the country should the emergency arise'.[21]

At the end of October, the Canadian Air Minister, The Honourable Charles Power, relayed at a press conference that there were 'no plans at present to make use of women pilots who hold flying licences'.[22]

Speaking to *Newsday*, Helen Mroczkoska, the first Civil Aeronautics Authority-trained woman pilot, expressed confidence that there was no doubt that women could attain excellence in aviation on par with the ability of men: 'The Civil Aeronautics Authority is doing a good job getting pilots ready for the planes that are going to roll from the assembly line of factories all over the country.'

'However, if the need ever arose, it is my opinion that women could assume even the rigorous role of the bombing and pursuit plane pilot.

Women could be as relentless and as ruthless in the defence of their country as any man could.'[23]

By December 1940, the number of pilots in the Air Transport Auxiliary in England had risen to 243, of whom 26 were women pilots. As the year closed, Helen learned that her younger brother had enlisted with the Royal Tank Regiment in the British Army. Cadet Albert Testemale, 28, had begun training for active military service. The Second World War was hitting close to home, and Helen was more determined than ever to serve.

Comingling Elation with Grief

A New Year's snowstorm in 1941 grounded all aircraft at Toronto Island Airport and those of the Norwegian air training centre. Little Norway had attracted about 120 Scandinavian aviators and soldiers when it set up camp in the autumn of 1940. Now they sat out the blinding snowstorm which swirled over the airport, Lake Ontario and city.

On the last day of 1940, one of Helen's pupil pilots, Mabel Maxwell of Port Credit, passed her final exams for a pilot's licence. Celebrating New Year's Eve was a moment of sweet poignancy as Mabel had realised a lifelong ambition.

Speaking to the *Toronto Star* Mabel explained how 'I saved and since last May I've been able to go up for an hour or two each week. The test worried me, but it wasn't hard and now I'm certainly thrilled.' Flying a Stinson 105, she completed 'four landings within 150 feet of a mark, a figure eight over a prescribed course, and a spin from 3,000 feet in order to qualify.' There was a strong wind blowing but she managed to nail her landings and master her aerial tasks.

Chief Instructor Pete Lennie related that 'she never missed a landing. I'd trust her to take a plane anywhere.' Mabel Maxwell became the first woman pilot to complete training with Air Transport and Training, and the eighth in Toronto. At the end of January, she completed her final exams and became a full-fledged pilot. Going forward, she planned to save and work for her commercial pilot's rating.[24]

There was further good news for Helen when she heard that one of her first Royal Canadian Air Force provisional pilots, Paul Henderson, known as 'Little Fella', had been assigned to a fighting squadron in Scotland.

Early in January that year, the aviation community worldwide was shocked to hear that one of Britain's greatest pilots, Amy Johnson, had parachuted to her death in the icy waters of the Thames estuary near London.

Amy had been ferrying planes and women pilots to and from their assignments with the Air Transport Auxiliary. On 4 January 1941, she flew from Prestwick airport to deliver an Airspeed Oxford to Kidlington near Oxford. The poor weather forced her to land at Squires Gate near Blackpool and she spent the night with her sister Molly. The next morning, on Sunday, 5 January, she was determined to complete her assignment despite the snow flurries and low visibility along her flight path. She left Squires Gate airfield at 10.45 am. Her flight was planned to take one hour. 'All right,' were her parting words, 'I am going over the top.'[25]

She had proposed to fly above the weather. 'The weather was bad with a cold mist and low racing cloud', described Flight Captain Alison King who was responsible for arranging the auxiliary ferry schedules in the Operations Division. 'Because of the occlusion lying over most of the country, it is reasonable to suppose that, due to the icing conditions in the cloud, Amy had gone above it into the clear.'[26]

Alison King noted that Amy Johnson's navigation was superb, despite having no wireless.

> This time there was no hole in the clouds and, as she tried to fly down blind through them, she must have found her wings were icing, the engines spluttering, and the Oxford getting out of control, thus forcing her up into the clear sky again, looking, still desperately looking, for that small gap to dive through to safety.
>
> One can imagine the small aircraft as it skimmed over the uneven, lumpy expanse of cloud, with the mockingly

> good visibility all around and the blue sky above, so alone and tied to the air by the icing conditions beneath.[27]

Ferry pilot Rosemary Du Cros explained that 'the top of an 8/8th cloud cover is like a vast, flat, white snowfield with no landmarks'. Cloud coverage is measured across eight equal segments of the sky with 0/8th referring to a clear sunny day, and 8/8th denoting a completely overcast, cloudy day.

> To fly a compass course over it without wireless requires a carefully plotted plan with accurate information about the wind direction and strength higher up; quite impossible to obtain at a small airfield like Squires Gate, Blackpool, during the war. Weather was rather a secret subject then because no one wanted to broadcast to the enemy what their weather was going to be like.
>
> Amy would have cast about all over the white field, looking for a darker place which showed the cloud was thinner there. If she ventured down into the cloud ice formed on the aeroplane. It was snowing in many places that day, and we at Hatfield had washed out flying.[28]

Alison described the scene that unfolded in the Hatfield Operations room when Commander Pauline Gower came in to enquire, 'Have you heard where Amy's got to?'[29]

'Nothing more was seen of her plane until 3.30 pm when it came down over the Thames estuary. Her aircraft had carried significant petrol for only a four and three-quarter hour flight – the exact time which elapsed between the take-off and the crash.'[30] Witnesses saw a parachute come down in the estuary.

Royal Navy Lieutenant Commander W.E. Fletcher with the trawler HMS *Hazlemere* died in a gallant rescue attempt when he and other rescuers dived into frigid waters to find her in the wreck.

Sometime after, Alison King met a young officer from the *Hazlemere* who recounted in graphic detail the crash and attempted rescue. The moment was very fresh in his mind:

> with its yellow fog, icy air and the heaving dark waters and the aircraft diving, almost silent like a rush of air, down like a huge bird to settle so near them. He told of the aloneness and terrible vulnerability of the parachutist as she came down to meet the leaping water, the mockery of finding her luggage floating afterwards and how they salvaged it, sick at heart that they had lost not only the pilot but their own captain.[31]

Her father, John William Johnson, noted that Amy had joined the Air Transport Auxiliary six months prior to the accident.

> She knew it was a risky job, but she felt she had to do something for Britain, and flying was the job she knew best.
>
> Our only comfort is that she gave her life for her country. We always knew her career might end this way. But she never spoke of such a possibility. She was always absolutely confident.[32]

The Air Transport Auxiliary rules prohibited pilots from 'flying above 2,000 feet and required visibility of at least 2,000 yards and a cloud base at 800 feet to ensure they could always see the ground – and the ground defences could recognise them – and navigate safely.'[33] The Auxiliary pilots were also not permitted to conduct night flying.

Amy Johnson will always be remembered as the first woman to fly alone to Australia in a light plane, a Moth. She learned to fly at London Aero Club at Hatfield, earning an 'A' licence in 1929. In 1936, Amy flew to Cape Town and back, breaking three records all held by Flight Lieutenant Rose, and received a gold medal from the Royal Aero Club.

That Amy Johnson, a brave, brilliant and determined pilot, tragically perished while ferrying warplanes was a sharp reminder of the dangerous work being undertaken by Air Transport Auxiliary pilots in Great Britain. Her death tore a huge hole in the fabric of the aviation community. Amy's long distance flights and numerous flying records, for which she fought with quiet courage and fortitude, broke barriers for women pilots around the world.

Rising to Become Chief Flying Instructor

In Toronto, Helen was appointed chief flying instructor with Air Transport and Training in February 1941, becoming the first woman to hold such a position in the Toronto aviation field. Her appointment arose when chief instructor Pete Lennie joined Trans-Canada Air Lines. Pete Lennie departed for Winnipeg, Manitoba, to start a three-month course in preparation for his role as a commercial pilot.

'The responsibility isn't new', noted the *Star*, 'however, as she held a similar position at the Kitchener-Waterloo Flying Club and taught to fly a number of Royal Canadian Air Force pilots now fighting planes over England.'[34]

For the second time, the promotion was bittersweet and a reminder that her career goal of joining Trans-Canada Air Lines continued to be elusive and beyond reach.

In an article headlined *Women in the War*, the *North Bay Nugget* reinforced the vital roles of women. 'In this war, women are not entirely content with sitting back of the lines. Many branches of military activity now have women in important posts. One is chief aeronautical engineer at an important Lakehead factory working on war orders. Now Helen Harrison takes on the job of chief instructor.'[35]

Around the same time, a sweet nod to Helen was made in an aviation announcement. Gordon Munro, an air engineer and flying instructor, had been appointed flying instructor to the Kitchener-Waterloo Flying Club. Gordon was following Helen's career trajectory. His path to the flying club also began at the Cub Aircraft Company in Hamilton and included a stint instructing for the air force.

'Instructor Munro follows in the footsteps of a former Hamilton aviatrix, Miss Helen Harrison, who is now an instructor at the island airport in Toronto', declared the *Spectator*.[36]

With her trademark cheerfulness and positivity, Helen easily stepped into her new role. The Air Transport and Training Company was beginning another class of women pilots and instruction for Norwegian pilots with Little Norway.

'Upwards of a dozen men in uniform are flying steadily with Air Transport and Training at Island airport', reported the *Star*. 'Half are Norwegians who ferry over from Little Norway and fly the Stinsons with instructress Helen Harrison, hoping that a private flying licence will advance them when they undertake air crew training.'[37]

Helen's joy of flying over Lake Ontario with pupils, and the dizzying heights that her full-fledged pilots achieved were frequently tempered with news from overseas.

In March, Helen received a shocking blow. Tragically, on 25 March 1941, Helen's protégé Flying Officer Charles Paul Henderson, 20, was killed in active service in an air crash in England. 'Flying Officer Henderson was full of the high spirit of youth', observed the *Star*. He was the second-youngest flying officer in the world at the time.[38]

She later learned that her fellow instructor, Captain Jack Desmond Dalrymple, at Haller Aviation in South Africa, had died in the service of his country. The 29-year-old pilot with the South African Air Force perished when his Avro 621 Tutor 721 collided with Tutor 709. The air crash occurred on 10 March 1941 at No. 3 Air School.[39]

Learning and Instructing by Trial and Error

One of Helen's pupil pilots at Air Transport and Training was Alan Galbraith Wingate, who became an accomplished pilot and Second World War veteran. Another student was Lou Wise.

At the Air Transport and Training Company, Royal Canadian Air Force air-frame mechanic Lou Wise was given an opportunity to remuster as a pilot with flying lessons. Lou, who grew up in Toronto, was stationed at No. 6 Service Flying Training School in Dunnville. On his forty-eight-hour passes every two weeks he took lessons at Island Airport with Helen Harrison.

On 5 April 1941, he found himself at the helm of a Stinson 105. Over several weeks, he became versed under Helen Harrison's tutelage with straight and level, medium turns, effect of controls, faults and corrections in turns, take-offs and landings. By 1 May, he had amassed three hours and ten minutes of dual instruction. On 31 May, his logbook showed several flights that day: the first of thirty minutes, the second of twenty-five and the third, a further thirty minutes. Lou recalled:

> Early in the second flight, Miss Harrison said, 'I'll do a complete circuit and verbally review everything that needs to be done or considered during a circuit,' which she proceeded to do. She took off and climbed at the correct airspeed and rate of climb. The first turn was exactly at the proper place. Everything about the circuit, up to and including the landing and roll-out, was executed with exact precision. Then she taxied the Stinson back to the end of the runway and said, 'Now I want you to do a circuit, and I won't say a word.'
>
> That is one flight I'll never forget. If there was anything that could be done wrong, I did it. In fact, I probably invented a few new wrong things right on the spot. Finally, I managed to complete some sort of base leg and get turned into final – wrong height, wrong airspeed, wrong throttle setting, wrong rate of descent, downwind checks not properly completed. Everything wrong. And to top it off, we were so far out over Lake Ontario you could hardly see the airport in the distance beyond the trees of Centre Island and Hanlan's Point.

> All this time, Miss Harrison had stuck to her word. She hadn't said a thing. But in many situations, there is a last straw, and I suppose the thought of having to fly a cross-country trip to get back to the airport was Helen's last straw. She spit out the words, 'I have control,' through tightly clenched teeth and literally snatched the controls away from me. She put on full throttle and got the Stinson moving quickly as it would to go across the beach and the island and into landing position. She landed the aircraft, braked hard and turned off the runway. Coming to a full stop, Miss Harrison then proceeded to let me have it.
>
> I had just turned twenty and I expect that Helen Harrison was four to six years my senior. I hadn't exactly lived a cloistered existence but I wasn't quite used to hearing ladies use such colourful language. Helen Harrison proceeded to cuss me out. It was a classic performance. Never before nor since had I been so roundly roasted.
>
> She finally ran out of ear-scorching words and said to me, 'Now taxi back to takeoff position and try again.' I proceeded to take off and fly a circuit with a silent Miss Harrison beside me. Everything about that circuit was as good as it had been bad before. Not a thing went wrong. After I landed and turned off the runway, Miss Harrison spoke to me for the first time since the tongue lashing. 'Now why in the name of Heaven didn't you do it that way the last time?'[40]

Lou continued to fly with Helen Harrison until 20 October 1941, by which time he had logged thirteen hours and fifty minutes of combined dual and solo flying. After earning his flying wings, Lou was presented with a silver cigarette lighter, engraved with a dedication to the most promising pupil.

He served with No. 111 (F) on the Curtiss P-40E Kitty Hawks on the West Coast following the Japanese entry into the Second World War. In mid-1942, he served in Alaska following the Japanese invasion of the Aleutian Islands.[41]

Building a Cohort of Pilots ready to Tackle any Flying Job

Helen's class of women pilots was instrumental in building a cohort of pilots who were ready to tackle any flying job. Each ten-week class graduated several fully-fledged pilots who were brimming with confidence, enthusiasm and patriotic duty. Their love of flying grew with every hour in the sky.

By July 1941, the city of Toronto and district had thirty-seven women pilots. Four of them held instructors' licences and one had earned her transport licence. The *Toronto Star* reported:

> Once they were girls who worked in offices and gazed wistfully out of windows up at the sky. They were lone eagles, getting instructions wherever and however they could, barely tolerated at airports, laughed at by some. They skimped on clothes and lunches, endured the jeers of overweening males, invested every penny in precious flying.[42]

Women pilots were coming into their own and preparing to form a Canadian girl pilots' association.

A half-dozen women met at the island airport and sent letters to all women pilots listed in Toronto and western Ontario.

'We don't want uniforms or to go marching around', said chief flying instructor Helen Harrison. 'We're not going to ask to be sent to war – we just want to get together to help one another.' Helen was recognised as the first woman to crack the instructor field in this part of Canada.[43] The group included new instructor Violet Milstead who was teaching at Paterson and Hill at Weston.[44]

Marion Gillies had passed her instructor's exam and was waiting for official word from Ottawa before signing with her father's aviation company, Gillies Flying Service at Barker Field. Before becoming an instructor, a pupil was required to have 250 flying hours and travel to Trenton for a test by Royal Canadian Air Force instructors. 'When Marion Gillies went up for hers, it was the first time she had ever put on a parachute.'[45]

The highest licence was that of a transport pilot which was held by Daphne Shelfoon, whose husband was serving with the Royal Canadian Air Force. It took 500 hours in the air to earn this licence.[46]

Quietly training with Helen was Mary Bishop, a young office worker. Her uncle was Canada's Air Marshall William Avery Bishop, VC, a world-famous First World War flying ace. By mid-July, she had been taking flying lessons for a month with the Air Transport and Training School on Toronto Island. Her ambition was to become 'a qualified pilot in preparation for the time when Canada, like England, will need women in the auxiliary air service'.[47]

At the time she was training, Captain H.H. Balfour, Britain's under-secretary for air, had arrived in Toronto on a tour of Royal Air Force training stations. Captain Balfour's party had arrived at Toronto Island on board a Royal Canadian Air Force amphibian monoplane after inspecting the Royal Air Force bombing and gunnery school at Picton, Ontario. Captain Balfour cordially agreed to pose for a picture with Mary Bishop. 'Is Billy Bishop really your uncle?' he asked after they were introduced by a reporter for the *Star.* 'Yes, sir,' Miss Bishop answered, 'and I'm trying to follow as well as I can in his footsteps.'[48]

Flying pupil Mabel Maxwell was pragmatic about her career options as a pilot. 'None of us expects the Royal Air Force will ever accept girls', she said. 'But the time might come when there will be a shortage of male commercial fliers and then we'll be ready.'

This, concluded Miss Harrison, is the reason she started the class. 'We are going to be ready for any eventuality.'[49]

Founding the Canadian Women's Pilot Association

Atfero, the North Atlantic Return Ferry Organisation, ensured delivery of war planes from American factories to the Atlantic coast where British pilots would fly them across the Atlantic. The domestic ferry service was also intended to provide training for pilots.

Canadian women pilots continued to exert quiet pressure. The momentum grew for a national association when several women pilots from Hamilton and Toronto accepted an invitation from women pilots in Western Canada. Elianne Roberge, president of the Flying Seven which represented eighteen women fliers, had issued invitations for eastern and western pilots to join forces. Helen Harrison was prominent in the new organisation.

After their August meeting, every registered woman pilot was polled. The qualitative results would inform the national group of their training levels and willingness to ferry planes if the opportunity arose. The results would be presented to the air defence minister for the potential employment of women pilots in ferrying jobs to release men for the Royal Canadian Air Force.

At the same time, unfortunately, the up-and-coming Air Transport and Training School had been forced to suspend its operations at Toronto Island airport. The school's pioneer operator, Bob Redmayne, had been advised by the Toronto harbour commission to vacate the island by the end of August. The school had by this time trained many pilots for the Royal Canadian Air Force and Trans-Canada Air Lines.

Bob Redmayne tried to reach a compromise 'whereby he could curtail his flying to fit in with operations of the Norwegians'. His appeal was fruitless. The order to vacate had come from Ottawa.

'Termination of his month-by-month agreement cost Redmayne heavily', reported the *Toronto Star*. 'From nothing, he built his student roll until he had nearly 300 names on his book when he had to close down. He spent large sums on advertising and owned four modern aircraft.'[50]

With this closure, Toronto Island airport became, for all intents and purposes, a military airport used exclusively by the Norwegians.[51]

This was a poignant moment for Helen as she left her pupil pilots, the up-and-coming flying school, and the beautiful island airport just offshore from the city of Toronto.

Attesting to her popularity and expertise as an instructor, Helen was immediately appointed chief flying instructor for the London Flying Club. She returned to the familiar airport where she had worked previously for six months in 1939. Here she was slated to train Royal Canadian Air Force airmen.

Her ambition was to become a bomber ferry pilot. Since her application to be an Air Transport Auxiliary ferry pilot in August 1940 was not accepted, she worked diligently to boost her qualifications.

By this time, Helen had amassed 2,400 flying hours. She was the only woman in Canada to hold a transport pilot's licence and the British transport licence. She had worked steadily, without pause, as a flying instructor for the past five years in England, South Africa and Canada. She kept her licences current, passed all the medical exams, and ensured her own fitness to instruct.

Helen Harrison's voice was becoming heard as news media sought her perspective on the changing climate for Canada's women pilots.

'Indifference and prejudice are keeping women from a vital role in Canada's wartime aviation', she expressed in an interview in the *Edmonton Journal*. 'Women have proven themselves as capable as men at flying and many qualified women fliers are available today for routine duties such as ferrying planes.'

'Thousands more could be trained to be good fliers, but opportunity is lacking.'[52]

'I think I must have been the first woman in the world to hold commercial licences in four countries', she said later.[53] She had applied to the Royal Canadian Air Force because she believed the administration was more progressive than old England.

'When I applied to the Royal Canadian Air Force, I was rejected because I wore a skirt', she said. 'I was furious. I just couldn't believe it. I had 2,600 hours, an instructor's rating, multi-engine and instrument endorsements, a seaplane rating and the experience of flying civil and military aircraft in three countries. Instead, they took men with 150 hours.'[54]

In the end, Helen was refused entry as a flying instructor by both the Royal Canadian Air Force and the British Commonwealth Air Training Plan.

'I was madder than heck', she said. 'I tried to get a women's auxiliary air force group going but there just weren't enough qualified pilots to make any sort of impression on the military or government.'[55]

Chapter 8

Championing the Need for 'Atta Girls' in Great Britain

I'll never forget that night. Soon after dark, the main fuse for the lighting blew out. We got that replaced. Then the northern lights appeared. It was the first time I had ever witnessed the aurora borealis and from a plane it is weird and entrancing. The distant light shot up out of nowhere in the north to give the appearance of the first crack of a strange dawn.

Just before daylight, we were heard or were spotted by radar and suddenly through the darkness tracer bullets came up in front and around us. There was sudden consternation on board. Carlisle rushed up to me and the radio operator came running out of his compartment. The firing was probably coming from either a German submarine or one of our own friendly ships. I thought maybe the pilots in the mass meeting in Montreal were right after all and the Germans were going to make a test case of me.

From the coast of Ireland to Prestwick, Scotland, was a tortuous air route. The route went one way and then another – without any real pattern – and the route was

> changed daily to make it difficult for enemy planes or submarines to intercept. At the end of 12 hours, we came to a stop on the runway. Carlisle, under the regulation, made the landing.
>
> Jackie Cochran, *The Stars at Noon*

Across the Atlantic, the need for pilots to ferry planes was accelerating rapidly. Initially the Air Transport Auxiliary began with eight women pilots which expanded to fifty a year later. The 'Atta Girls', fondly named for their can-do attitudes, were ferrying aircraft as quickly as they were manufactured. The Air Transport Auxiliary soon became known as 'Anything to Anywhere'.

During the worst of the London blitz, on the week ending 15 September 1940, fifteen women pilots ferried 400 aircraft and logged 800 flying hours. On average, each pilot ferried twenty-six planes during a fifty-three-hour work week.

'That's an achievement which surely will figure one day in the annals of the Battle of Britain, side by side with the daring exploits of the Royal Air Force', reported roving correspondent Rosette Hargrove in the *Kingston Whig-Standard.*

'There was some idle talk about the glamorous wealthy girls, all owning their own planes, who had rushed to join the Air Transport Auxiliary at the outbreak of the war', relayed the correspondent. 'Nothing could be further from the truth … but for sheer hard work and endurance, they do their share and more.'

The pay for women ferry pilots was £6 a week for junior officers, £7 10s for seniors. 'Out of this, however, they have to feed and house themselves as well as supply all their kit.' Being civilian pilots, they had no access to free medical or dental care, nor other advantages, so the 'legend that they are being paid exorbitant wages is absurd'.[1]

When the number of pilots in the women's section reached eighteen, Commander Gerald d'Erlanger said: 'They fly as neatly and precisely as men; they feel that their first duty is to deliver sorely-needed planes on schedule, and so they fly carefully.'[2]

Advocating for a Similar Air Transport Auxiliary in North America

'I was overwhelmed by what the English women were doing in the Air Transport Auxiliary', observed American aviator Jacqueline Cochran, who, like Helen, had started her working life in a beauty salon.[3]

Jackie burst into the forefront of aviation when she set a new women's speed record of 331.7716 mph over a 1,245-mile course on 6 April 1940. Her time was 20 mph faster than the previous record held by the pilot Ernest Seibert.[4]

In her choice of activities, Jackie Cochran pursued the furthest and highest aviation goals. 'To live without risk would have been tantamount to death', she once remarked.[5]

Watching the Air Transport Auxiliary in action in England, she believed that 'women could deliver any types of airplanes from small trainers to twin-engine bombers anywhere from Alaska to the Panama Canal zone'.[6]

During a luncheon with General H.H. 'Hap' Arnold and American recruiting committee leader Clayton Knight for the British Ferry Command, Jackie Cochran asked if she could help with recruiting. Her conversation marked a significant turning point for women pilots in North America.

'General Arnold, in an impetuous moment', she wrote, 'turned to me and asked why I didn't do some of this flying to England yourself to dramatize the need. That was all I needed to be off and running. Of course I'd do it,' she stated, 'I jumped at such a chance.'[7]

That was the opening she needed, and she began to form a plan to fly a plane across the Atlantic.

What worried her more than the ocean crossing or Nazi planes, Jackie noted, was the exam she was required to pass in Canada before being permitted to make the trip.

'The exam had me plain scared and I boned up for six weeks before taking it', she explained. The examination was 'like the regular check-out American transport pilots have to take every three months to prove their reactions aren't slowing up or their knowledge rusting'.[8]

She thought the exam would be very stiff. To prepare, she arranged with Northwest Airlines to fly a twin-motored transport plane with a check-out pilot. Working out of Boston for six weeks 'he put the needles in me and put me through the regular captain's check-out', she said.[9]

> For instance, he'd lean over and cut out one of the motors suddenly when I wasn't looking. He did that once on a black night just when I was making a steep turn – and if I had been asleep then, maybe neither of us would have woken up again.
>
> The favourite little wrinkle was to give you a difficult problem to work out under the hood – that means, flying blind – and while you're working on it, keep firing at you on the intercommunications system with a stream of bright, chirrupy, attention-arresting gossip. The check-out pilot tries his hardest to divert your attention to test your powers of concentration. This one kept talking about a lot of things I was interested in, too, drat him – baseball and this and that. I was brought up politely and taught to answer when spoken to. It made everything complicated.[10]

Specifically, the test was intended to assess how quickly a pilot could react to sudden situations and how rapidly a pilot could co-ordinate their knowledge with the immediate problem.

> I went out with the chief pilot while he gave the periodic check flights to several of the captains on the line. It was an eye opener. I had been on many test flights but never had I seen anyone get the rough treatment those captains received. They had to be good. Getting them purposely lost and requiring them to locate themselves on instruments at night and to come back on the beam towards home base was not simple.

> Putting the plane into a difficult position while flying on instruments, then stopping one engine while the pilot was working his way out of this trouble was a tough experience.[11]

She practiced by completing sixty take-offs and landings, ten of which she completed while blind in the rear seat of a Harvard trainer. After this, Jackie felt confident she was ready to pass her check-out and fly a bomber. 'I was wrong', she wrote. 'Red tape and sexist insinuations stood mountainously in my way.'[12]

In Canada, preparing for her trans-Atlantic flight, Jackie's check-out test 'included take-offs under all conceivable conditions, flying under all conceivable mishaps and finally landings under all conceivable conditions'.[13] For three days she went through various flight tests overseen by Captain Cipher. By the third day her right arm was sore from pulling the hand brakes while taxiing the plane. This turned out to be a major issue. She was shown Captain Cipher's check-out report which noted that she passed all her tests but 'was not physically strong enough to handle the handbraking under all conditions'.

'The administrative officers sided with Captain Cipher and suggested that I take the title of Captain but not take off or land. A stronger man than I would do it for me. I was furious', she wrote in her autobiography.[14]

Jackie Cochran received word from the top brass that she was authorised for a ferry flight across the Atlantic. Then 'all hell broke loose', she wrote, as the 'pilots called a mass meeting and threatened to strike'.[15] Captain Grafton Carlisle, with several trans-Atlantic flights to his credit, was satisfied with flying with Jackie Cochran as well as the radio operator.

Assigning a woman to do a man's job was a direct challenge to their competence, they said, and if she would be shot down by enemy fire, then it would be the Air Transport Auxiliary's responsibility for the loss of one of North America's leading woman pilots.

> The upshot of the meeting was that the authorities appointed me First Officer for the flight but required that the navigator,

> Captain Carlisle, who was also a fine pilot, take the plane off the ground and land it. That, I thought, ended the battle of the sexes, although in a rather unsatisfactory way.'[16]

As first officer, Jackie's first task was to check the plane, which she did early in the morning of 14 June 1941 so she could pick up her permit from the American Consulate.

Walking onto the Dorval airstrip in Montreal, Jackie Cochran and her co-pilot Captain Carlisle along with their radioman were disturbed by the condition of the Lockheed Hudson 14 bomber plane they were to ferry. The bomber hadn't yet been outfitted with a life raft and the wrench used to activate the oxygen system was missing. Jackie bought a wrench from a nearby mechanic for ten dollars.

That afternoon, the Hudson roared down the runway and soared into the air. Once aloft, Jackie took the controls from Captain Carlisle and piloted the plane towards a refuelling stop in Gander, Newfoundland.

Late in the afternoon on the pre-flight check, she discovered the oxygen wrench was missing again, and one window was broken in the pilot's cabin. 'The window was repaired but no wrench seemed available. Again, I saw one protruding from a mechanic's pocket and this time, through force of orders, he turned it over to me', she related.[17]

The first take-off was a failure due to the Hudson being overloaded with gasoline. The second try was successful, and the bomber launched into the dusk over the grey Atlantic. Captain Carlisle, true to his word, turned over the controls to Jackie. The night flight to Prestwick in Scotland was unforgettable.

> Soon after dark the fuse blew. The lights went out, and while we were able to get them back on, something went haywire with the port engine. It didn't quit. We just couldn't close the gills on it. In the dark, however, I saw the aurora borealis, the northern lights, for the first time, and let me tell you, from an airplane they are weird but entrancing.

> Then we hit the soup. Overcast is never fun when you find yourself in it for four hours. I glued myself to the instruments. Just before daylight we must have been spotted because suddenly, tracer bullets came up in front and around us. The three of us jumped. The firing continued and I thought of the angry words from the pilots' meeting – would the Germans try to make an example of me? But the bullets stopped flying as mysteriously as they began.
>
> The coast of Ireland in the distance was the friendliest sight I had seen in weeks. But it wasn't over yet. The route from Ireland to Prestwick was a tortuous air tangle guaranteed to protect us from enemy intelligence. It had no pattern and jumped one way, then another. Twelve hours from Gander, I handed the controls to Captain Carlisle for the last time, and he brought us in easily.[18]

After the clearance of the plane in Prestwick, they flew south to London, arriving on 20 June 1941.

'It is a marvellous machine' she informed the huddle of reporters when she arrived. 'I had a wonderful trip.'

While in England, Jackie met with many women pilots of the Air Transport Auxiliary. 'I think they are doing a magnificent service', she commented.[19]

In flying a bomber across the Atlantic, she put in practice a theory that she had long held 'that women should have definite air piloting jobs in wartime'.[20] Describing this further, she noted that her bomber flight accomplished something more significant than setting another record. She realised that it showed that 'women pilots could handle noncombat military flying'.[21]

After ten days in London, which was badly battered she observed, she returned to New York and immediately started advocating to form a similar auxiliary in the States. This, she said, would relieve a shortage of manpower if the US became involved in the war. She stated:

> In flying, women can hold their own against men. Every woman who can fly a plane to factories or repair stations would relieve a man who could be used in action.
>
> Those Air Transport Auxiliary girls are flying many different types of planes, including some that are hard to handle, all over the country. And you should hear the enthusiasm of some of the men about the work of those woman fliers.[22]

Sparking Enlistment in the Air Transport Auxiliary with Vigour and Enthusiasm

The New Year of 1942 opened with news stories that illustrated the steps forward being made by women pilots in Canada towards their self-determination.

Behind the scenes in Britain and the United States, Jackie Cochran had agreed to organise a group of American women pilots to join the British Air Transport Auxiliary.

On 24 January 1942, it was reported in North American media that she had announced plans to recruit twenty-five women pilots to ferry planes for the RAF. One paper, the *Portland Press*, reported that 'she will start a tour of 12 states for the purpose of selecting from the 3,258 licensed pilots' in the US.[23]

According to the *Press*, 'She said that at least 500 of them are competent to pass the conversion course, the first step in qualifying for the ATA. She said she thought she would round up 75 for a start, drawing on them for the final 25.'[24] She explained that the women 'will go to Canada for preliminary army flying courses to prepare for the flight check'.[25]

On 29 January 1942, Helen wrote to Jackie Cochran at the Civil Aeronautics Authority in Washington, DC expressing her interest in joining a Women's Ferry Service for overseas duty in England.

'I believe my services would be of great value in this movement', Helen wrote. 'It occurred to me that you might require a representative here in Canada, as I understand the girls are to be given a course in Montreal, Que., before going overseas.'[26]

Along with her summary of her flying career, she noted that her two Canadian references were Mr Desmond Murphy, an inspector with the Department of Transport in Ottawa, and Wing Commander D. Joy, also an inspector with the Department of Transport in Toronto.

On 16 February Jackie Cochran enthusiastically responded by letter:

> If you would like to be one of the girls to go to England and can pass your check in Montreal, I would be delighted to have you. I am at the present time on a tour through the middle west and western part of the United States, returning to New York shortly. If you are interested in an interview, I will be glad to see you on my return.[27]

Without hesitation, Helen submitted her application with her summary of experiences on 18 February. She listed the twenty-two types of aircraft which she had flown since learning to fly in 1933.

Her certified logged time was 2,520 hours and her unlogged time was 100 hours. In the past year, she had flown 880 hours. In total, she had flown 1,435 solo hours in aircraft of 80 hp and under, and 1,150 solo hours in single-engine planes of over 80 hp. Her flying time included ten hours on multi-engine aircraft.

She included five testimonial letters from her previous employers:

The Cape Town Air Taxi Company certified that Helen Harrison was employed as an instructress from January 1937 to April 1937. Managing Director J. Williamson noted that 'she was engaged in the instruction of civilian pilots and also on the training of government pupil pilots. … She is hard-working and her capabilities as an instructress are definitely good', he declared.[28]

A Royal Air Force squadron leader, W.C. Kennedy, who was attached to the South African Air Force, had tested Helen to determine her suitability to give *ab initio* and advanced training to reserve pupils on light aircraft and found her satisfactory.

'She obtained very good results with her pupils that came under my observation, during the time she was instructing at the Cape Town (Wingfield) and Pretoria flying clubs', he wrote. He noted that she completed an instructor's refresher course at Robert's Heights in 1937 'which she completed to my entire satisfaction and was categorised as a "B" instructor'.[29]

The Sheffield Aero Club Ltd also confirmed that Helen Harrison was employed as a pilot and flying instructor between February and April 1939, with Club secretary Percy E. Smith writing:

> Her ability as a pilot is unquestionable and in the performance of her duties, she gave every satisfaction being equally adaptable to the requirements of both *ab initio* and advanced pupils. Her disposition is bright and cheerful, she has personality and should do well in whatever future capacity in aviation she finds occupation.[30]

Haller Aviation Ltd, with its flying schools in Port Elizabeth, East London and Grahamstown in South Africa, was equally positive. Managing director George R. Haller declared that 'her work was entirely satisfactory', and his company could 'thoroughly recommend her for *ab initio* and advanced instruction'.[31]

African Flying Services in Johannesburg also commended Helen Harrison's work as a flying instructor and pilot. In 1938, she had managed the flying school in Kroonstad in Orange Free State. She also had full control of the government training school at Grahamstown in Cape Province.

'Under our local regulations', described manager E. McConnell, 'the standard of instructional flying here is very high indeed, and as an instructor we have never had the good fortune to employ a better one. Her whole-hearted cooperation and hard work is much appreciated. We wish her success wherever she may go.'[32]

On 3 March 1942, Helen boarded a Lockheed Lodestar passenger plane in Toronto and flew to New York to be interviewed by

Jackie Cochran. The passenger manifest for the Trans-Canada Air Lines' flight listed her as a flying instructor, aged 32 years, 5 feet and 10 inches tall, with light brown hair.

During the interview at Jackie's cosmetics business, Jackie described the working conditions in Great Britain, which included blackouts, rations, hard work and long hours. She wanted to make it clear to all prospective pilots that this was not a glamour job.[33]

Shortly after the interview, Helen was selected to undergo training and to complete the flying check in Montreal. She became the first Canadian woman pilot to be selected for consideration to ferry planes with the Air Transport Auxiliary. She made tentative arrangements to leave the London Flying Club on 15 March and noted to Jackie that she could not remain idle for too long a period.

'I am eagerly looking forward to beginning my duties with the Air Transport Auxiliary',[34] she wrote to Jackie in letter dated 6 March. Helen was chosen for group three which included six other American women who were all summoned to Montreal on 17 March 1942.

The first round of exams was conducted by Captain Harry Smith of Brunswick, Georgia, and formerly of Manchester, England. His brother Captain Tom Smith of Texas oversaw the final exams. Helen was among the first eighteen candidates to crack the Harvard machine test. The exams were so difficult that many trainees failed to pass despite having spent many hours in the air and having piloted several types of planes. A third of the pilots who came to Montreal to try the course failed.

'I can tell in the first 30 minutes if a girl is going to be able to do the job', Captain Smith told a *Star* reporter. 'There's a set procedure and if they don't fit in, they are told immediately they are "washed out" and might as well go home.'[35]

After careful and rigorous testing, only four women qualified of six candidates in cohort one. In group two, only four of seven women passed. In the third cohort of six women, candidates Helen Harrison, Ann Wood and Polly Potter passed. Helen had 2,600 flying hours by this time.

Upon successful competition of their training and flight checks, thc first group signed their English Ferry Pool Service contracts. The contract stipulated that pilots must have a minimum of 350 logged hours, an excellent flying record, and, preferably, a commercial licence. A private licence would do, if their records were satisfactory. Applicants were ideally required to have map reading and experience with compass flying exercises, as these were preferable to instrument flying for this type of work. And finally, pilots must pass a flight test on a Harvard or Yale trainer, and be between 21 and 35 years in age.

Helen Harrison, Ann Wood and Polly Potter packed their suitcases and prepared to wait for their departure, details of which were kept under wraps.

In a letter dated 1 April, Jackie Cochran's personal assistant Mary Nicholson advised Helen that the Air Transport Auxiliary's schedule was delayed due to weather conditions and lack of equipment. A new rule stipulated that a maximum of 200 pounds of personal luggage could be brought to England.

From Montreal, Jackie Cochran departed in advance for England as she wanted to be there to meet each group when they arrived, either at Liverpool or at Maidenhead. As the Battle of the Atlantic raged, Jackie flew on a British Overseas Airways flying boat to England via a southerly ocean crossing. From Canada, her route included refuelling stops in Baltimore, Bermuda and Lisbon, Portugal.

The seventh and last group of selected pilots included Jackie's secretary Mary Nicholson, who was one of the earliest women to be licensed, in 1929.

Mary firmly believed that women were in aviation to stay. She made that clear in a paper she prepared for a symposium on women's life and work held at the Women's College of the University of North Carolina. As she was training in Montreal, her mother delivered her address with this final paragraph:

> In England women have become a vital part of the air transport auxiliary which is charged with the duty of flying

> planes from the factory up to the airports on the battle lines. Many of these girls flying there today are from the United States. It is not too much to imagine that women will be given an even greater part in protecting the freedoms of our democracy. And if they are called upon to give this service, the women of America will not be found wanting. Upon these ideals the future of our nation is based … The past record of femininity in blazing sky trails has left no room for argument on the subject. We are in it to stay.[36]

Arriving in England to Ferry Planes for the Air Transport Auxiliary

In the spring of 1942, trans-Atlantic passage to England was arranged for all pilots. The women pilots were separated into groups of two, three or four pilots, and their departures were staggered to ensure safe arrival. The German U-boat peril during the Battle of the Atlantic was one of the most frightening aspects of the war.

Fresh in everyone's minds was the tragic loss of life the previous year when the SS *Nerissa*, a Canadian troopship, was struck by three torpedoes from German submarine *U-552*. On the night of 30 April – 1 May, 207 souls lost their lives including 81 Merchant Navy men, 73 Canadian Army servicemen, 10 Royal Canadian Navy men, 8 Royal Air Force members and 11 Air Transport Auxiliary pilots from America. The *Nerissa* which had departed from Halifax, Nova Scotia, sank 80 miles from Ireland. At this point in the war, the tragedy resulted in the largest loss of life sustained by the Canadian Army.

A few months later, the Air Transport Auxiliary suffered another devastating loss of ferry pilots. Twenty-two airmen lost their lives when their Consolidated Liberator encountered low visibility and crashed on the Isle of Arran after taking off from Heathfield (Ayr). The ferry plane was delivering pilots to North America who would ferry new planes across the Atlantic for Atfero, the North Atlantic Return Ferry

Organisation. The crew who died on 10 August 1941 included pilots for the Royal Air Force Ferry Command, the Air Transport Auxiliary and the British Overseas Airways Corporation.

Jackie Cochran's women pilots sailed on seven different ships, some which voyaged in large convoys and others which steamed independently across the Atlantic.

'We went in small groups of two, three, four. Someone asked why', recalled one of the pilots, Roberta Sandoz. 'The answer was, so you won't be all lost at once.'[37] From Montreal, they sailed from the mouth of the St Lawrence River to Canadian ports such as Halifax and Sydney in Nova Scotia.

The first group of pilots who all signed their contracts on 10 February 1942 sailed from Halifax on 9 March on the Canadian Pacific steamer SS *Beaverhill*. On board were pilots Virginia Farr from New Jersey, Winnie Rawson Pierce from New York, Dorothy Furey from Louisiana and Louise Schuurman also from New York. Louise, originally from Holland, had emigrated to the US as her father was a Netherlands consul general. The *Beaverhill* joined convoy HX.179 with twenty-two vessels and convoy escorts.

One of the passengers, Dorothy Furey, had been informed that the previous convoy had lost six of its ten ships. This was nerve-wracking news.

The *Beaverhill* had mustered in the safety of the river downstream of Quebec until the 'Canadian submarine spotters judged the least bad moment to make a dash through the blockade of the Gulf of St Lawrence'.[38] The Atlantic voyage was completed without any mishaps and the pilots sailed into Liverpool on 23 March. Two days later, they were training on site in London.

In Halifax, the second group boarded the SS *Tetela* which sailed independently to Avonmouth near Bristol on 11 May. On board were pilots Grace Stevenson from Oklahoma, Virginia Garst from Kansas, Hazel Raines from Georgia, Suzanne Ford from New York, and Helen Richey from Pennsylvania. On 25 March, Helen Richey cabled her parents, saying that her group 'arrived safely, feeling well'.[39]

Passengers on the MV *Indochinois* included the third group which comprised Helen Harrison, Ann Wood of Maine, Polly Potter from Oregon and Evelyn Hyam of Massachusetts. They had been briefed on the wartime ship routine which included 'lifejackets at all times, no stopping if other ships in the convoy had been torpedoed, even to pick up survivors'. Not forgotten by the passengers was the fact that three ships were lost in the Gulf of St Lawrence the week prior to their departure.

The initial sailing from Montreal was delayed by three days due to a German submarine in the St Lawrence River which had stealthily ventured upriver as far as Quebec City. On the night of 11/12 May, *U-533* had torpedoed the British freighter *Nicoya*, and the Dutch freighter *Leto*.

When the *Indochinois*, with twenty-three passengers, was cleared to head downstream, it was delayed again at Trois-Rivières as the previous week's wrecks were hauled out of the shipping lanes downstream. Ann cabled her mother to let her know her ship was still afloat. After watching a group of Flying Fortresses pass overhead, she wrote in her diary: 'Perhaps someday it will be my chance to have a crack at one of those crates.'[40]

On 16 May 1942, the *Indochinois* sailed past the Heights of Abraham in Quebec City, entered the Gulf and joined convoy QS.1 which comprised eight ships. On the small Free French boat, Helen conversed fluently with the captain and staff in French and her fellow pilots in English.

'The food was good, plentiful (four meals a day) and French. The atmosphere was convivial, to put it mildly.'[41] The U-boats left the *Indochinois* alone during the nine-day crossing to Liverpool.

When the *Indochinois* docked at Liverpool on 25 May, no one greeted them. Helen was familiar with the British currency and rail system and arranged transport for the group to London. There they had no way of contacting the Air Transport Auxiliary headquarters. When she asked for a phone number she was refused with the comment, 'Don't you know there's a war on?'

She called her contacts at the Hatfield Flying Club and was able to reach Jackie Cochran who picked up Helen and her fellow pilots the next day and brought them to White Waltham for training. A captain at White Waltham heard of Helen's experiences as an instructor and thought she had arrived to instruct the ferry pilots. 'That was not what Helen had gone overseas for – she wanted to fly the planes herself, and she refused to instruct for the Air Transport Auxiliary', noted author Joyce Spring.[42]

Helen had arrived in England just as her brother Cadet (Jim) Albert Testemale was posted to India with his regiment.

The fourth group of pilots departed from St John's, New Brunswick, on the M/S *Mosdale*, a Norwegian freighter. Americans Margaret Lennox, Florida; Mary E. Zerbel, California; and Una J. Goodwin, Oklahoma joined several other passengers, five of whom were pilots with the Royal Norwegian Air Force. The *Mosdale* arrived in Liverpool on 29 June.

Sailing on the Norwegian fruit carrier M/S *Olaf Fostenes* was the fifth group. A trio of pilots comprising Catherine van Doozer and Evelyn Hudson both from California, and Edith F. Stearns of Oregon departed from Halifax. The *Olaf Fostenes*, which sailed independently, arrived in Belfast, Ireland on 28 June.

Pilots Opal Pearl Laster-Anderson from Illinois, and Nancy Jane Miller from California voyaged on the Canadian Pacific passenger liner SS *Winnipeg II* from Montreal. Opal, one of the few mothers in the Air Transport Auxiliary, bade farewell to her little son Norman. They arrived safely in Liverpool on 30 July.

Also docking in the Liverpool harbour on 30 July was the ship bearing the final four Air Transport Auxiliary pilots from North America. On board the faithful M/S *Mosdale*, which plied the trans-Atlantic crossing without fail, were pilots Mary Nicholson of North Carolina, Roberta Sandoz of Washington, Emily Chapin of Idaho, and Myrtle 'Mikki' Allen of New Jersey.

Captained by Gerner Sunde, the *Mosdale* encountered no enemy activity on the crossing. According to Roberta Sandoz, the ship zigzagged slowly with bursts of speed, which conveyed an impression of great danger to the passengers. The five women pilots sought refuge under a lifeboat where they played poker all night.

'But we still had the feeling we were going off seeking adventure', she recalled. Steaming into the harbour, the ship 'came into Bristol in the lane cleared between wrecked ships. Some were stern up and some were on their side, but it was a sobering moment for us, because we realised this wasn't an adventure, it was the real thing.'[43]

By the beginning of August, Jackie Cochran's pilots had survived the treacherous Atlantic crossing, set their boots on English soil, and were busy training and flying with the Air Transport Auxiliary.

'I've got a good bunch of girls', she announced to *International News Service* correspondent Kathleen Harriman. 'They're the best in North America.'

On arrival in England, they were issued with the official Air Transport Auxiliary uniform. Their full set of flying equipment included helmet, goggles, gloves, flying suit, boots, parachute, etc. which was issued against their signature and required to be returned on completion of assignment.

'They were a smartly turned out lot', Harriman reported. 'Some wore navy slacks, others the skirt adaptation of the Air Transport Auxiliary uniform. Each one had Air Transport Auxiliary wings on her jacket.'[44]

The seriousness of their Air Transport Auxiliary work was brought home when they learned that several young ferry pilots had recently lost their lives. Flying Officer Graham Lever, Third Officer Bessie Sawyer, and Third Officer Bridget Hill had lost their lives when the Air Transport Auxiliary plane they were in crashed into a bungalow. A fourth Air Transport Auxiliary officer, a woman, was injured. Twenty-six people were injured when they rushed to the house to extricate the passengers. It was 'believed that the petrol tank in the machine exploded when it contacted the fire in the kitchen of the house'.[45]

The first five of Jackie Cochran's pilots, who had arrived in April, knew that it could 'be dangerous, and that three British women pilots already lost their lives'.[46]

Flight Captain Alison King recalled the arrival of the North American pilots:

> They had come with much experience and many flying hours, and they had taken a big and voluntary decision to leave their own wide shores for what might be a tottering island. They had come to fly unknown aircraft in unknown treacherous weather that was reputed to be mainly fog. They had spent weeks being screened and undergoing medical checks and other formalities, and further weeks of training in Canada so that they would be equipped to fly what was needed of them.
>
> They had spent long dreary days of inactivity and insecurity, crossing the ocean in convoy and each morning there had been a diminishing number of ships round them – unexplained.

She noted the bewilderment that both the North American and English pilots felt when they met each other:

> there were, no doubt, the usual polite questions, 'Did you have a good trip?' and the hearty, meaningless reply, 'Fine, Fine' – no mention of course of the fear of being the next ship to be sunk. And then the questions from the North Americans, 'How are things here?' and our reply, 'Oh, not bad at all,' with no words about the bombing, the incessant nights wide-awake, the strain. British reserve? American bewilderment! Not the best mixture for a good beginning.[47]

Chapter 9

Flying as a Ferry Pilot with the Air Transport Auxiliary

To be airborne over the Pennines on a clear spring morning with a delivery to Colerne, Kirkbride or even Lossiemouth, jumping off point for Scapa Flow on the murderous North Atlantic, was to be blissfully cut off from the rest of the world.

Alone in the cockpit, past and present would recede until existence became once more a pinpoint in time, concerned solely with the immediate present of gauges, weather, navigation and finding that next landmark.

But when the cloud came down, so did the dreadful pall of death. Ferrying aircraft around well-defended Britain was, bizarrely, one of the most lethal activities on offer to either men or women in the war. Nearly one in ten Air Transport Auxiliary women pilots died. They flew without radio, and this was tightrope walking without a safety net: no weather actuals, no check calls to the nearest Royal Air Force or Met station, no radio beacon to home in on.[1]

G. Whittell, *Spitfire Girls*

Every effort was made to house the North American unit together. Jackie Cochran had particularly stressed to the pilots at the outset that although their work was,

> intensely interesting it must be recollected that it is being carried out in a country that is at war ... The fullest implications of this must be realised, [as] factors such as rationing, blackouts, etc. and the general shortages which are corollary to a country at war will mean a considerable difference in living conditions to those to which you have been accustomed.[2]

She noted that with the food ration cards, service posts and a few unrationed items, the pilots managed.

The Air Transport Auxiliary had been growing rapidly since it started in November 1940 with fifty pilots, of whom eight were women. When Third Officer Helen Harrison joined, the Auxiliary was 2,000 strong with over 500 fliers. The number of women pilots had at this point exceeded fifty. Helen recounted:

> I remember my first night back. Jackie had put three of us up in a hotel and the air raid siren went off. We were the last ones down to the shelter because we stayed behind to fix our hair and put on our make-up. We learned not to do that again.[3]

The pilots soon became accustomed to the bombings in England and learned to simply carry on. As Jackie Cochran remembered:

> there was a lot of carrying on, partying, worrying and theorising that you were spending your last night alive, so why not make the best of it? You'd be sitting at a dinner party, eating, drinking, playing backgammon, and you'd hear the bombers overhead. They'd swish right over and those planes would make a terrible noise.[4]

Jackie Cochran recalled sitting on the front steps of her house at 41 Orvington Square, behind Harrod's, with a blanket wrapped around her and watching the bombs rain down in the middle of the night. In witnessing a bombing blitz in London, she wrote in her book *The Stars at Noon*:

> the sky at night was full of flashing planes, searchlights, and anti-aircraft fire accompanied by the incessant sound of the sirens and explosions of bombs.
>
> The panes in my windows were broken from nearby bomb explosions. A house went to pieces a block up the street and then another hit came just a block below me. I concluded that the damage around my quarters was not heavy. I wondered whether Providence let St Paul's Cathedral stand up while most everything around it was flattened. It seemed to me also that some mysterious force was at work to save the Parliament buildings, palace, bridges and the power plants. London was pretty much a shambles at that time. People slept to capacity in the subways and cellars were at a premium.

The month of June was rainy, and this washed out flying at the new Air Transport Auxiliary training grounds at Luton. It had moved there after the de Havilland factory at Hatfield switched from building Moths to Mosquitos. Training meant ground school, navigation and mechanics with Captain Sloper, and elementary flight training on Class I and II planes.

In the Air Transport Auxiliary, a structured training program of successive, specialised courses enabled pilots to fly nearly every aircraft in Great Britain. Ferry fliers were trained to meet the wartime conditions: flying without wireless, navigating by maps and physical landmarks, and relying on the fundamental principles of flight and aircraft design to pilot a vast number of different planes. Flight Captain Alison King:

> It meant converting trainees on new types in easy stages so that they could eventually fly any type at any time. It meant that at the peak, a pilot could and did fly any one of well over 100-odd types in any one day – perhaps four in one day, from a four-engine bomber to a new type of fast jet, and then a pre-war light aircraft with a third of the approach speed of the jet flown but an hour before.
>
> The danger in the scheme lay in the fact that if in trouble, such as having to go round again urgently, or violently needing to brake, the pilot *might,* in the instant action that must be taken, forget which aircraft she was in and reach for the throttle in the wrong place, or a brake lever where it was not, and precious, vital moments would be lost.[5]

All aircraft were classed by engine type, so that after a training course based on one of several similar types, the trained pilot was able to fly them all. 'The gradual "growing up" of a pilot was carefully watched and nurtured', noted King.[6]

Ferry aircraft were divided into six groups according to their size, power and difficulty of flying. Class 1 included light single-engine planes such as the Tigers, Magisters, Fairchilds, Puss Moths, etc. Class 2 comprised single-engine fighters such as the Barracudas, Hurricanes and Spitfires, etc. Class 2 plus included additional training for some of the trickier single-engine fighters such as the fast wreckers like the Typhoon and Tempest, and the quirky American Tomahawk which liked to ground-loop.

Class 3 included the light twin-engine planes including the Avro Ansons, Airspeed Oxfords, and de Havilland Dominies. Class 4 included advanced twin-engine aircraft including the de Havilland Mosquito including all variants, North American Mitchells, Lockheed Hudsons, etc.

The fifth group comprised four-engine bombers, and the sixth group included flying boats. No woman ever achieved a Class 6 licence, but not many male pilots held this licence either.

Training in the different conversion courses incorporated real-time ferrying jobs. Pilots graduated through the classes as the production of warplanes increased and more and more different aircraft arrived in the United Kingdom.

Pilots began on the Miles Master, a Royal Air Force training monoplane that was equivalent to the Harvards used at Montreal's Dorval airport. A short apprenticeship ferrying Master planes with Wasp, Mercury and Kestrel engines followed. From the Master, the pupil pilots moved on to Fairey Battles and Hawker Hurricanes.

The new pilots were accelerated through training, flying a new type of faster plane every few days. The Supermarine Spitfires remained tantalisingly out of reach. Every step of the way, pilots and crew in the Royal Air Force closely watched the women pilots as they progressed through the classes of aircrafts.

Third Officer Harrison studied at the Advanced Flying Training School at White Waltham which provided conversion courses for Class 3 and 4 planes, and lecture courses for Class 5. Ground school included meteorology, map reading, navigation and mechanics. Specific classes taught pilots where to expect barrage balloons.

As an aerial deterrent, barrage balloons were sent aloft at strategic locations to protect cities, ports, factories and coal-fired industries. Balloons were tethered to cement blocks on the ground which were set in a circle. They bobbled aloft at 5,000 feet. During the Battle of Britain and the bombing blitz, these were lines of defence against the Luftwaffe as their trailing metal cables would severely damage or destroy any aircraft which ran into them. Attackers who attempted to shoot down a balloon could be caught in an explosion of hydrogen. German bombers were forced to fly above the balloons, reducing their bombing accuracy.

New pilots to England were required to complete twenty-five cross-country familiarisation flights along fixed routes. These were intended to create an imprint in their minds of a giant aerial map of England. Particular attention was paid to railways and Roman roads since these were the best lines to help pilots fly out of trouble. Pilots were required to memorise routes and destinations as they were considered at risk of being captured by the enemy. Destinations of aircraft being ferried were kept confidential.

Jackie Cochran was astutely aware of the challenges her pilots faced in their Air Transport Auxiliary training. Wartime navigation was 'no cinch'. 'When we ferry three or four different planes to three or four different destinations on the same day, we must be on the alert.'[7]

Third Officer Harrison did not require the full familiarisation training as she brought considerable experience flying over England. After nine cross-country flights, she was promoted to fly the Hurricanes.

During her training in 1942, Helen recalled making a forced landing on a field seemingly 'no larger than a dime'. Carburettor problems forced her Fairchild down. The field was so small that they couldn't fly the plane out but dismantled it to remove it.

> If I do say myself, I picked the only decent field available and got my Fairchild plane down perfectly. Not the slightest damage was done to the craft at all. After my instructor saw the field, he said it was the only one in the vicinity and a tough one to land on.[8]

That Helen safely landed an ailing plane in a small field was another example of her superb flying skills. 'She had not really completed her training, but her ability to land the aircraft safely under such adverse conditions won Helen her first commendation.'[9] 'Her last course was the hardest, but she passed with flying honours.'[10]

Her companion Ann Wood noted that training was two or three months long, and the women made multiple trips through various areas to familiarise themselves with the airports, factories and cities.

As soon as the women had successfully completed the training course, the Air Transport Auxiliary assigned the pilots a service number. Third Officer Helen Harrison was assigned W.75. After graduating, pilots were issued with a numbered flight authorisation card classifying them for Class 1 ferrying. Each pilot kept their card with them. Records of conversion courses were marked on the cards, showing the bearer to be endorsed on additional aircraft.

'If the pilot passed all three stages of training satisfactorily, she took a deep breath, patted herself on the back, and knew she was now a ferry pilot', explained Flight Captain Alison King.[11]

By mid-September, Jackie Cochran's North American women pilots were flying full time with the Air Transport Auxiliary. Five days later, the Auxiliary celebrated its third anniversary, noting that it had delivered its 100,000th aircraft and had flown 30 million miles.

Using Aircraft Notes to Fly Planes

All pilots were equipped with a remarkable set of pilot notes. The Air Transport Auxiliary produced the *ATA Handling Notes* which were white-covered books, one for each type of aircraft. All marks of a type of aircraft were included in one book which was meticulously kept up to date. Aircraft mechanical details were presented first and these included details such as fuel systems, cockpit controls and undercarriage retracting gear, etc. Secondly, it included instructions for starting engines, preparing for take-off, cruising, landing, etc. The notes also included careful instructions for emergency action in the event of problems such as hydraulic failure.

Pilots who were qualified on specific planes were provided with *Ferry Pilots' Notes*, which were small cards held in a stiff cover by a shoelace. The blue-covered flip-pad of succinct notes for each plane was small enough to be tucked into a pocket. These *Ferry Pilots' Notes* contained essential information on each type of aircraft a pilot was qualified to fly.

'That was all, but they were brilliant', wrote ferry pilot Ann Welch. 'No long-winded instructions on how to fly, just important facts such as approach speed, how to manage the fuel, and emergency systems for recalcitrant undercarriages.'[12]

Ann succinctly observed that the pilots were so busy each day that these notes were being read at the same time their assignments started.

> Sometimes, given a new type (of plane) with no spare time before last light, one read 'engine starting' while being driven to dispersal; 'take-off procedures and speeds' while the engine was warming up; and things like 'flaps and landing speeds' while in the air.
>
> It worked, probably because we were flying every day with little else to think about but the next airplane.[13]

Helen found the blue notebook of small cards so comprehensive that she did not need the white notes.

> With it you could fly anything. It told us how to inspect the aircraft, the procedures for take-off and landing, how to fly straight and level, and so on. You'd be up there and think, 'Now, how do you land it. Well, I'll look in my Blue Book!'
>
> As I was taxiing, I would read the recommended take-off and climb speeds and when I was at my cruise altitude, I would see what speed I let down and land at. That wasn't always the wisest thing to do because sometimes you were so busy map reading and trying to figure out where you were that you arrived at the airport before you had the numbers for landing.[14]

There were notes for all the 130 aircraft types which contained technical details such as stall speeds, flap operation, wheel operation, and range. Critical details had been compressed into these brief notes. And they included additional advice not included in the manufacturer's notes such as 'the Tempest's exit handle needed pulling extra hard', and 'the tail wheel lock on the Dakota was under the throttle, not, as marked, next to the oil controls'. For the Mosquito the notes read, 'Watch your step. They're inclined to bite'.[15]

The appearance of a new type of aircraft always generated suspense and excitement among the ferry pilots. There was the anticipation that they would be called upon to ferry it somewhere at a moment's notice without any previous instruction. Pilots needed to be able to fly 100 plus different types of aircraft at any time. On an average day, Helen may have jumped from a Taylorcraft to a Spitfire and then to a Wellington.

Nailing the Landings

Every day there was always the element of surprise. When pilot Ann Welch received her assignment to fly a Hurricane one day, she was astonished to find a gleaming new Mark II 'bristling with cannons and smothered with overloaded tanks' awaiting her on the airfield.

'They might at least have given me an old one to practice on', she wryly noted.[16]

Fortunately, the grim wet weather provided her with time to familiarise herself with its cockpit and controls. She undertook the drills repetitively while on the ground. The next day the dreary rain continued, and she was grateful for the Air Transport Auxiliary policy that stated that 'the pilot was responsible and must decide when to go – or turn back – and this decision was respected'.[17]

The following day, Ann Welch was given a chit to deliver a Hurricane from Brooklands:

> We went in a bus, eight of us, hot and nervous, reading our notes all the way there. We arrived near lunchtime, and as the machines were not ready, we went to eat in the old clubhouse. It was a relief when the telephone rang to say the Hurricanes were now ready.
>
> We each climbed into our aircraft and soon, with a great roar of Merlins, were taxiing out to take off and climb away over the camouflaged racetrack, banking. My Hurricane, bound for Scotland, felt stiff, new and most expensive with its four cannons, but this time with no overloaded tanks.
>
> The ground crew grinned when I told them it was my first, and as they pulled the chocks away my thousand

> horses galloped off at what seemed uncontrollable speed in the vague direction of the take-off point, with me mentally trying to catch up.
>
> I turned into the wind and opened up. Almost immediately we were in the air with a marvellous surge of power. Now, undercarriage up. The selector to bring up the wheels did not move. A second and more determined attempt brought no better result, except that the effort made my poor Hurricane behave like a drunk porpoise in full view of everyone.
>
> Before going on to the Spitfire we were expected to do a number of drama-free Hurricane landings, and I wanted to get three out of this trip. It was not going to be easy to get to Scotland before dark with the stuck selector keeping my speed at 150 mph.[18]

Ann went into Shawbury to refuel, and the ground crew attempted to free the selector. With a weather depression moving in rapidly, a patchwork solution was devised. During the flight, the selector refused to move. She had no recourse but to fly on to Silloth airport in Scotland with legs dangling. The new Hurricane landed with only a 'wump' square on the runway. Turning off at the intersection, she watched a Hudson come in, overshoot the runway, bounce and prance off.

'Each time it touched there were wild squeaks from the tires and jets of smoke. It ended up in long grass three feet from the main road. My little moment was forgotten in the excitement', she penned.[19]

On an assignment from Prestwick, she luckily flew another Hurricane to a southern destination, while other pilots in her group were given Tigers to ferry.

> A sky of washed blue had spread over the whole country, and visibility was fifty miles everywhere, even around Liverpool. This time the undercarriage went up like silk and my purring Merlin floated me south, without need for maps, over a September countryside looking as though

> England was just a big familiar garden. Again I landed at Shawbury for petrol, splashing down the runway through shining pools of rain still left from the day before; then up again to cross the vale of Evesham, its trees bright with fruit, down low over the house where my parents were living, and then fast over the tip of the Cotswolds, to race along the valleys of Thames and Isis to the Berkshire Downs cream-coloured with corn. Far ahead was London sprawling pink and grey to the horizon, with my destination a small grass oasis among those houses. I landed this kindly Hurricane on the smooth grass of Hanworth and went to get some tea.[20]

Mosquitos Become the Newest and Fastest Planes to Launch Into the Air

Respectfully, the Air Transport Auxiliary pilots understood and knew from experience that ferrying a military plane from point A to point B was much less demanding than flying the same aircraft in aerial combat where lives were at stake. The ferry pilots had learned the fundamentals of flying, and how principles of flight were transferable from aircraft to aircraft.

When the Mosquitos rolled out of the factories, they were considered to be the newest, fastest things to launch into the air. A Royal Air Force officer was thrilled that his squadron was among the first to get these wonderful aircraft and be the first to fly them.

As Rosemary Rees Du Cros recalled the story, a signal came that three Mosquitos were being delivered by the Air Transport Auxiliary, and as soon as they were sighted, everyone came out to the airstrip to watch them land.

> They were looking up saying, 'Um, fast; certainly, is quite an aeroplane, that'.

> Well, the first Mosquito landed and taxied up to the control tower and when the pilot got out, she was a very pretty, little blond girl. The second Mosquito came in and the pilot emerged, and he was a man with only one arm. Then the third Mosquito landed, taxied up and out climbed the pilot – a small, elderly woman clutching a knitting bag. Well, that was perhaps a slight exaggeration by the gallant officer, but it is a fact that Air Transport Auxiliary was manned entirely by people who for one reason or another could not be used in the fighting services.[21]

One Auxiliary pilot noted that they,

> had learned how to handle big powerful engines, different kinds of constant-speed propellers, hydraulic systems, etc. We had available all the performance data for every type of airplane – temperatures, pressures, power settings, airspeeds. We could take off, cruise and land with the best of the boys – perhaps even a little better than some. Their job was to fight with the airplane – taking off and landing were only means to this end. Our job was limited to flying the airplane, and we worked at it.
>
> But we couldn't blame the Air Force boys for finding it hard to understand.[22]

Training, Flying and Ferrying

During this training period, Helen was on call at various stations. Once all the courses were passed, she was assigned to operate from one base.

The logistical challenge of coordinating the ferry pilots and transport of planes was the job of the Operations Officer and her staff at each Ferry Pool.

Her formidable task was three-fold: first, to move every aircraft to its ultimate destination with as few intermediate stops as possible and by the shortest route; second, to return all pilots to base the same day, if possible; and third, to apportion the work among the pilots so that flying hours, experience and advancement in types would be even and fair.[23]

The daily coordination of ferrying also had to account for weather conditions, the available pool of pilots and their categories that day, and other challenges that arose.

The Air Transport Auxiliary pilots were based at fourteen ferry pools from Hamble, near Southampton, and as far away as Lossiemouth near Inverness in Scotland. The No. 1 Ferry Pool at White Waltham was close to the Brooklands factories for Vickers-Armstrongs, Langley which produced Hawker planes, and Woodley which manufactured Miles planes.

Once pilots received their chits or assignments, there could be much waiting around for the weather to improve. At White Waltham, the pilots kept a lookout for the spire of Shottesbrooke Church, a mile away on the other side of the airfield, as it was a good measure of visibility.[24]

Once their ferry jobs were completed, an Air Transport Auxiliary taxi such as an Avro Anson or Fairchild Argus came by to collect them and bring them to their next assignment or home. The air taxis also delivered urgently needed parts for grounded aircraft. Ferrying jobs took place during daylight hours due to the blackouts at night.

The ferry pilots formed about a third of the Air Transport Auxiliary. The ground support staff throughout all fourteen ferry pools included flying instructors, ground school instructors, ground engineers, motor transport drivers, medical staff with doctors and nurses, crash rescue teams and administrative staff. Air cadets and sea cadets were hired as messengers and auxiliary crew members. Although the Auxiliary expanded rapidly, it was a well-oiled machine that ferried 'anything to anywhere'.

'The superb confidence displayed by these women is astonishing when one considers that they never flew the same aircraft twice', observed author Joyce Spring, 'and they flew dozens of marks of each type of military aircraft.'[25]

When Jackie Cochran returned to the US after leaving her North American pilots, including Third Officer Helen Harrison, she informed the press that she was 'proud of the fine work being done by the more than a score of North American women pilots now in England'.

> Those who arrived in the spring and early summer are already ferrying combat equipment. One alone has ferried more than 50 Hurricanes and Spitfires during the last month. In this all-out struggle, women must more and more take over non-combatant burdens to free men for combat service. England has pointed the way in this respect.[26]

Jacqueline Cochran had been named the director of women's flying training in the US. Using the Air Transport Auxiliary as a blueprint, she was tasked with creating a pool of trained American women pilots,

> from which will be drawn, as needed, personnel for non-combat flying purposes, to release as many men pilots as possible for combat and other important duties.
>
> I am delighted that the more than 3,000 licenced women pilots in America are going to have an opportunity to prove their competence to serve in their chosen field in the war.[27]

Jackie Cochran had written to Helen's parents and told them how proud she was of Helen. 'She is a steady, cautious pilot and her behaviour is excellent', she declared.[28]

Observing the Daily Routine of an ATTA Girl

Third Officer Helen Harrison and several other Air Transport Auxiliary pilots, including Ann Wood, were posted to Ratcliffe Airfield, the home of No. 6 Ferry Pool, north of London at Leicester. They were billeted at Ratcliffe Hall where Sir Lindsay Everard, an MP for Melton Division and chairman of the Royal Aero Club and honorary air commodore of 605 County of Warwick Squad, lived with his wife Lady Everard. The couple were providing 'digs' for eight or nine pilots with the Ratcliffe ferry pool. The North American pilots greatly appreciated the Everards' hospitality in the face of meagre rations. 'A feature of the house was that everyone dined together with the family at a long refectory table served by Smart the butler', she recalled.[29]

Their location was close to Manchester where the Spitfires were manufactured at Castle Bromwich. They rose at 8 am and after breakfast they either boarded a bus to Ratcliffe airfield, or made the ten-minute walk. Upon arrival, the pilots picked up their chits or assignments, checked on the weather and anti-barrage balloons. An Anson flew the pilots to their assigned plane factory where they collected a plane for delivery.

Pilots in the Air Transport Auxiliary usually flew alone. Once aloft they were on their own as they had no radios. It was up to each pilot to problem-solve any flying difficulties, weather challenges or equipment malfunctions.

The weather in the British Isles was a constantly changing variable and it tended to blow in from the west. Ferry pilots viewed three-hour forecasts for the route they were planning to fly. The ferry pool Meteorological office also displayed maps which showed areas below Air Transport Auxiliary minimums. Locations that were below the minimum 800-foot ceiling and 2,000-yard visibility were indicated.

Knowing the exact locations of barrage balloons was a complete *must*. These protected areas such as aircraft factories from low-level air attacks. At the Castle Bromwich Spitfire factory, barrages were placed on three sides of the runway. Planes taking off were required to make a sharp 180-degree turn immediately to avoid the massive water-cooling towers 3 miles away.

Ann noted that during training, some planes made check rides impossible because they were single-seater fighter aircraft such as Spitfires or Hurricanes with no room for test pilots.

The Air Transport Auxiliary pilots needed to learn very quickly how different aircraft operated in a short period. Often, they studied the operation of a specific aircraft the night before a ferrying job. Helen was awarded the rank of second officer on 27 August 1942.[30]

While she flew with rarely any accidents, an experience with a Hurricane on 3 September 1942 brought her to the attention of the commanding officer. This one was not as pleasant as the first visit. 'I ran my plane off the runway. I was flying a Hurricane and couldn't get the flaps down on the downwind leg.' She was landing a Hurricane IIC (HV.920 registration) at Litchfield at 4.15 pm.[31]

As she explained, she should have decided to land without flaps. Instead, she circled to make another approach:

> I overshot the active runway and landed on the wrong one which was too short. I ran off the end and into the mud and put the plane up on its nose.
>
> When I got back to White Waltham, I was called up on the mat. 'Well Miss Harrison,' said my Commanding Officer. 'I would think with your experience you would know better what to do. What is it, 2,000 hours?'
>
> I told him in no uncertain terms that of course I knew what I should have done, that of course I was sorry, no one could have felt worse than I did. I think he was quite shocked that I spoke to him like that instead of 'No sir. Yes sir.' I didn't hear any more about it and shortly after I got my Second Officer stripe.[32]

The notes in the accident report stated: 'Flaps failed to lower owing to stiffness of flap selector lever. Pilot landed with flaps up but approached too fast in the wrong runway and overshot.'[33]

On average, the Air Transport Auxiliary pilots ferried two planes a day. In the winter, the women pilots were busier. Flights were frequently delayed due to weather conditions, but pilots flew up to five collect-and-delivery jobs. They ferried twelve days straight, followed by a three-day rest period.

Even though she mostly ferried Spitfires at Ratcliffe, Second Officer Harrison's flying was varied.

'Some of her trips involved much more than the short Spitfire hops', wrote Joyce Spring. 'She mentioned one trip where she picked up an Anson in the north of England and ferried it to Wales. The Air Transport Auxiliary pilots were allowed to plan their own routes.'

In a letter home to her parents, Helen wrote that the pilots were 'well cared for' and their meals were good. 'All the girls are most enthusiastic about the ferrying job', she stated.[34]

Captain Jackie Cochran wrote to Helen's mother Gertrude that the food situation was monotonous in England, but it was healthy with plenty to eat:

> I feel that all of us went over with the anticipation of never having quite enough to eat, which certainly is not the case. Naturally, one misses the fresh fruit, particularly citrus, and people who like candy get only a very small amount a month. In mailing packages, I would suggest that you send chocolate as that is one thing that is rather scarce.
>
> I saw Helen just before I left and she was looking exceptionally well and is very happy in her work in England. She is doing fine work, and I am proud of her.[35]

Gertrude replied:

> It is very gratifying to hear from those in authority that she is doing well. She is of course absolutely in her element, happy in her work and appreciating the advantages of the training she is getting.
>
> I propose sending her a parcel in about a fortnight's time and shall not forget the tip about the chocolate. We are very close pals and although I naturally miss her, I am happy to know she is doing her bit and really enjoying it.[36]

Meeting a Passionate Supporter of Women Working in War

On 26 October 1942, Second Officer Harrison and her fellow pilots found themselves meeting First Lady Eleanor Roosevelt and Lady Clementine Churchill when they arrived at White Waltham Airfield in Berkshire. Eleanor Roosevelt had been touring Britain as an ardent supporter of women taking on war work, and to learn about the huge civilian and military efforts underway.

During the introduction, Colonel J.J. Llewellin noted that the Air Transport Auxiliary overall had flown 30,000,000 miles. Comprised 2,824 members, the Auxiliary included 540 pilots, nearly 100 of them women.

He thanked Eleanor Roosevelt for 'sending so many of her countrywomen across to the assistance of British pilots'. It was recognised that the 'Atta girls' were crucial to Britain's air defence as they ferried aircraft around the UK.

The First Lady acknowledged that while the US introduced a ferry service, it did not use women to the extent that Britain had employed women.

> Those who have come from our country will be very grateful for the experience which has been gained in Britain.
>
> The example set here will give other women a courage to do things which they have not in the past considered open to them.
>
> We look to you to do something to make the world a better place for the people who are coming after, and to prevent those people from going through a similar ordeal to that through which you are going.[37]

Following the introductions, First Lady Roosevelt talked with Second Officer Harrison's flight group. 'She was very charming', Helen reflected, 'speaking to many of us.'[38]

At the main headquarters, roving reporter Anne Robertson Coupar, who was covering Eleanor Roosevelt's tour, immediately grasped the magnitude of the work undertaken by the Auxiliary.

'On the windswept tarmac of an aerodrome in the Home Counties, I saw more types of planes than I had dreamed existed', she reported. 'They were the machines ferried by pilots of the Air Transport Auxiliary-Trans-Atlantic Service.'[39]

Throughout her tour, the First Lady become known as the 'American women's ambassador'. In an earlier interview, she declared that 'they are now finding that women are very much needed and there has been a sudden very great interest in what women can do, and I think there is a great deal for me to learn while I am here.'[40]

While at White Waltham, the reporter interviewed Flying Establishment Officer Captain Stocks, a Leeds man, who managed all pilot personnel.

> [He] told me that the women fliers were as keen and as efficient as the men and thought nothing of taking up a big bomber alone and flinging it about the sky. The women never know when they're finished. They'd go on working all night if you'd let them.[41]

Becoming a Spitfire Pilot

'At first I thought, "What a thrill to fly a Spitfire", but when you ferry three or four of them in a day the glamour wears off', Second Officer Harrison acknowledged.[42]

The Spitfire belonged in the air. It had six central instruments, the same as any operational plane, comprising of an airspeed indicator, artificial horizon, rate of climb indicator, altimeter, turn indicator and gyroscopic compass.

Lettice Curtis had her chance one day when she flew a repaired MK I from Cowley airfield next to the Morris Motor Works in Oxford. Comparing it to the Hurricane, she noted that:

> the Hurricane was dogged, masculine and its undercarriage folded inwards in a tidy business-like manner.

> The Spit [called] for more sensitive handling, was altogether more feminine, had more glamour and threw its wheels outwards in an abandoned extrovert way … Only for bad weather did I prefer the Hurricane, where the shorter, more downward sloping nose and slightly larger canopy, contributed to just that much better ground visibility.
>
> For women, the whole package was perfect.[43]

Without exception, the Air Transport Auxiliary women pilots 'longed to fly Spitfires not because of what they'd seen and heard, but because they loved them when they got their hands on them and how they felt'.[44]

The power crammed into the Spitfire spoilt pilots who moved on from them to early jets and found them sluggish. The responsiveness of the Spitfire 'gave meaning to the cliché that you didn't fly a Spitfire, you wore it'.[45]

Or as pilot Diana Barnato Walker put it: 'You moved, it moved.'[46]

Prior to taking control of a Spitfire, ferry fliers studied the Pilots' Notes. They were also warned, as pilot Ann Welch described, about the 'ease with which a twitchy first take-off could be achieved by over-use of the sensitive elevator'. Even then, pilots still twitched in the air while flying a Spitfire. Ann Welch clearly remembered the bliss of flying one. Once in the air 'the Spitfire's delight in flying gave me sheer pleasure: some airplanes are harsh or reluctant, others without character, but the Spitfire was perfect and when I came into the circuit at my destination, she floated back on to the ground like a feather.'[47]

In June 1942, Ann flew her 100th Spitfire, actually a Seafire, 'distinguishable as the airspeed indicator was in knots instead of mph.'

> Flying those lovely airplanes was so instinctive that one day I was thinking it would be perfect weather for flying, only to realise suddenly that I was 1,500 feet over Winchester in a Mark VB. Maybe we took them too much for granted, although they rarely let us down.[48]

Helen recalled how one time she:

> was zooming along in a Spitfire when the ceiling closed in.
>
> I brought the plane down close to the ground because I couldn't see a thing and the regulations forbid ferry flying over 2,000 feet.
>
> I was tearing along just 50 feet above the ground. Every minute a cloud would drop over me and I couldn't see anything. I kept thinking about all those hills in England that I might bump into. And about all those churches that Englishmen always build on their hills. I didn't want to crash into a church. However, I made the airfield and (was) just a little shaky.[49]

Chapter 10

Knowing the Sightline to the Theatre of War

The only way to be sure of reaching Colerne was to carefully plan a route so that I could follow roads and railways all the way; and stick to it rigidly, even round a double loop in the Savernake Forest railway line. When everything was ready, I watched for the promised improvement as the trees at the end of the field appeared and disappeared in veils of light snow. Then they reappeared for a little longer. Visibility was not up to 700 yards and cloud base, if you called the amorphous weeping greyness a base, about 300 feet, perhaps 400 feet. Now was the moment to go.

My Merlin started with its comforting rumble, and I taxied out at once, doing my checks on the way, to take off uphill towards the trees which were still just visible. A minute later the second Spitfire roared into the air, but the trees disappeared again for the third, so it was taxied back to the hangar. My plan worked. I flew as slowly as possible, flaps down. It was not possible to fly with the wheels down on a Spitfire for extra drag as the undercarriage leg obscured the oil cooler. The weather did not improve, but neither did

> it worsen, and I picked my way along the roads and railway tracks at 140 mph, flying the last mile along a lane uphill to the aerodrome.[1]
>
> Pilot Ann Welch, *Happy To Fly*

On 22 February 1943, Helen Harrison was awarded the rank of First Officer. The rank of First Officer in the Air Transport Auxiliary ranks was conferred to pilots who had been Second Officers for at least eighteen months, and who had attained at least a Class 4 qualification. She wore two gold broad stripes on a dark blue background. The blue background was reserved for flying staff on pilot's contracts.

On 19 March 1943, Canadian pilots Violet Milstead and Marion Orr departed from North America to commence their service with the ATA. Their ship sailed in an Atlantic convoy that reached Avonmouth in Bristol, England on 9 May 1943. Transferring to the RAF, they reached White Waltham and immediately started training. The pair crossed paths with their colleague First Officer Helen Harrison as they commenced their ferrying assignments.

Vi Milstead earned her instructor's licence when she was 21 and managed a wool shop when she was not flying. With 1,000 hours flying time, she passed the rigorous tests in Montreal and was accepted as an ATA pilot. Marion Orr's position as a flying instructor literally went up in smoke when the St Catherine's Flying Club burnt down. Alongside Vi, she too qualified to be an ATA instructor after completing the flying checks at Dorval airport.

In England, the pair shared a room in a hotel and took a bus daily to the airfield. During the summer, they ferried planes for twelve days at a stretch with two days off during each two week period. In the winter time, the pilots received a three-day rest each two week period. Violet admitted that it took her some time to get used to the climate and the food.

Of Violet's first flying trip, the *Toronto Star* reported: 'Britain appeared to her as a small island, full of trees, towns and railways.'[2]

Equalising Pay for Women Ferry Pilots

There were cheers in the House of Commons on 18 May 1943 when Sir Stafford Cripps, minister of aircraft production, announced that women pilots of the Air Transport Auxiliary would receive the same rates of pay as male pilots. Women pilots engaged in full flying duties would begin receiving equal pay, rank for rank, as men similarly employed.[3]

Women pilots started receiving equal pay at the beginning of June 1943, and the Air Transport Auxiliary became one of the first Equal Opportunities Employers in the UK. Although in a written Commons answer, Cripps tempered this breakthrough with the caveat that 'the decision regarding the women pilots of the Air Transport Auxiliary was based upon the particular circumstances of their employment and not upon any general acceptance of the doctrine of equal pay'.[4]

In the House of Commons, Miss Irene Ward, Member of Parliament for Wallsend, asked: 'Is he aware how gratifying it is that this decision has been arrived at without pressure from women members of the House?'[5]

'They paid us the same as men', exclaimed pilot Betty Ann Lussiar, 'and advanced and promoted us just as if we were real citizens. It was the first time I saw equality with men, and that really amazed me.'

By Women's Day on 1 June, there were 100 women pilots ferrying planes around Great Britain, from Spitfires to Lancaster and Stirling bombers. The Air Transport Auxiliary ferry pilots were cognisant of how their fortuitous equal pay may have been perceived by other personnel supporting the transport sector.

'What we did might sound glamorous', pointed out ATA pilot Molly Rose, 'but we were not frivolous about it. We were only too aware how short we were of fuel and pilots, so we did not rush around the sky doing aerobatics. It was serious work because England had its back to the wall.'[6]

Pilot Rosemary Du Cros remembered the nights they often spent at bomber stations during their delivery runs:

> When one spent the night, one heard the thunder of the take off in the dark and next morning in the Mess there was a dreadful pall of gloom and sadness for those who had not returned. One felt apologetic for being there, for being alive, for not having to take the terrible risks which they did.[7]

Paying the Supreme Sacrifice in Defence of Freedom

On 22 May 1943, American pilot Mary Nicholson, 38, was flying a Miles Master when it developed an oil leak in bad weather. A few miles west of Birmingham, the engine froze and the propeller flew off. Being too close to the ground, Mary didn't have room to parachute down. She attempted to land in a small field. Tragically, she lost her life when the plane crashed into a stone barn.

The *Winston-Salem Journal* wrote:

> The flying activity of Miss Nicholson in Britain grew out of the demands of war and was closely linked with the war efforts of the United Nations. She was serving her country and the cause of the United Nations when she lost her life, and thus she becomes one of the true heroines of World War II.
>
> Those women who have become fliers have long since demonstrated that the airplane is not a device for the use of man alone, and that women are capable of assuming even greater roles in the skies if need be in the protection of democracy. And there are many of the Mary Webb Nicholson types, no doubt, who would respond to such a call spontaneously, joyously, dauntless and unafraid.[8]

Mary had been based at Maidenhead, west of London, where she lived with a host family.

In a letter dated 8 June to Captain Jackie Cochran, Helen wrote: 'We were all very upset about Mary Nicholson. One thing I know, she spent a very happy time here.'[9]

On 23 June, Captain Jackie Cochran wrote to Helen and expressed her grief at the tragic accident. 'I was terribly distressed over Mary Nicholson', she wrote. 'I presume you were aware she worked for me for several years and I was very fond of her.'

'For that matter,' Captain Cochran continued, 'I am devoted to all you girls over there and every night in my prayers I hope you will all be safe.'[10]

Experiencing a Close Call in a Lysander

'I did have the odd narrow escape', First Officer Helen Harrison admitted. 'I'm not superstitious. I can't afford to be. And I don't carry any good luck charms. But I do get scared now and then.'[11]

On 30 April 1943, First Officer Harrison found herself at RAF Llandow, west of Cardiff in Wales. Llandow is nestled on the Bristol Channel 50 miles away from her parents' first home in Llantilio Crossenny in Abergavenny. Supermarine Spitfires equipped the Royal Air Force's No. 53 Operational Training Unit based in Llandow. The air base served as a training centre for foreign pilots, including Canadian pilots who were stationed in April 1942.

The No. 53 Operational Training Unit relocated to Kirton in Lindsey in Lincolnshire by 9 May 1943. The preparations to ferry Spitfires to its new site may have been the reason First Officer Harrison was in Llandow on 30 April. At 4.40 pm, Helen began taxiing a Spitfire Mk VC, registration LZ.880. 'In turning around on a perimeter track, the tail of the aircraft hit a large stone, concealed by grass on the edge of the track, causing damage to the rudder stern post.' The Air Transport Auxiliary accident report noted that First Officer Harrison was uninjured and found that the Auxiliary and pilot were not responsible. The aircraft was deemed 'repairable on site by unit'.[12]

Helen said she never encountered any enemy aircraft while ferrying but did have a close call landing a spy taxi, a Westland Lysander. 'I nearly ended everything one day', she said of her assignment.[13]

Every plane has a thrilling story to tell, and this Lysander was no exception.

The Westland Lysander was designed for military liaison and cooperation duties, including artillery spotting and intelligence gathering. Its seat was elevated giving the occupants an eagle's eye view of the sky and landscape below. It had the capability to land and take off from places normally unrecognisable as airfields. This contributed to its fame in ferrying Allied agents in and out of enemy-occupied Europe.

In terms of design, it was an oddball in a rather affectionate way. The high-lift devices operated in alignment with the aircraft's position and speed. As the aircraft slowed and its angle of attack increased, lift exerted by the airfoil action of the slats was harnessed by gears to deploy them forward automatically. The pilot had no control over when the slats and flaps deployed or detracted. Its design and mechanisms were similar to that of an A-model Tiger Moth, with which Helen was familiar.

It required a three-point take-off. A thorough ground school and flight briefing was essential before pilots could begin flying them. For the ferry pilots, there was no time for in-depth training. Fliers briefed themselves from the small notebooks provided by their leader. They also relied greatly on their extensive aeronautical knowledge and experience to coalesce in their minds the unique operational features of specific planes to quickly complete their ferrying assignments.

Lysanders were initially employed in combat duties at the beginning of the Second World War, seeing action as spotters and light bombers. Despite occasional victories, they became easy targets for the Luftwaffe, even when escorted by Hurricanes. Then they were withdrawn from front line service. The Royal Air Force continued to use them on air sea rescue duty until April 1942. The Lysanders were painted matte black and flew with 138 Special Duty Squadron and 161 Squadron of the Royal Air Force. In all, Lysanders transported 101 agents to and recovered 128 agents from Nazi-occupied Europe.[14]

The Lysander IIIA, registration V.9814, that Helen was tasked to ferry was destined for the boneyard, an inglorious ending for a remarkable aircraft that was vital to the Allies. At Sherburn airfield in North Yorkshire at 3.10 pm on 5 June 1943, Helen prepared for take-off:

> I had been told it would leap off the ground, but I had difficulty and once airborne, I couldn't get the trim handle to move and had to struggle to keep the nose up.[15]
>
> …
>
> As soon as I got airborne, I knew I was going to crash. I couldn't get the kite to level out and plunged straight into the ground.[16]

She had struggled to align the lift mechanism in trying to gain altitude:

> As soon as I could, I turned back – thinking at least the crash wagon would be there to pick up the pieces. I had one hell of a job keeping the thing in the air and didn't dare throttle back or the nose would go down. I knew I couldn't land with all that power on so, on final approach, I took a deep breath, throttled back and just before touching down I heaved back on the control column as hard as I could and put a burst of power on.[17]
>
> …
>
> I had to make a crash landing, hitting the ground at 110 miles an hour.[18]
>
> …
>
> Everything collapsed. No prop, no undercarriage. I slid off the runway and then dead silence. No crash wagon and the stink of gas. The door wouldn't open. I wondered if I would end up in the graveyard with the plane. Finally, a mechanic

> came, broke the Perspex and hauled me out. A transport car came and took me to the hospital.[19]
>
> …
>
> The plane was nose heavy because of faulty ballast conditions. The plane was damaged, and I was shaken up and suffered from shock, but after a night in the hospital, I was back on the job the next day.[20]

'Next time I was on leave I sure celebrated!'[21]

From the rear of the Lysander, an 18.7-pound ballast 'had been taken out of the tail by the pilot who had been in the plane before [her]'.[22]

The hospital staff and Air Transport Auxiliary officials couldn't believe she had escaped with no injuries. It was a standard procedure that medical checks were conducted after any accident. Importantly, they also included expert assessments and treatment of any post-traumatic stress injuries. Immediate attention was given to any mental trauma that could potentially emerge later. The Auxiliary pilots were eligible for admission and treatment at most Royal Air Force hospitals. Medical personnel with the Air Transport Auxiliary were available for consultation for all personnel throughout the organisation.

She had been ferrying it to a graveyard for aircraft as it was designated to be scrapped. 'I just saved them the job for it was about to be broken,' she smiled, 'but I admit I was scared.'[23]

In *Daring Lady Flyers: Canadian Women in the Early Years of Aviation*, author Joyce Spring notes:

> One of the most worrisome aspects of this situation for the Air Transport Auxiliary pilots was that their flying was done under conditions where they walked up to a plane, saw it for the first time, got into it and flew away in it. They had no way of being sure what the condition of the plane was, so this accident of Helen's was just one routine risk these women faced every day.[24]

Investigating the accident, an inquiry board discovered that the previous pilot had not reported the removal of the ballast. The official accident report noted that:

> on take-off the pilot found the aircraft nose heavy and unable to correct this owing to the jamming of the trimmer, in consequence a heavy landing was made causing the undercarriage to collapse. Subsequent tests showed a possibility of the trimmer jamming on this type of aircraft when considerable backwards force is applied to the control column.[25]
>
> …
>
> [The] investigation disclosed maladjustment of the trimmer so that when the indicator was at 'take-off' the actual setting of the tail plane was nose heavy. Moreover, the previous pilot had removed the two ballast weights to compensate for the carrying of a passenger and had noticed on take-off that the machine was nose heavy, but he did not report either of these facts when leaving the aircraft at Sherburn.[26]

The accident report concluded that the Lysander was a write-off.

The Board could make a distinction between blame and responsibility. The board, in determining the cause of, and assessing, the accident, could make one of five decisions: (a) pilot not responsible and commended; (b) pilot not responsible; (c) pilot responsible; (d) insufficient evidence to determine responsibility; or (e) pilot to blame.

The Board cleared First Officer Helen Harrison; she was not held responsible and was commended.

Returning Home on Furlough

At the end of the summer 1943, Commander Pauline Gower allowed some of the North American women pilots to go home on leave. Many of the British pilots had homes and friends to return to on their days off. The North Americans were not so fortunate. Helen's sister-in-law Sally lived in Staffordshire, and she had friends from her early years.

Helen and five colleagues boarded the SS *Aquitania* in Greenock, Scotland. Joining her for the seven-day voyage were Virginia Farr, Mary Zerbel Ford, Grace Stevenson, Ann Watson Wood and Dorothy Furey Bragg. The six pilots arrived in New York on 28 July.

Helen took a train to Montreal and hitch-hiked to Toronto to join her sons and family. Her crisp distinctive uniform quickly helped her get a ride. While at home on furlough after sixteen months in Britain, she was besieged by news reporters keenly interested in her stories and experiences with the Air Transport Auxiliary.

In an article entitled 'Ferries War Planes to Job', she declared to a *Toronto Star* reporter that 'every one of us 100 Air Transport Auxiliary pilots would jump at the opportunity of flying planes in action. If Russian girls can do it, we can too. If women are called for combat pilots, there will be a rush to get the job done.'[27]

At this point in her career, she informed the *Toronto Star* reporter, she had flown thirty-two different types of aircraft as a ferry pilot. Helen explained:

> There is no likelihood of women making up air crews and going into action, but we girls often discuss it. Personally, I'd like to fly a Mosquito bomber. I have ferried several of them.
>
> It's an interesting job, ferrying planes. There's always a certain challenge, a big responsibility. A huge bomber has to be brought safely to an operational base. We need sound judgement for the ferry job for we do not use instruments.
>
> We do our own navigation, and as we don't use radio, we have to use our own judgment. We don't fly when the ceiling is 800 feet or when visibility is less than 2,000 yards. After all, there are barrage balloons to cope with.[28]

The *Star* noted that Helen 'has never encountered enemy aircraft while ferrying a plane. In fact, she has never seen a Nazi plane at any time'.[29] In an August 1943 article entitled 'Man's Superiority Fades', the *Globe and Mail* reported on a press conference with Helen. It opened its feature with:

Man's last vestige of superiority walked resignedly to the open window and jumped out when First Officer Helen Harrison came into the room. It's just as well that Man's last vestige, etc. didn't wait around for the details. He'd have done a much grimmer job on himself.[30]

The *Globe and Mail* went on to quote Helen talking to the audience of reporters:

> the Mosquito is my favourite bomber, of course. I like to call it a Spitfire bomber. That Spit's a dream. It's the best fighter I guess, but I like the American Mustang too. The Mosquito though, I had it doing 350 level and it wasn't flat out.

Effervescent, entertaining, personable Helen Harrison almost became an instructor at the Toronto Flying Club but was ruled out at the last minute because – that's right – she was a woman.[31]

The paper's article included a photo of Helen Harrison with her friend, C. Ernest French, president of the Toronto Flying Club, which conveyed a network that transcended hiring practices. The newspaper noted that C. Ernest French 'wanted to know about the latest models overseas'.

In her interview, the *Globe and Mail* reported:

> What she was talking about were the planes she's flown overseas in her capacity of ferry pilot attached to the Air Transport Auxiliary. Now she is one of more than 100 women, including girls from Poland, Argentina and England. Helen has about 350 flying hours to her credit; has flown 32 different types of aircraft from fighters up to but excluding four-motored bombers.

> 'We use an Anson to taxi people around at times,' she said. 'One time there were some pilots, a couple of paratroopers, and one of our girl pilots crammed into the Anson when they met a twin-engine German bomber. It fired a burst at them and,' the audience (of reporters) leaned forward attentively, 'and scared the hell out of 'em.'
>
> Just to put the final cruncher on man's last vestige, etc., Helen Harrison concluded: 'Men ferrying planes over there used to get more money than we. Our commandant beefed loud and long. Now we get the same. Why not? We do the same work.'[32]

First Officer Harrison described how her greatest excitement was not necessarily in the air, but in meeting other pilots in England. In one of her letters home, she wrote about meeting the second pilot who flew Winston Churchill to Russia and elsewhere. 'He was a most personable chap and very interesting to talk to.'[33] Oftentimes she bumped into a Canadian flyer, 'a seasoned veteran whom she had taught to fly'.[34]

In a letter to Jackie Cochran in 1943 while Helen was on furlough in Canada, she wrote, 'You will be glad to hear that all the American girls are doing a very good job of work here and are getting on very well. I was fortunate to get my Class 4 plus conversion on Hudsons last month. I had to sign on for an extra six month's kit. I think the added experience is worth it.'[35]

'Needless to say, I just love the job, and I can't tell you how grateful I am to you for all you've done.'[36]

Raring at the Chance to Pilot a Bomber Across the Atlantic

At the end of their leave, First Officer Harrison and her five companion pilots were unexpectedly given the chance of a lifetime when they reported back to Dorval airport in Montreal.

Earlier, the North Atlantic Return Ferry Organisation had been reorganised to form the No. 45 Group of the Royal Air Force's Ferry Command at Dorval. While personnel comprised Royal Air Force crews, it relied on civilian crews of the Air Transport Auxiliary and British Overseas Airways who flew regularly in both directions.

The Royal Air Force had received nearly 900 Mitchells which were replacing the Douglas Bostons, Lockheed Venturas and Vickers Wellington bombers. The North American-built aircraft had entered active Royal Air Force service on 22 January 1943.

Dorval airport was a hive of activity as heavy planes arrived daily from US factories and were flown to Great Britain via the northern 'Snowball' route. Between 3 and 4 September, a blitz movement of 200 Boeing B-17 Flying Fortresses ensued at Dorval.

'While waiting for their assignment, the girls were given the opportunity to fly some of the aircraft at Dorval, and so impressed the airport authorities with their knowledge and skill.'[37]

'When I was on leave, I had taken a course on the Mitchell – I went out with an officer here and there', she explained, noting that she garnered all the flying experience she could obtain while on leave.[38]

The Royal Canadian Air Force Command officials offered the six pilots a chance to work their passage back to England as co-pilots. They 'underwent the necessary training and briefing for the long distance flight with enthusiasm'.[39]

Helen recalled having gone out for dinner on a muggy September evening in Montreal. Returning at 4 am to her hotel she checked the front desk for messages. As she read a message the night clerk had handed to her, she exclaimed, 'Oh my God, my flight leaves Dorval at 6 am. That's less than two hours – I'll never make it.' Her companion, an air force doctor, told her, 'You've got to!' and helped her pack while she changed into her flying gear. Immediately, her friend rushed her to the airport, driving 'like a whistle'.[40]

'I'm really looking forward to the flight', she told a reporter by phone when she reached the Dorval airport, before boarding the twin-engine bomber. 'I've never flown the Atlantic before, even as a passenger. To think I am going as co-pilot is like a dream. Then, too, it will be the longest flight I have ever made over water.'[41] The flight course was 3,200 miles.

First Officer Harrison checked in and was taken to the aircraft. All the other crew members were on board and the engine was warming up.[42]

> I thought I was going to be a supernumerary passenger, but the captain needed a co-pilot, and I was the only passenger who happened to be a pilot. He wouldn't let me do a take-off or landing. It was mainly gear up, and gear down and doing the fuel consumption calculations. … I was happy as a lark and higher than a kite.[43]

The twin-engine B-25 Mitchells were a safe and forgiving aircraft to fly. When engaged in warfare, these were operated by a crew of six. It flew at a cruising speed of 230 mph although its maximum speed was 272 mph. Its range was 1,350 miles. Its brakes were very effective, and more than a slight touch could send a pilot through the windshield.

First Officer Harrison with a captain and crew took off in Mitchell FR185 as dawn broke on 14 September with the good wishes of the Montreal airport staff. Her fellow pilot, Grace Stevenson of Oklahoma, followed as a supernumerary co-pilot in Mitchell FV958. Four of their colleagues had just flown across the Atlantic the previous day.[44]

As co-pilot, Helen was expected to perform the greater part of piloting the plane on the long ocean crossing to England.

From Dorval, the route of the bomber convoy hugged the Canadian eastern coast towards Goose Bay, Labrador. This Royal Canadian Air Force airport had become the largest airfield in the Western hemisphere as it was a key stopover on the European route. Her crew overnighted while the plane was being refuelled and checked. The Goose Bay air facilities were crucial to ensure the successful ferrying of planes to and from England. Heading northeast the next day, the planes veered across Greenland, and landed in Reykjavik, Iceland.

The captain of the Mitchell was an American, Helen as co-pilot was Canadian, the navigator was Australian, and the radio operator was English. The captain was billeted at the American base and the others at the Royal Air Force base.

> As I was the only female there, the Royal Air Force had to rig up accommodations for me – an old radio shack with an old coal stove which didn't give out much heat, a cot with a couple of blankets and a toilet which wouldn't flush. I was so cold. I went to bed with my flight suit on over my uniform and my boots and gloves on. I grumbled about the Royal Air Force food and accommodations and asked why they didn't have a base like the Americans. I was told that while the Americans were flushing their toilets, the Royal Air Force were sinking German subs. I didn't complain again.[45]

Due to nose-gear problems in the Mitchell, they stayed for four days.

From Reykjavik, Helen swept into the British Isles. The only significant issue was the high engine noise. Helen related that 'the most difficult part of the flight was using the tube to go to the bathroom. I got a little damp! The captain and I had a laugh about that'.

The 3,200-mile flight was completed without mishap. Arriving in Scotland, she became the first Canadian woman to perform a cross-Atlantic ferry flight. Her logbook had reached 2,900 flying hours in 32 aircraft.

The six Air Transport Auxiliary pilots made history as they were the first women to officially ferry fighting aircraft across the Atlantic Ocean.

Picking up Conversion Courses

On her return to England and over the next few months, Helen ferried mostly Defiants, Spitfires, Wellingtons, Blenheims, Dominies, Hamdens, Beaufighters, Barracudas and Warwicks.

When asked about her flying highlights by the *Toronto Star*, she replied, 'Oh, I love any kind of flying but Spitfires and Mosquitos are my favourites. There's nothing like them.'[46]

She had ferried several Mosquitos by this time as well as the Mustangs with their Merlin engines. She did not fly the Mustangs with the Allison V-170 engines. The North American P-51 Mustangs were considered the best all-round fighter plane of the Second World War.

In the same interview she recalled,

> one of the Spits I flew had a Priority 1 chit. When I collected it from the maintenance unit to take it to a fighter squadron it had a sign on the control column which said, 'Guns loaded'. I was sure tempted to give just a little burst but managed to control myself.

Helen's eighteen-month contract, which expired on 31 October 1943, was renewed for another term.

A few days before Christmas 1943, she shared a room with Ann Wood at the Red Cross Club in London when they had a few days off. Ann wrote of Helen, 'she is of all the best-natured soul and when happy far too generous'.[47]

Landing at Home After a Glorious Run

In the midst of the Second World War, the tragic losses in the flying community mounted. All pilots heartbreakingly knew of fellow pilots who had not returned from the skies. Helen's colleague in South Africa, instructor John Meiring who worked alongside her for Haller Aviation succumbed.

On 8 February 1944, he was flying with the Fourth Squadron of the South African Air Force. Captain John William Meiring was killed in action in a Supermarine Spitfire Mk VC, registration JK922, when it was shot down by flak near Bariscaino, Italy. The 28-year-old was laid to rest at Ancona War Cemetery.

In March 1944, Helen requested a leave of absence for family reasons.[48] Her mother had written, and she decided to go home to attend to family matters. She voyaged to Canada on the *Queen Mary* from Gourock, Scotland, a port near Glasgow.

At the end of May 1944, it was reported that Helen's brother Lieutenant Albert Testemale was wounded in action in Burma, now Myanmar. He was serving in the Royal Tank Regiment of the Royal Armoured Corps in northern Burma. In the jungle warfare that ensued in the Southeast Asian theatre, tanks were used to drive back the Japanese attacks, and counter-striking Japanese positions. The Burma campaign was successful in denying the enemy any control of vital oil resources.

When Helen was ready to return to the Air Transport Auxiliary in August, she wrote for instructions.

'She was shocked to be told that after D-Day on 6 June 1944 they were not taking on any more overseas pilots', notes author Joyce Spring. 'She offered to pay her own fare, but they still refused her.'[49]

'I was devastated', she recalled. 'I knew I would never get another chance to fly those fast military planes. I was also due for the Class V conversion course and lost out on that too.'[50] The Class V course covered four-engine aircraft including the Halifaxes, Lancasters and Fortresses.

D-Day Marks the Beginning of the End

The Normandy invasion on 6 June 1944 led to the liberation of France and denied Germany any further exploitation of France's manpower and economic resources. The D-Day victory was a turning point as it enabled the Allies to make a headlong advance into the interior of France. By D-Day, the Air Transport Auxiliary was at its peak. The auxiliary comprised twenty-two bases around the UK. Its full complement of 659 ferry pilots included 108 women. They were among the 3,555 staff who worked nonstop around the clock to transport planes.

Beginning in September 1944, Air Transport Auxiliary pilots began ferrying aircraft across the Channel. As the Allied armies moved through France and towards Germany, ferrying aircraft began to ease.

In February 1945, the Royal Air Force Balloon Command removed its 2,400 balloons, thus opening the skies for easier flying. The Balloon Command itself was decommissioned.

Time with Air Transport Auxiliary Draws to a Quiet Close

'My time with the Air Transport Auxiliary was the most exciting and interesting of my career', mused Helen.[51]

Her Air Transport Auxiliary history sheet had described her as a 'first class officer, keen, steady pilot and with a cheerful personality.' First Officer Harrison believed there was nothing unusual about her abilities or glamorous about her work.[52]

Her pilot's personal record noted that she had completed training up to Class 4 plus. She left with the rank of first officer and 'the written comment from her CO that she was a good officer and a sound pilot who flies with accuracy and care'.[53]

During her employment with the Air Transport Auxiliary from 1 May 1942 to 22 May 1944, First Officer Helen Harrison flew thirty-four different types, not counting the different marks of Spitfires. She flew both single and twin-engine aircraft including Avro Ansons, Fairey Battles, the challenging Bristol pair of Beaufighters and Blenheims, Bristol Fairchild Bolingbrokes, Douglas Bostons, Douglas C47 (Dakotas), Handley Page Hampdens, de Havilland Mosquitos, de Havilland Tiger Moths, North American Harvards, Hawker Hurricanes, North American Mustangs, Westland Lysanders, Airspeed Oxfords, Supermarine Spitfires and Vickers Wellingtons and others. She did not fly any of the four-engine aircraft.

She logged approximately 500 hours while in the service of the Auxiliary, which was considerable, given that most ferry flights were about 20 to 30 minutes in duration.

As her time with the Air Transport Auxiliary came to close, First Officer Harrison realised that her favourite aircraft was the Mosquito bomber:

> It's smooth, light, easy to handle yet powerful.[54]
>
> …
>
> You could control it nicely; it was a fast airplane – for those days. The Spit was a nice airplane, but it could be tricky on a crosswind landing. The Mustang was a real dandy.[55]

In fulfilling a dream, she flew 400 miles an hour in a Mosquito during delivery trips in England.[56]

Unlike combat pilots, the Air Transport Auxiliary pilots 'flew without radios, instrument training or weapons in aircraft that were nonetheless legitimate targets for any Luftwaffe pilot who saw them, and they flew in any weather except the certifiably foul.'[57]

'We didn't have any radio so we couldn't communicate with one another,' recalled pilot Ann Wood.[58]

They flew continuously. The women Air Transport Auxiliary pilots were assigned to fly badly damaged planes to maintenance units for repair or to boneyards.

With pride and confidence, they handled assignments to fly new types of aircraft on short notice, and often with only the Pilot's Notes with which to familiarise themselves. Often, they only had twenty minutes in an unfamiliar cockpit during which they correlated the flying instructions tersely packed into one card with the instrument panel and the airstrip looming ahead. 'Nothing similar was ever asked of combat pilots. It was a sustained aerial stunt that one seasoned British Airways instructor called, simply, "mind boggling".'[59]

Being a female Air Transport Auxiliary pilot was not a career of glory but one of grit and determination. The losses of female pilots during the war were fewer than one in ten. According to author G. Whittell in *Spitfire Girls*, the male pilots 'lost nearly one in three of those enrolled by February 1940, a rate comparable to that of Fighter Command.

But still it was death on a significant, non-civilian scale, close to what the Romans called decimation, and it took some getting used to.'[60]

By the end of the Second World War, 170 Air Transport Auxiliary pilots, 158 men and 15 women, had paid the supreme sacrifice in the defence of our freedoms and in pursuit of peace. Mary Webb Nicholson was the only North American woman pilot of the Air Transport Auxiliary not to return home.

At the end of the Air Transport Auxiliary's mission, its 1,318 pilots including 168 women had ferried nearly 309,000 planes. This included 57,286 Spitfires, 29,401 Hurricanes, 9,805 Lancasters and 7,039 Barracudas.[61]

The total number of flying hours amassed in this unknown war service reached 414,984 hours. The Anything to Anywhere pilots had flown all over the British Isles, Europe and across the Atlantic.

The pride of serving in the Air Transport Auxiliary was best exemplified by pilot Ann Wood, who said in 1946: 'I will always deem it the greatest privilege of my life to have served the British government in its hour of need.'[62]

The vital work in ferrying planes by First Officer Helen Harrison and her fellow pilots defied all expectations.

Air Transport Auxiliary Pilots Played a Soldier's Role

At the Air Transport Auxiliary closing ceremonies at White Waltham airfield near Maidenhead on 30 September 1945, Lord Balfour, the undersecretary of state for air, observed that:

> the men and women of the Air Transport Auxiliary were civilians in uniform who played a soldier's part in the Battle for Britain, and who performed though the war a task of supreme importance to the Royal Air Force.[63]
>
> They did not fight the enemy with guns, but they fought and beat an enemy which can kill just effectively as the

> bullet. Snow, fog, ice and storm were faced daily and only triumphed over through skill and courage as they kept the ferry moving.[64]

Lord Beaverbrook, minister of aircraft production, emphasised:

> Just as the Battle of Britain is the accomplishment and achievement of the Royal Air Force, likewise it can be declared that the Air Transport Auxiliary sustained and supported them in battle. They were soldiers fighting in the struggle just as completely as if they had been engaged on the battlefront.[65]

Twenty-five women pilots led by Pauline Gower Fahie joined representatives of all Air Transport Auxiliary departments at the ceremony. The Auxiliary was a unique organisation. 'Never before had civilians participated to such an extent in aerial warfare,' observed pilot Rosemary Rees Du Cros. 'One can be fairly certain that they will never again.'[66]

The Air Transport Auxiliary, a glorious experiment 'worked beyond everyone's dreams', declared Flight Captain Alison King.[67] The positive impact of the Auxiliary in opening doors for women pilots would be felt in the years to come. As the sun went down on this unprecedented chapter in modern aviation history, one salient fact remained unassailable.

The late Air Transport Auxiliary pilot Mary Nicholson summed it best when she observed: 'The past record of femininity in blazing sky trails has left no room for argument on the subject. We are in it to stay.'[68]

For many pilots, the motto of the Air Transport Auxiliary, *Aetheris Avidi*, eager for the air, carried many pilots forward into the peacetime years around the world.

Part Three

Chapter 11

Pursuing Flying Dreams in Post-War Canada

Trust me – for the pure joy of flying there is nothing to equal the life of a bush pilot.

Bush flying is different. Every flight is unique, and there is magic in each of the flying seasons. During spring break-up, when the northern lake ice disintegrates in a roar of protest, across the country float planes are slipped into the cold, clear water to begin their long summer of work.

Each trip has a purpose, a challenge to a pilot's flying skills. An overloaded aircraft in a lake too small for a necessary take-off; landing in a grey overcast almost too low for safe visual flying; charging home through blinding rains or snowstorms when fuel is low and head winds high; and the sense of helplessness when trying to turn a weather-cocking plane out of the wind. Then there are the terrible winds with their mind-numbing cold, the swarms of voracious blackflies and harpoon mosquitoes. Yet above all there is the unquenchable warmth of companionship with those who have shared that splendid isolation and discovery of our Canadian north.[1]

J.A. Foster, *The Bush Pilots*

Returning to Canada from the Air Transport Auxiliary, First Officer Helen Harrison's passion and commitment to flying had not diminished in the slightest.

In an interview for the *Toronto Star*, Helen enthused: 'I can't keep away from it. I just love it. I even convinced Mother that flying was safe and took her for a ride one day. But Dad, I haven't won over yet. He won't go up. He leaves all the flying business to me.'[2]

In the Canadian aviation sector, returning pilots sought career opportunities in commercial flying, at flight schools, within transportation and in other flying fields related to flying. She began to seek a pilot chauffeur role with a chartered flying company.

'Her Air Transport Auxiliary history sheet describes her as a "first class officer, keen, steady pilot and (with a) cheerful personality" but First Officer Helen Harrison feels there is nothing unusual about her abilities or glamorous about her work', wrote a reporter.[3]

'The future for women pilots in Canada is, I believe, definitely brighter now that the war is over. It is entirely up to the individual girl herself, of course, to make her opportunity in aviation. Each one must find an opening and convince the aircraft manufacturer or airport owner that she can do the job.'[4]

After the Second World War, Helen's brother Captain Jim Testemale remained behind in India until he returned to Vancouver in 1950. Before he left the subcontinent, she visited him and flew in India. This Far East experience increased her hours and added depth to her resume.

After her return to Canada, Helen learned that her former employer in South Africa had been liberated as a prisoner of war. George Haller, who founded Haller Aviation, had become an officer with the South African Air Force. Patrolling by air the Mediterranean sector in February 1942, 'he tangled with an overpowering squadron of German M-Es far out over the sea. Hitting the silk from his disabled ship, Haller floated down, inflated his rubber dingy and spent the next two days floating in the Mediterranean under a fierce tropical sun.'[5]

Sighted by an Axis patrol, he was brought ashore near Benghazi in North Africa. George Haller was held a prisoner of war at five prisons: Camp 9 A/H at Spangenberg, Stalag Luft II at Sagan, Camp 21B at Schugen, Stalag Luft III(N) at Sagan, and Marlag which was north of Bremen. He was on a forced march from Marlag to Trenthorst on 10 April 1945 when he was liberated. Returning to South Africa, he resumed Haller Aviation and began an aviation export business.[6]

Despite her matchless experience as a pilot, First Officer Helen Harrison had returned to Canada to challenging employment opportunities for female pilots.

An Opportunity Briefly Arises South of the Border

While she was with the Air Transport Auxiliary, Helen maintained correspondence with Jackie Cochran who had been appointed Director of the Women's Flying Training Program for the US Army Air Force. In her letter to Helen on 23 June 1943, she shared her plans to develop a class of women pilots.

> There is no higher position any women could possibly hold within the Air Forces, and I am going to keep trying to have a class made up of Allied nations. If this should materialise, you naturally would have an opportunity to serve here with the American girls. It certainly will give me considerably more opportunity to present this idea to the people who can make this possible.[7]

In a September 1943 press release, Jackie Cochran described the growth of the Women's Airforce Service Pilots who were trained to work with the US Air Force. In October 1944, as the war wound down, she announced the deactivation of the Women's Airforce Service Pilots program which curtailed her plans to develop a women's flying unit.

She stated: 'The reduction in the flying training program and the changing war situation's bearing on availability and deployment of pilots make it evident that the Women's Airforce Service Pilots will soon become pilot material in excess of needs.'[8]

In a letter to women pilots, she expressed: 'It is with deep regret that I found it necessary to recommend the inactivation of the entire program. But … how great is our satisfaction to know that over 1,000 women have learned to fly "the Army way".'[9]

Jackie Cochran thought the women pilots could be commissioned into the US Army. 'I lost the battle for militarisation of the Women's Airforce Service Pilots in Congress in the summer of 1944.' The waves of protests were 'strange':

> We were putting male pilots on bread lines, we were teenaged schoolgirls, stenographers, clerks and factory workers piloting military planes … we were wasting millions of taxpayers' dollars to train women in a frivolous program. All of it was untrue. All of it was demoralising and very destructive of the truly heroic dimensions to which the Women's Airforce Service Pilots had risen. I was disgusted.[10]

The program was disbanded five days before Christmas in 1944 in a storm of protest. The Women's Airforce Service Pilots did not receive any benefits.

However, this program, along with the women's branch of the Air Transport Auxiliary in Great Britain, did prove to the public and to the air forces the ability of women to fly every type of military aircraft. In the US, the women pilots flew the highly sophisticated P-51 Mustang, Boeing's B-17 Flying Fortress, and Boeing's legendary B-29 Superfortress bomber. Jackie Cochran noted that 150 women flew the B-29 with only one minor incident and not a single fatality.

In *Women and Flight*, author Carolyn Russo writes 'In all, 1,074 women flew more than 60 million miles in the service of their country; thirty-eight were killed. When the Women's Airforce Service Pilots were disbanded in 1944 a few women found jobs in general and business aviation, but the great majority of them pursued different careers.'[11]

Across the border in Canada, the Royal Canadian Air Force disbanded the Women's Division in addition to the Canadian Women Army Corps and other women's organisations.

Helen's goal of becoming a commercial pilot with airlines such as Trans-Canada Air Lines seemed even further from reach. But Helen remained steadfast and indefatigable. With steely determination underneath her cheerful demeanour, she remained resolutely focused on her flying career. She put the disappointment of not returning to the Air Transport Auxiliary behind her, although it ached poignantly.

The media conveyed her confidence, enthusiasm and buoyancy in news stories across the country.

'A tall, blond girl whose resemblance to Barbara Stanwyck has often been noted, Helen has 3,000 flying hours to her credit', reported one newspaper.[12]

'But I think there should be many openings for women as instructors, first of all – and after they have gained enough experience, more advanced jobs as demonstrators.'[13]

For women pilots and instructors, it was a period of digging deep within themselves to find the courage, stamina, resilience and persistence needed to restart a career in aviation where there were few openings. The war had interrupted civil flying. Post-war, the nature of civil flying had irreversibly changed. Lifelong dreams were reshaped, but not for Helen.

Conditions for working women after the war were tough. On the home front, it was estimated that 700,000 women worked in Canadian factories producing everything from bombs and gun carriages to parachutes and aircraft engines. In the civilian labour force, another 400,000 women found work opportunities. When the Second World War ended, many women found themselves out of work.

Historian Jean Bruce wrote:

> They basically just disappeared under this tidal wave after the war. Once the men came home from the war and most of the working women returned to their houses – there was

> always that little kicker phrase about 'serving only for the duration' – then equal pay and childcare and expanded roles in the armed forces and workaday society became irrelevant.[14]
>
> In effect, it took another 20 years before the issues really surfaced again.[15]

The experiences of women who worked and served during the Second World War 'empowered women and led them to seek professional opportunities in the workforce'.[16]

In the US, staunch advocate Jackie Cochran spoke about the need to include women pilots to achieve post-war aviation goals. She spoke at a national aviation conference in Oklahoma City in November 1944: The *Capitol Hill Beacon* noted that she 'declared she was a realist and not a feminist in the belief that America would have been better prepared for war had women played a greater part in the development of aviation before the war. She 'praised the wonderful job accomplished by the WASPS who have flown every type of airplane.'[17]

With the approaching deactivation of the WASPs on 20 December, she emphasised that women pilots will 'be a post-war asset to this country, somewhat alleviating a lack of airmindedness. You won't keep these women out of the air', she said. 'People never stay grounded once they learn to fly.'[18]

'If She Can Do It, I Can!'

'Although she has had no luck and has decided to return to England, Helen has managed', reported *The Gazette*, 'in a rather oblique fashion to stay near flying fields and the air activity she loves.'[19]

Driving passengers in a taxi to Malton airport, Helen Harrison picked up a pilot from his hotel and was surprised to discover he was Flight Lieutenant George F. Buzz Beurling, a famous Second World War flying ace. As a flight commander with a Royal Canadian Air Force spitfire squadron, Flight Lieutenant Beurling had set an aerial combat record when he downed thirty-one enemy planes over Malta.

'He recognised her and was furious to think that a woman of her ability and experience couldn't find a job flying', wrote Joyce Spring.[20] Eventually her contacts at the airport paid off and she became a pilot chauffeur for a businessman.

In December 1945, Helen became the chief test pilot and demonstrator with Percival Aircraft Ltd which planned to assemble passenger aircraft in Toronto. In England, Percival Aircraft had built Mosquito bombers and other high-speed planes in its factories. Their Proctor plane had been designed earlier as a Royal Air Force communications aircraft during the Second World War. The new Proctor V was a later development of the pre-war Gull and Vega Gull.

Hiring a former military pilot instructor and Air Transport Auxiliary ferry pilot was a strategic move by Percival Aircraft.

> Demonstrating airplanes is one field where women have a definite advantage over men because of the psychological factor of a woman handling a plane. The average man or woman seeing a woman pilot at the controls says: 'This must be a safe, easy-to-fly plane when a woman can pilot it. If she can do it, I can!'[21]

'I am starting with a four-place, single-engine Proctor,' Helen announced 'but will do some demonstration of twin-engine planes also. My specific job is to bring the company's planes before the Canadian public.'[22] Helen recognised that her role was to instil confidence in new light aircraft.

In late January 1946, Helen launched a cross-country 1,240-mile flight from Toronto in a Proctor V. 'At Minnesota, the plane was quite a sensation', she recalled. 'In fact, things were going so well that I told someone I'd better touch wood so I wouldn't have a forced landing before Winnipeg.'

No sooner than she had said this, she rued her words. Aiming for Winnipeg, she detected engine trouble emanating from under the cowlings of the Proctor. Fifty miles south of Winnipeg and just after 4.00 pm, Helen and the flight engineer were forced down at St Jean Baptiste:

> It was very tricky. I was about 1,500 feet up when the engine began to pack up. It was missing badly, and we were losing height. There was a road below us, but it looked pretty narrow. It was just a side road off the highway. To make things worse, there was a crosswind blowing over it.[23]
>
> I set the plane down on the road, which was clear of snow except for a few drifts. I was thinking I'd made it safely when we slithered off the road into a ditch. The ditch was filled with six feet of snow, and we tipped on our nose. I was amazed that the prop wasn't damaged.[24]

She said her teeth were chattering in the -15 degrees Celsius temperatures by the time they reached the farmhouse of a French-Canadian family. Helen took the next train from Letellier, Manitoba while the engineer stayed with the Proctor.

'This is my first visit to Winnipeg', she informed a reporter when she alighted from a train at the Canadian National Railway Station, 'and it's a trip I'll never forget.'[25] The next day, Helen was a guest of the Winnipeg Branch of the Women's Canadian Press Club at The Lodge.

A few days later, Percival Aircraft Ltd announced that Helen Harrison, 'who holds the distinction of being the world's first military aviatrix', had been chosen to demonstrate *Glamor Girl*. This was the company's first British-manufactured plane to be shipped to Toronto for assembly.

The sky-blue aircraft was unveiled in February 1946 to Ontario aviation enthusiasts. The low-wing monoplane, equipped with a 210 hp de Havilland Gipsy Queen II engine, boasted a top speed of 150 mph. Importantly, it could be adapted to skis and floats.

'When *Glamor Girl* underwent the whirling manoeuvres of test-flight a short time ago', reported the *Edmonton Journal*, 'Miss Harrison found her a "grand ship".'[26]

'We're Here!' proclaimed Percival Aircraft's first ad in the *National Post* on 23 February 1946, announcing the plane's arrival. Photos of John F. Carroll, acting manager and a former Royal Canadian Air Force fighter pilot, along with pictures of Helen and the chief ground officer A. Graves were featured.

In April, when temperatures were considerably warmer, Helen and John F. Carroll landed in Calgary on their cross-country tour to demonstrate the plane. One weekend, she made a flight over the city but ran into engine problems. Repairs delayed the take-off for the next leg of their journey to the coast.

The first post-war pleasure plane to appear in Canadian skies flew over the majestic Rockies into Vancouver. Helen was at the controls with John F. Carroll sitting next to her. The pair soared over the Fraser River valley with its steep forested mountains on both sides. The glaciated peak of Mount Baker, the new world Fuji-Yama from Helen's childhood days in Steveston, shimmered in the bright sunshine on their left. Straight ahead the Strait of Georgia and the Gulf Islands beckoned.

The striking beauty of Vancouver, seen from the air for the first time, did not fail to evoke a sense of wonder and awe in both pilots. Their plane had become part of the magnificent, intoxicating vista of sea, mountains and sky that surround Vancouver. Touching down after a 3,000-mile tour, Helen Harrison had returned to her birthplace after an absence of many years.

Later that spring Helen was heartbroken to hear of the tragic death of one of her South African flying colleagues, Captain Rosamund Everard-Steenkamp. After Helen's move to North America, Rosamund had served with the South African Women's Auxiliary Air Force, flying officials to military centres. She joined the Air Transport Auxiliary in Britain on 7 February 1944 and ferried aircraft up to 31 October 1945. Notably, while with the Air Transport Auxiliary, Rosamund became the first woman to fly a jet aircraft in Britain, a Meteor Mark III, which had the capacity to reach speeds of 606 mph.

A widow of a fighter pilot, Rosamund continued ferrying after her Air Transport Auxiliary service. Stationed with the Royal Air

Force at No.1 Ferry Pool, she was delivering a Spitfire XIV from Hamble to a Shropshire station on 19 March 1946. The aircraft crashed at high speed near Kidderminster in the Wyre Forest. Captain Rosamund King Everard-Steenkamp, 33, was buried at Maidenhead cemetery.

In her advocacy for women pilots in South Africa in the late 1930s, Rosamund had highlighted Helen Harrison as one of the few international women pilots breaking barriers.

Inspirational Women Break Down Barriers

In the Near Year, updates from her community of Air Transport Auxiliary pilots kept Helen in the loop. She followed the news of where her fellow pilots had landed following their intense ferrying work together.

Tragically, the ferry pilots learned that on 2 March 1947, Air Transport Auxiliary Commander Pauline Gower Fahie, 36, had soared on her final flight. After delivering twin boys, she succumbed to a heart attack. Her sons Paul and Michael both survived and were healthy. Left to mourn were her husband, Wing Commander William Cusack Fahie, who she married in 1945, her father Sir Robert Vaughan Gower, and close family members. Tragically, Pauline's close friend and flying partner Dorothy Spicer Pearse had been killed with her husband Richard in an airliner crash in Argentina in December 1946.

Earlier in the New Year, Jackie Cochran's North American pilots absorbed the news that one of their own had died. The death of Helen Richey, who at 37 years old was the same age as Helen Harrison, touched a raw nerve. Helen Richey had fallen into a deep depression at the demise of her flying career, which she had struggled to maintain after the war. The large number of ex-war pilots who had returned to North America meant that she saw no prospect of continuing with her life's passion. The cause of her death on 7 January 1947 was an apparent overdose of barbiturates.[27]

'Floats Harrison' Rediscovers a Love of Seaplane Flying

The open skies for flying on the West Coast convinced Helen to begin the next chapter of her life there. In the spring of 1947, Helen returned to her birthplace in Vancouver with her three sons and her parents.

Helen's first job was to instruct at the fledgling Vanderhoof Flying School which was going to be opened by brothers Bill and Glen Lee. The pair, with two other brothers, were widely known throughout BC as Lee Transport Company. The previous year, they had purchased a plane and started a chartered freight service and had planned to open a flying school in BC's interior.

Helen had taught the younger brother Glen. Once they had obtained their licences, the pair planned to fly to Estevan, Saskatchewan, to purchase a second plane. Helen, having heard their flight plans, tried unsuccessfully to discourage them.

The pair took off from Vancouver airport at 5.46 am on Wednesday, 28 May 1947. The *Vancouver Sun* later reported:

> Their fight plan called for them to land at Penticton. But they stopped at Hope due to gathering clouds. Minutes after they took off from Hope at 11.45 am, their two-seater Fairchild Cornell crashed directly on the Hope-Princeton Highway, nine miles east of Hope.
>
> They took off on the flight from Vancouver Airport in spite of the pleas of a woman flying instructor. Weeping, she told how Glen had just got his pilot's licence.
>
> Gathering clouds and a dead-end mountain pass, then a looming telephone wire as they attempted an emergency landing on the highway, brought death to the Lee brothers. The thin strand caught the wing or undercarriage of their plane as they nosed in and spun it about. It crumpled to the gravel roadway, broke in two.[28]

When she learned that they were determined to go, she had warned them particularly not to fly up the valley.

Pilots flying on visual flight rules in mountainous terrain learned how to maintain visuals in poor weather and follow valleys safely. Valleys usually include the watersheds of rivers and creeks, and in the mountains tend to narrow as they rise in elevation. The risk in flying up valleys is that if clouds are low and the ceiling is dropping, a pilot may not have enough room to turn around. Pilots are trained to fly along the right side of a valley, which provides room to bank to the left and execute a 180-degree turn if the route is not passable. The direction of rotation of most aircraft engines makes it easier to turn left.

The arrival of planes on floats and skis had opened the vast interior and far north of the West Coast. The wilderness of Canada, with its myriad lakes and rivers, offered many ready-made landing sites. Pioneer pilots and bush planes flew into untouched regions thanks to these unlimited waterways. The BC coastline also offered access to floatplanes.

During the inter-war years, floatplanes established themselves as workhorses of the north. They carried surveyors to unknown terrains, flew prospectors and miners to exploration sites, and ferried large loads of equipment parts and personnel to remote areas that were inaccessible by other means of transportation. Floatplanes were versatile, spry and, above all, glorious to fly unfettered through Canada's north.

The Canadian north and Alaska served as the cradle of floatplane flying from which air charter services grew. From these nitty-gritty, can-do charter flying services that literally operated on a wing and a prayer grew some of the largest international airlines.

In teaching student pilots to fly these stalwart workhorses, Helen was better equipped than most instructors. Her work as an Air Transport Auxiliary ferry pilot had involved navigating without the use of maps, radios and in the most death-defying wartime conditions. Her two-year sojourn flying and instructing in South Africa was instrumental in providing Helen with a foundational knowledge. Across the high veld of the interior African plateau, she gained invaluable experience of flying at high altitudes, through rugged mountain ranges and in wildly varying and violent weather conditions.

In British Columbia, her tremendous skills learned in Great Britain, South Africa and Singapore coalesced to strategically position her for this new chapter of her life.

Recognising that instructing in the art of floatplane flying could rejuvenate her career and infuse new adventures, she obtained her float rating from Rosalie 'Rolie' Moore before she went job hunting.[29] Rolie Moore was the president of the famous Flying Seven group of women pilots and an instructor with the Aero Club of BC.

In September 1947, Helen became the first woman instructor in Canada giving lessons on floatplanes when she was hired by the Duncan Flying Club. On Vancouver Island, she was both an instructor and vice president of the club. Her skills were literally second to none, noted the *Vancouver Sun*, continuing:

> She has seen much of the world from the clouds. And she has flown more than a half million miles. In South Africa she earned a reputation as a skilful stunt pilot. During her time with the Air Transport Auxiliary she flew every type of military aircraft.
>
> She flew any time, in any kind of weather, without any guardian fliers with her.[30]

A week later, the *Sun* extolled the rise in floatplane flying: 'As much of BC's commercial flying is done to mining and logging camps whose only airstrips are interior lakes or sheltered bays, amphibians and floats are used extensively, so it is necessary for commercial pilots to be able to handle these types of aircraft.'[31]

With Helen Harrison teaching in Duncan, young women began flocking to the flying lessons being offered. They enrolled in flying clubs around BC and across the country. Teaching on floats, part of her instruction time was spent at Youbou on Lake Cowichan. 'It's more of a challenge because wind and water play a part in take-off and landing', she explained.[32]

Helen provided her pupil pilots with the essential skills she had learned in the challenging conditions of Singapore where sea, currents and winds met the wide open skies.

First Flying Instructor Soars

As Helen's career soared to new heights as one of Canada's first instructors on floatplanes, she reflected on her earlier trip to Singapore where she learned the hard knocks of seaplane flying. Her first instructor and mentor Jack Sale had thrown open a door for her. Through his guidance, she had discovered the sheer exhilaration, unfettered freedom and ultimate challenge of flying on floats.

Revelling in her newfound work at the Duncan Flying Club, the year 1947 ended with a heartbreak for Helen. Flight Lieutenant John Alexander 'Jack' Sale, her first instructor in England and Singapore, had died.

Jack was the chief instructor at the Singapore Flying Club from 1935 to 1942. As a Royal Air Force pilot, he had survived the atrocities of the Second World War in the Far East and returned safely home to England. He died in London on 5 November 1947 during surgery.[33] Retired Flight Lieutenant Jack Sale had packed a lifetime of adventures in horse racing, yacht sailing, barnstorming, stunt flying, aviation instruction and war flying in his 40 young years.

Months later, on 28 May 1948, Helen was crushed when she heard that Flight Lieutenant George Frederick 'Buzz' Beurling, 26, was killed in a plane crash at Rome's Ube airport. The Canadian flying ace had lifted Helen's spirits when they met fortuitously in Toronto. His confidence in her buoyed her efforts to kick start her post-war aviation career.

Stringent Licensing Regulations Force Closure of Flying Clubs

At the beginning of 1949, new licensing regulations introduced by the Canadian transportation department were viewed as too stringent. The requirements were beginning to have the effect of strangling flying clubs in small communities.

At a meeting on 16 May 1949, the Duncan Flying Club informed the BC Aviation Council that 'the club had been forced to cease operations because of "unreasonable and stringent demands of the Department of Transport".'[34]

The department had previously requested that the Duncan Flying Club hire a full-time engineer to service its two planes, which it could ill-afford. 'Previously, the planes were flown to Cassidy landing strip near Nanaimo for their weekly inspection or an engineer came from there to Duncan.' Another regulation required civilian flying students to undergo seventy-five or eighty hours of ground school training.[35]

The closure of the Duncan Flying Club's school forced its instructors, including Helen, to look elsewhere for employment.

In 1949, she was hired to fly lumbermen and company officials for the Kent Logging Company of Vancouver in its Cessna 170. Based at Galiano Island, Helen became the only female pilot in the area. 'I had no trouble', she said of her work flying for Kent. 'I had my share of sweeping snow off the floats.'[36]

'When this job came to an end, she spent the next twenty years instructing or acting as interim manager at flying clubs whenever she could find work.'[37] Helen soon earned a reputation as the best float instructor in the province. According to her, even BC Airlines sent their new pilots to 'Floats Harrison' as she was known. 'But they wouldn't hire me.'[38]

Federal Subsidies Revived Interest in Flying Across Canada

New federal funding for flying clubs and schools in the summer of 1949 revived interest in flying across Canada. The subsidies included a $100 grant to each school for each qualified pilot trained, and a $100 grant to each pilot when he or she qualified for a private transport licence. If a pilot was accepted into the Royal Canadian Air Force reserve, an additional $100 grant would be provided.

It was estimated that 1,500 pilots and nearly forty clubs would have benefited from federal grants. At that time, it cost an average flying pupil about $285 to $300 to qualify for a private flying licence.

'Since the war, flying clubs have been in financial difficulties and many have operated at a loss', news media reported.[39]

In mid-June 1949, the celebration of National Flying Club Week provided an opportunity for flying clubs to entice young budding pilots to take up flying.

'Thousands of young Canadians have an intense yearning for the freedom and skilled accomplishment of flying as pilots', enthused the *Nanaimo Daily News*. 'This plan makes available to student flyers of all ages cash grants which will contribute substantially to the cost of their training and flying practice.'[40]

The new subsidy program for training pilots rejuvenated flying schools around the province, and Helen manoeuvred onto the rising wave.

Parade Highlights Air Power on Floats

Vancouver's complement of air power roared past excited children at the Pacific National Exhibition on 29 August 1949. In a 'Fly Past', more than sixty aircraft thundered over the exhibition grounds.

Three Tiger Moths and an Anson Mark V led the BC Aero Club's fleet of Stinsons, Fleet Canucks, Moths, Cornells and Piper Cubs. Vancouver U-Fly and Associated Air Taxi flaunted their float-equipped planes. BC Airlines paraded their Seabee amphibians. A de Havilland Beaver on floats rumbled by, wagging its wings.

Nearly half of the planes were on floats, which also included a Custom Waco on floats, an Aeronca sedan on pontoons, Cessnas and Luscombes on floats, and a Grumman Goose amphibian. Several Supermarine Stranraer flying boats were demonstrated by Queen Charlotte Airlines.

The breadth of floatplanes and seaplanes hinted evocatively at the far ranges to which they flew: the northern lakes and waterways beyond the rugged mountains of Vancouver; the mist-shrouded archipelago of the Haida Gwaii, formerly known as the Queen Charlotte Islands; the vast boreal hinterlands with its myriad wildlife; and the dazzling icefields of

Atlin, Kluane and Alaska. Onlookers were captivated by the possibilities: the unknown destinations to which these floatplanes ventured, and the untold adventures that could be unlocked by planes on pontoons.

The 'Fly Past' organisers dreamed that more people would start to include flying in their lives. They also hoped that the airshow would become 'an annual event growing in size with the advancement of the air age', reported the *Vancouver News-Herald*.[41]

Chapter 12

Sustaining a Joy of Flying

Veteran woman pilot Helen Harrison has pioneered in the field of aviation and blazed a wide trail for other women to follow. For the past nine years she has been in BC and has decided that home is best after all.

Helen is in charge of float training at the Aero Club of BC and is the only woman flying full time commercially in the province. Pupils have complete confidence in their instructress. With 6,000 flying hours to her credit, 4,000 of them on teaching, Helen is an old hand at the game.

She places people with a fear of flying in three categories: those who think it will be like a roller-coaster ride; those who think they will become dizzy from the height; and those who think the plane will drop like a stone if there is an engine failure. Once they have been up, she claims, all fear of flying vanishes, and they see what a pleasure they have been missing all these years.

The veteran's advice to women who want to enter aviation is: 'get lots of experience and get it when you are young'.

My opinion is that it is up to women to make their own way in aviation,' she said. 'I've been earning my living at it for 22 years and haven't had any trouble.'

If women would go ahead and qualify themselves for commercial flying positions, Helen believes they would get them – in time. But there are not enough going after them now, she says, thus restricting women's orbit in the air. 'There is prejudice against women, but we've just got to break in and keep plugging,' she says.

Helen is a woman who literally 'lives her work'. She admits her twelve-hour working day and also her weekend flying leaves her little time for other diversions. The pilot pooh-poohed the idea that she is in a glamorous profession.

It is interesting work, and I am in love with it, but flying is routine.[1]

Judy Thormahlen, *The Province*

Flying clubs were spreading their wings further and faster. Since the war, hundreds of new airports were built across the country. As navigational aids were installed, aircraft companies began building stronger, durable, safer and more flexible bush planes. Cessna, de Havilland, Piper and Fairchild produced aircraft that were more suited for Canada's remote, wild and rugged regions. The Canadian western province of British Columbia with its Rocky and Coastal mountain ranges, and remote hinterlands invited pilots with experience in bushplanes and floatplanes.

Cranbrook Flying Services in the East Kootenays, in southeastern British Columbia, first beckoned Helen. Here she immersed herself in the life of the town of Cranbrook and volunteered with search and rescue flights whenever she could.

In February 1951, two students passed their flying exams while eight students were progressing under tutelage by chief flying instructor Helen Harrison. In early July 1951, four flying students received their private licences. At the end of August, three more students earned their private pilot licences.

Now married to John Taylor Dixon, Helen scaled back her time devoted to instruction. She taught during the spring, summer and autumn months when the weather was more conducive to flying.

In the lounge of the BC Aero Club at Vancouver Airport, a newly formed chapter of the Ninety-Nines welcomed many women pilots throughout the province. The Ninety-Nines was founded by the late Amelia Earhart and ninety-eight pioneer women pilots in 1929.

By the time the chapter was formed in BC in 1953, the Ninety-Nines had expanded to 1,200 members around the world. Its purpose was to facilitate 'a closer relationship among women pilots and unite them in any movements that may be for their benefit or that of aviation in general'. Helen Harrison of Cranbrook was among the fifteen BC charter members of the new chapter.[2]

Instructing Throughout British Columbia

In a step forward to standardising flight training, flying instructors across Canada undertook a ten-day refresher course. The courses were held on the threshold of the jet era. In Lethbridge, Alberta, Helen completed the second Air Industry and Transport Association course in 1953 along with dozens of instructors. Joining Helen in the course were five professional instructors including Elizabeth Kerr, Dawn Dawson, Mary Willcox, Phyllis Drysdale and Vera Strodl, the latter a compatriot Air Transport Auxiliary pilot.

The support pledged by the Canadian government for cadet training turned Chilliwack into a national training base. Many young cadets received their first flying instruction in the summer of 1954.

Sixteen air cadets began training at the Chilliwack municipal airport in a course sponsored by the Royal Canadian Air Force and the Air Cadet League of Canada. Helen Harrison Dixon, chief flying instructor, was assisted by Ray Scott of Vancouver U-Fly and Sherwood Moffit of

Cascades Air Service. Beginning at 6.00 am each day, the cadets spent thirty hours flying: the first twelve hours on dual instruments and the final eighteen hours flying solo.

After completing the twenty-seven day course, new cadet pilots demonstrated their flying skills in the BC zone eliminations for the Webster Memorial Trophy.

> This was the elimination round to determine the best Canadian amateur pilots. Pilots flying light aircraft executed forced landings, precision turns and other qualities of good airmanship. Safety, precision, and perfection of judgement rather than stunting ability, were the basis of competition.[3]

After the Chilliwack program finished, Helen turned her gaze towards northern BC. At the beginning of August 1954, she flew her two-seater Cessna 140 north to Prince George as she was bringing a satellite flight school. The local flying club boasted fifty-five members including two hospital nurses. Helen's plane complemented the local flying club's sleek Luscombe Silvaire, registration CF-GYM, which was used for dual instruction. The club also offered the cheapest rental fees in Canada for this type of plane at eight dollars an hour.

The course for twenty enrolled students was offered by Skyways Air Services of Langley Prairie. Fledgling pilots from all walks of life enrolled in the ninety-day government-approved course. The cost was $700, but half of the fee was covered by the federal government which was promoting civilian flying.

At the beginning of August 1954, Helen's logbooks attested to a substantial 5,700 hours in the air. She 'enjoyed with a handful of other women pilots, the distinction of having flown every military aircraft used in the Second World War, with the exception of four-engine types', enthused the *Citizen* at the start of her course. The *Citizen*'s article was featured on the first page, one of the rare times a daily newspaper had placed coverage of a woman's aviation career so prominently.

> Reading almost like a Jane's *All the World's Aircraft*, her logbooks show time on Spitfires, Mosquitos, Wellingtons, Mitchells, Bostons, Hurricanes, Mustangs, Dakotas, Oxfords, Harvards, Hampdens, Bolingbrokes, Fairey Battles, Lysanders, Tiger Moths and others.
>
> Flying and living, she found, requires a certain amount of easily negotiable coin of the realm and so she decided to become a professional.[4]

To instil confidence in her nervous pupil pilots she assured the *Citizen* that she had soloed hundreds of flying students, including her husband and her youngest son. She hoped to have women students before the 1954 flying season ended.

After Labour Day, ten club members qualified for their pilot's licence, and seven others had completed their required examinations and flying tests. Training planes included a Piper PA-18 Super Cub, the Luscombe Silvaire and a Cessna 140 supplied by Skyway Air Services.

'Conducting a two-month, accident free-training period, including twelve hours aloft with their instructress, eighteen hours of solo flight and periods of ground instruction, fourteen members of the Prince George Flying Club have received their private pilot's licences', reported the *Citizen.*[5]

Before the first snowflakes arrived in mid-October, the successful and proud pilots were presented with their certificates at an 'enjoyable supper dance at the airport club rooms on 15 October 1954'.[6]

Since the Prince George airport did not have flight controls at the time, pilots were verbally instructed to stay out of the way of the large passenger planes that came in a couple of times a day. These small planes did not have radios which meant that pilots simply taxied towards the runway, and after completing pre-flight checks, wiggled their tail fins to indicate to the control tower they were ready for take-off. A green light from the control tower signified permission to take off. When landing, pilots flew by the control tower to look for a green light for landing.

Lands Dream Job as Chief Float Instructor

As winter gales subsided and clear skies arrived on the West Coast in 1955, Helen had realised her dream job in becoming the chief flying instructor in charge of float training at the Aero Club of BC. 'I just got the job I wanted so badly in Vancouver.'[7]

The Aero Club clubhouse beside the Vancouver airport, filled with maps, photographs and artifacts, was a mecca for fliers from around the province. Founded in 1912 by several pioneers, it was the oldest club in Canada. In the early years, the club began building their first aircraft, a plane on floats. It took two years to complete, and only two minutes to crash after its maiden take-off.

By May 1956, the Aero Club had over 1,000 members, 16 aircraft and a staff of 17, including 4 full-time instructors. The previous year, the Club had graduated 100 private pilots, 22 commercial pilots, 20 instructors and 15 airline pilots.

Pupil pilots started their training on a Fleet Canuck and graduated to a Cessna 140 floatplane and a Beechcraft Bonanza.

Helen continued to advocate for women to pursue training and qualify for commercial licences. 'There are not enough women going after flying jobs now', she commented to the *Windsor Star*.[8]

Interest in flying was taking off. Helen supervised a similar ninety-day course in Williams Lake that summer. At this point in her career, she had 6,000 flying hours to her credit, of which 4,000 were instructional hours.

During National Flying Club Week, the unsung work of non-profit clubs was highlighted. 'During the Second World War, these clubs operated twenty-two elementary flying training schools for the British Commonwealth Air Training Plan, graduating pilots to advanced training units.'[9] Helen's instruction at the Kitchener-Waterloo Flying Club was part of this.

'Canada's record in civil and military aviation sparkles with achievement', wrote the *Vancouver News-Herald*. 'The Royal Canadian Flying Clubs are one of the chief contributing factors in making that record possible and in keeping Canada one of the world's most air-minded nations. These clubs are performing a national service of the highest order.'[10]

Sky Becomes Unlimited for Women Pilots

A year later, with nearly 6,500 flying hours, Helen figured in another new story. By mid-1956, over fifty women in the province were licensed to fly, including several who had completed further training and earned sufficient hours to obtain their commercial licences.

The District Superintendent of air regulations, D.D. Murphy, highlighted two BC women who were 'natural born instructors'. He was referring to Helen, and Alberta instructor Gretchen Mathers. Speaking from experience, Helen stated that there were many opportunities for women in aviation, and 'definitely in the field of instruction'.

Aviation advocates had noted that the main deterrent to its popularity was the expense.

In June 1956, the *Vancouver News-Herald* ran a feature entitled 'The Sky isn't the Limit', in which news editor Margaret Ecker Francis interviewed Helen about her experiences. 'In its 25 years of existence, Vancouver's international airport has not produced a Jacqueline Cochran and Amelia Earhart, but women are finding a growing space in the skies over Sea Island', she wrote.

Margaret reported that in addition to pioneer trailblazer Helen Harrison, several young women were claiming their space in aviation. Aero Club manager Harry O'Reilly exclaimed that the sky is literally unlimited for women pilots. Nineteen-year-old Valerie Cheltenham accomplished what would have seemed impossible, a full-time flying job testing and demonstrating aircraft for Garner Flying Service.

'Encouraged by Mr O'Reilly and the example of Helen, she emerged with one of the most unique jobs ever done by a young girl', Margaret Francis wrote, 'Women like Helen paved the way for Valerie down at the Aero Club float wharf (on Sea Island) where she was directing students taking off and landing on the Fraser River.'

In her article she quoted Valerie who said: 'I fly more than 100 hours a month when the weather is good. It doesn't leave much time or energy for other things.'[11]

The *Vancouver Sun*'s Kathy Hassard, in an article entitled 'Women with Wings', reported that four other women who trained at the Aero Club had obtained commercial flying jobs elsewhere. In addition to Gretchen Mather, Eleanor Jones held her commercial licence in Langley for eight years, Betty Kerr taught cadets as an assistant in Kamloops, and Dawn Dawson launched her commercial flying career in Whitehorse, Yukon.

In her article, she noted that Harry O'Reilly described Helen as 'one of the most respected members of the flying profession'. She wrote that Helen was 'the much-in-demand float flying instructor at BC Aero Club and loving every moment in her career aloft. On terra-firma, Helen's the mother of three grown sons and even admits to a groundling grandson.'[12]

In 'The Sky isn't the Limit', Margaret Francis observed; 'For Mrs Dixon, who was formerly Helen Harrison and Canada's outstanding woman pilot, it was a rough, tough struggle to land herself where she wanted to be.'

Margaret wrote how she herself 'remembered the Air Transport Auxiliary, the glamor girls of the war, trim in their uniforms, always chic and attractive, their flying admired ever by fighter pilots. They could fly anything, anywhere.' In her interview, she quoted Helen saying: 'It was a great period of my life, Of course, I was lucky. I've had very few forced landings and only one crash landing.'

Margaret continued:

> after the war, the world apparently expected these 'powder puff pilots' as they were called in England, to go back to their hearths. Jobs were hard for the veterans to come by, and Helen drove trucks, buses, anything, until Percival Aircraft gave her a job testing their planes, across Canada ... BC offered opportunities, and she came home to run a float plane school in Duncan, to instruct in the interior and in 1954, to train cadets at Chilliwack. Just joined the Aero Club just over a year ago, instructing float aircraft in summer and wheels in winter.'

In her conversation with Margaret, Helen admitted: 'Yes, it's all been hard pioneering groundwork, people were prejudiced against woman pilots, but now they have been accepted as instructors and demonstrators.'

Margaret asked Helen if 'her students, who include men being trained for BC airlines resent a female instructor?' Helen replied, 'No, it's good for their male egos. They feel if a woman can handle an aircraft, they can, too.'[13]

Change Arrives 'In the Air'

The stories of women aviators across Canada in the news spoke to the continuing struggle to become commercial pilots.

Margaret Fane Rutledge, one of the charter members of the Flying Seven, became one of Canada's first half-dozen women to earn her commercial pilot's licence. In 1957, she spoke pragmatically about the realities facing pilots with commercial employment aspirations:

> Airlines have not accepted women as transport pilots and there's no sign they will. We have attained our greatest equality only in an emergency, as wartime trans-Atlantic ferry pilots.[14]
>
> Most women today fly for their own enjoyment, act as instructors, stewardesses or work in airport administration. A man will hire a woman pilot today pretty well only if he wants freight hauled to Knob Lake.[15]

Margaret's first job was a 'world first' as she worked as a radio operator for a tiny seaplane airline based 200 miles north of Vancouver. Unable to find a flying job, she became a radio dispatcher for Bridge River and Cariboo Airways. Her position, just before the outbreak of the Second World War, was based in Zeballos, a gold rush town on the west coast of Vancouver Island.

For two decades she worked on the inside of Canadian aviation. And optimistically, she felt that change was 'in the air' and fated to remain there.[16]

In 1957, Helen received a judicial separation from John Taylor Dixon and reverted to her flying name.[17]

A Family Matriarch Passes a Torch

On 27 January 1958, Helen and her family lost one of their most loving, ardent and loyal supporters. Gertrude Helen Marcella Testemale, 79, of Richmond, BC had passed away.

She had lovingly nurtured the family as it grew. She had organised and taken care of every detail during all their moves from England to South Africa, and onwards to the US and finally home to Canada. Gertrude supported Helen and her three sons unconditionally.

Without Gertrude, Helen would not have been able to pursue her goals as a single mother, pilot and instructor. Her mother made it possible for her to dedicate and focus on continually training, upgrading and studying for the difficult licensing exams. The rapid development of new aircraft, with refined aerodynamics, instruments and mechanics, meant that Helen had to be constantly studying and experimenting with new aircraft.

Gertrude was survived by her husband Albert, daughter Helen, two sons Percy Fulford and James Albert Testemale, four grandchildren and one great grandchild.[18]

Expanding Flying Instruction Throughout BC

In 1961, Helen earned a seaplane instructor's certificate in the US and continued teaching flying on floats. After seven years of instructing at the Aero Club of BC, she set up a new base in Kamloops from which she instructed various local clubs in the interior.

Tragically, her eldest brother Percy Fulford died on 23 November 1962 in Victoria after a lengthy illness.

Fast disappearing from flight schools were the old Fleet 80s, Aeronca sevens and Taylorcraft. In their place, new instructional aircraft began arriving with modernised controls for advanced flying. The new arrivals included the Piper Colts, Cherokees, and Cessna 150s, 172s and 182s.

In 1964, Helen became the chief flying instructor for McColl's Air Transport Limited at the airport in the city of Vernon. By this time, she had logged 12,000 hours on nearly 100 different types of aircraft.

She flew to Quesnel to conduct a brief refresher course for pilots. The *Quesnel Cariboo Observer* reported:

> Quesnel pilots took advantage of the visit last weekend by Helen Harrison of Kamloops for some advanced check-out in flying safety techniques. Pilots practiced short field take-offs and landings, as well as procedural checks. She said it was a tribute to their interest in safety that they were taking the refresher courses.[19]

Opportunities Begin to Lift for Pilots Overseas

In the New Year of 1965, British pilot Yvonne Pope was appointed co-captain for a regularly scheduled air service – a first in British history. The 34-year-old pilot began piloting a Dakota freight plane for Morton Air Services, a subsidiary of British United Airways.

In Canada, the news of the co-pilot appointment was excitedly received. 'It's about time! I've been advocating for it for a long time', exclaimed Dawn Dawson Bartsch, former bush pilot turned instructor in Calgary, Alberta.[20]

'They think it's a perfectly logical move to have women airline pilots', wrote reporter Linda Curtis in an article with the headline *Women Earn Wings Hard Way, Soon to Be Captains*'.[21]

Access to Technical Training Needed

At this time, a flying grandmother spoke about a key barrier affecting women pilots from working in the commercial sector. Doris Renninger, a 48-year-old New York pilot, had earned her helicopter licence.

Through her flying experiences, Doris reflected on the women pilots who came before her, and their struggles to work in commercial aviation sector. She recalled that in the Second World War,

> women ferried all kinds of planes – fighters as well as bombers – from manufacturing plants to aircraft.
>
> Right now, there are sixty-seven licenced women pilots who have commercial, air transport and instrument rating, required for a commercial pilot's licence. These women did this at their own expense, on their own time.
>
> They think that someday there may be a breakthrough, and women pilots will be hired as commercial pilots.[22]

She observed that women did not have access to technical training provided to male pilots. 'But I think if women had the same opportunities to learn the technical aspects, they could qualify.'[23]

What had been forgotten was that barriers lowered in the Second World War had been raised post-war when women were not admitted as pilots in the US Air Force and naval air forces as a result of US legislation. Consequently, women pilots could not access technical training and specialised flying experience, which was primarily offered in military service, and lost ground. Women pilots also bore the full costs of training, exams and keeping their licences current.

'Women have a lot to offer both as commercial pilots, and as astronauts', she said. 'They have patience and endurance – two excellent qualities for piloting aircraft.'[24]

Learning More About Flying with Every Flight

After a summer teaching in Quesnel, Helen returned to the Chilliwack Flying Club in December 1966 to become its first woman chief flying instructor. Thirteen years earlier, she had overseen a flying cadet school in Chilliwack. Returning to the Fraser Valley, Helen had now earned

12,950 flying hours, nearly 10,000 in instructional flying time. She held a Canadian Senior Commercial licence valid for all aircraft, single and multi-engine, for land and sea, up to 1,250 pounds gross allowable weight.[25]

In a December 1966 article entitled 'Helen Flies Million Miles', the *Chilliwack Progress* reported that Helen's flying career totalled more than twenty-five years. The *Progress* summed her career: 'She has flown Spitfires in World War Two, co-piloted a two-engine Mitchell across the Atlantic, and she includes among her students a flyer who currently is a department of transport inspector in Edmonton.'

Commercial trainee Stewart Purvis told the *Progress* that he liked Helen for the reasons that: 'She is thorough, and she is boss in the air.' Fellow trainee Stuart Jones echoed the same sentiments to the *Progress* reporter, adding, 'She's great!'

The Progress observed that 'Helen Harrison has flown a long way – perhaps 1,500,000 miles.' Noting her flying career in England, South Africa, the United States and Canada, the *Progress* reporter asked: 'Is there anything more she can learn?'

Helen told the reporter: 'I am sure of one thing after all these years, I can learn more about flying every time I go up.'[26]

The active Chilliwack club used a low-wing Cherokee and two Cessna 172s. Training planes like the Cessna 152 or 170 were durable and resilient and could withstand pupils' learning errors. They could be slopped onto a runway without bouncing in response.

Helen preferred to allow for three months for all the lessons to 'sink in'. A student under Helen's tutelage was able to fly solo in thirty-five hours. A federal subsidy of $100 offset their training costs. Regarding the cost of learning to fly, Helen informed the *Progress* reporter:

> Flying is a low-cost form of recreation, not out of line with costs associated with other forms of amusement like skiing and golf. The fact that each trainer plane costs as much as $14,000 and the high price of maintaining rigid mechanical upkeep are sound reasons why course prices are what they are.[27]

Since taking to the air as a teenager, Helen Harrison reflected to the *Progress* reporter on the changing times. 'The prejudice the world knows towards woman flyers has since lessened and today, instructors are much in demand, almost universally.' Training each pupil flyer, she said to the *Progress* reporter that a student must learn to develop good habits in the air. 'It is just as hard to break good habits as it is bad habits', she explained. 'This, and alertness, are basic.'[28]

The following month at a Soroptimist Club meeting, guest speaker Helen Harrison spoke of the continued difficulties women pilots faced in the commercial sector. After sharing her experiences in four countries and as a wartime ferry pilot, 'she emphasised the fact that airlines have not yet accepted women as pilots.' This was 'in spite of their unusually fine record though prejudice against woman instructors has been overcome'.[29]

On 9 March 1967, her father Albert Jules Testemale, 92, passed away. While her father was reluctant to fly during Helen's earlier career, he steadfastly supported Helen and her family alongside his wife Gertrude. He was survived by his daughter Helen and son James of Canim Lake, BC, four grandchildren, five great-grandchildren, and his sister Suzette, of Paris, France.

By mid-1967, the Chilliwack Flying Club was planning a large expansion of its facilities, including new planes, new quarters and 'high hopes for an extended, paved and lighted runway'.[30]

The latest change 'is the return of Peter Dick as chief flying instructor, a post he once held in the late 1940s', reported the *Chilliwack Progress*. 'Dick, coming from a flying job in the Edmonton area takes over from veteran woman aviator Helen Harrison, headed for Port Hardy on Vancouver Island.'[31]

The up-Island community of Port Hardy had hired Helen Harrison to instruct, and she left the Chilliwack Flying Club in July 1967. Port Hardy on the northeastern tip of Vancouver Island served as the terminus for flights along BC's Inside Passage. Secluded communities served by floatplanes included Bella Bella, Bella Coola, Ocean Falls and Prince Rupert in addition to many indigenous villages and work camps.

Her work at flying clubs around the province had fallen into a pattern.

> I can't tell you how many clubs I've cleaned up the mess for. I was often hired to get a club out of a financial jam and add a little life to it, but as soon as the club was prospering the Board of Directors would put a man in as chief flying instructor/manager.[32]
>
> It was frustrating, always having to step back and let a man do the job when I had already shown that I could handle it.[33]

Retiring on the Thirtieth Anniversary of Her Commercial Licences

While instructing in Quesnel in 1968, Helen Harrison was awarded the Back and Bevington air safety trophy for her immense contributions to air safety during the year. Helen's work in flying 14,000 hours as pilot-in-command of numerous aircraft models, without injury to pilots in training and passengers, was commended by the BC Aviation Council.[34]

As Helen continued to instruct pilots at the end of the 1960s, barriers began to fall in aviation. Thirty years after she earned a commercial pilot's licence in the United States and in Canada, Helen became witness to the first woman pilot appointed first officer.

On 30 April 1969, Norwegian Turi Widerøe made history as a first officer with Scandinavian Airlines. Leading up to her historic flight, she had flown de Havilland Twin Otters and Noorduyn Norseman seaplanes on mercy flights, and scheduled routes for Widerøe's Flyveselskap, north of the Arctic Circle.

At this time, a young Canadian pilot was beginning an aviation life of firsts. Rosella Bjornson earned her instructor's rating and was teaching at a Winnipeg flying club.

In Great Britain in 1969, Yvonne Pope Sintes had broken ground when she was appointed co-captain for a regularly scheduled air service.

And in the US, Emily Howell Warner mustered the courage to apply to Frontier Airlines in 1969. She had earlier lost all hope of being hired, after watching her former male students being hired.

These small steps by women pilots in the commercial sector were overshadowed temporarily by the historic landing of the first man on the moon on 20 July 1969.

On 26 August 1969, Helen Harrison retired and capped a remarkable thirty-four year career as a flying instructor and ferry pilot. With her final flight as an instructor, she had logged 14,000 injury-free hours as a pilot-in-command.

On the West Coast of Canada, Helen had acquired a reputation as the best floatplane instructor in BC and was affectionately nicknamed 'Floats Harrison'. She was an indefatigable and unforgettable pilot. In pursuit of her lifelong dream to be an airline commercial pilot, Helen had been thwarted at every turn at aviation's 'glass' ceiling. In an interview later in life, she discussed how she had 'applied at Trans-Canada Air Lines, Pacific Western Airlines, and Canada Pacific Air Lines. The answer was always the same. 'I was either too weak to handle the controls as one TCA captain told me, or the public wouldn't accept a woman as Grant McConnachie said. It didn't matter that I had thousands of hours experience flying heavy twins and floats in BC. I couldn't overcome my sex.'[35]

When asked how she found her work operating in a predominantly masculine occupation, she said:

> Well, I had to grapple. But I decided pretty soon, I'll tell you, if you wanted to be even with the men you had to be twice as good, definitely had to be twice as good as the men.
>
> And I think I ended up that way, being twice as good. And then they decided I knew what I was talking about and finally I got their respect because they knew what I was doing. It was interesting, no doubt about that.
>
> I've never regretted it at all. I enjoyed every minute of it I'll tell you that.[36]

In her retirement Helen continued to fly, for the sublime joy of being aloft in the wide open skies. Joining her in the cockpit on her ethereal flights over western Canada and the United States was her new pilot husband. In the year of her retirement, she married Donald McGlasson Bristol, an engineer from New Brunswick who had worked for Lockheed Aircraft Corporation.

Although she had flown almost everything with wings, she still enjoyed floatplanes more than any other kind of flying. At the end of her career, when she was asked which aircraft she loved the best, she declared, 'Cessna! Any Cessna!'[37]

Postscript

Recognising Achievements Through Investitures

In July 1974, Helen Marcelle Harrison-Bristol was invested as a Companion to the Order of Icarus, Canada's most select aviation order. Companionship in the Order honoured Canadian aviators whose airborne skills resulted in outstanding developments in Canadian flight.

A few days later, in the inaugural induction of Canada's brand new Aviation Hall of Fame, Helen Harrison-Bristol was inducted alongside many of the nation's 'great eagles'. During the ceremony, Helen's tremendous contribution to aviation was succinctly described. 'The career dedication of her flying skills to instruct an almost entirely male population of students, despite adversity, has substantially benefited Canadian aviation.'[1]

Helen was inducted alongside aviation trailblazers including inventor Alexander Graham Bell, a pioneer of manned flight who experimented with huge kites and rocket-powered jets; Raymond 'Collie' Collishaw who was credited with shooting down twenty-seven German aircraft in the First World War; Robert Cheetham Randall, a bush pilot who mapped and photographed unknown territory throughout Canada's far north; and Moretta 'Molly' Fenton Beall Reilly, who became the first corporate pilot in Canada.

Posthumous inductions in 1974 included William Avery 'Billy' Bishop, a First World War flying ace who was awarded a Victoria Cross for his valiant aerial combats, and George Frederick 'Buzz' Buerling, Canada's top Second World War flying ace.

Celebrating Historic Moments but Climb Still Ahead

During her retirement, Helen witnessed many significant changes and steps forward for women pilots. She continued her love of flying and was joined in the air by her husband Donald McGlasson Bristol, a retired Boeing engineer who was also a pilot.

Thanks to civil and women's rights movements, along with post-secondary education and greater independence, women began to fly in greater numbers. Women pilots built up more hours, became flight instructors and acquired ratings. The gender barrier for women pilots applying for commercial flying positions began to fall throughout the early 1970s.

On 14 February 1970, Yvonne Pope Sintes, a British aviator of South African origin, became Britain's first female commercial airline captain.

In 1973, Canadian history was made when Rosella Marie Bjornson became the first woman pilot to be hired with a scheduled commercial carrier in North America, and the first woman member of the Canadian Air Line Pilots Association. She said:

> The door had been closed to women with airlines. I realised that, and I wanted to be the best qualified and do the best job I could. I felt I had to be the best I could be for the women following me.[2]

Reporter Louise Brown with the *Toronto Star* observed that women had 'broken through the first barriers in commercial flying, but the seas remain a man's world'. In the US, Emily Howell Warner also made history in 1973 when she became the first woman pilot hired by a scheduled American passenger airline.

Five years would pass before another Canadian airline appointed a woman pilot to its commercial sector. On 10 April 1978, Air Canada hired Judy Cameron, 23, to its pilot-training program. Judy was one of 12 successful pilots to be hired from an applicant pool of 1,800 pilots.

Rosella Bjornson was the first and only woman among 2,800 pilots on Canada's national and regional airlines. By 1978, she had become co-pilot of a sixty-three-passenger F-28 aircraft and was halfway up the seniority waiting list for a captain's (or full pilot's job) with Transair. She told the *Toronto Star*:

> Back in 1970, when I was job-hunting, I felt the odds were against me. It was the start of women's lib and there was a lot of controversy among pilots and flying instructors about women flying – but I was out to prove them wrong.[3]

These were historic moments that Helen had waited a long time for. The climate that barred women pilots from the left seat had slowly been changing.

Recognising the Leadership of the Air Transport Auxiliary

American women pilots with the US Ferry Transport Command had realised that their vital role during the war had been forgotten. As a result of their ceaseless advocacy, the US Congress passed the GI Bill Improvement Act of 1977 which retroactively granted the trailblazing Women Airforce Service Pilots status as veterans.

Former Air Transport Auxiliary pilot Roberta Sandoz Leveaux recalled how out of place she felt walking into a 1978 Women Airforce Service Pilots' convention. Her Air Transport Auxiliary uniform was instantly recognisable:

> I shuffled around corners. Then people started asking me for my autograph. I was amazed. Women told me that we,

> the women pilots in the Air Transport Auxiliary had been in the vanguard. They said, 'you gals were the thin edge of the wedge, for women's rights'. … I came home with the feeling that we had undervalued ourselves.[4]

It was recognised that the women pilots in the Air Transport Auxiliary had broken ground for other women fliers in countries such as the United States. Former Women Airforce Service Pilot Dawn Seymour observed that:

> the Women AirForce Service Pilots would never have been able to have their program if it hadn't been for a select group of women pilots who joined the Air Transport Auxiliary.
>
> Because these women did such a great job, he [General 'Hap' Henry Arnold of the US Air Force] allowed Jackie to start her program. So, we are indebted to them. The Air Transport Auxiliary pilots are part of history and must not be left out. The Air Transport Auxiliary women pilots called themselves the 'forgotten pilots' but they cannot be forgotten pilots.[5]

Of the 300 American women who volunteered their service, only 25 pilots were first chosen to represent North America in Great Britian's Air Transport Auxiliary. Roberta Sandoz Leveaux recounted:

> 'We were a remarkable group. We were all mavericks, outspoken, dominant.
>
> We were unique. We were aware of our options when most women were not.
>
> I think most of us were so busy and we felt so useful,' she remembered. 'We were frightened to death by the war.'[6]

Retired Colonel Marcelyn Atwood of the United States Air Force wrote:

> Today's women military aviators view the Women Air Force Service Pilots' legacy as so much more. They proved

> women could fly any aircraft in the inventory and could do so under adversity.
>
> …
>
> Lastly, the Women AirForce Service Pilots proved that military aviation is not a gender-specific skill; the aircraft does not care what gender is at the controls.[7]

Becomes First Woman Director on Canada's Aviation Hall of Fame

Canada's Aviation Hall of Fame welcomed Helen Harrison-Bristol as a new board member in 1981. In doing so, she became the first woman to hold a board position in the Hall.

Helen, along with her fellow pilots, shared a sublime joy of flying which transcended earth-bound experiences.

On 27 April 1995, Helen Marcelle Harrison-Bristol rose on her final flight into the bright cerulean skies where she felt most at home.

Helen was predeceased by her husband Donald McGlasson Bristol, 82, who died in 1988; parents Gertrude and Albert Testemale; and brothers Percy Fulford and Jim Testemale who died in 1986. She was survived by her sons Robert (Eleanor) Barnes, Peter (Fran) Barnes, and David Barnes, numerous grandchildren and great-grandchildren.

Canada and the world lost a legendary 'crack' aviatrix who inspired generations of men and women to pursue the joy of flying. By instructing fledgling pilots of all ages and walks of life, she not only made an impact on the pilots she taught, but also on their families, subsequent generations and all who came to know her. The trajectory of her flying career not only encompassed four countries but also spanned a magnificent era of aviation innovation and design. Her role in fostering airmindedness in both civil and military aviation cannot be underestimated.

Her cheerful demeanour hinted at the pure and undiluted joy she experienced when flying. And she was pragmatic and believed strongly in making one's own way in the world. In her joy of flying and by sharing her passion for flight, she shaped a path forward so other pilots could aim for the stars and realise their dreams of flight.

With Thanks To

Canada's Aviation Hall of Fame, Hangar Flight Museum, Calgary, Alberta

Dwight D. Eisenhower Presidential Library, Museum and Boyhood Home, Abilene, Kansas

Hoover Institution Library and Archives, Stanford, California

New York Public Library, New York City, New York

City of Richmond Archives, Richmond, British Columbia

Royal BC Museum and Archives, Victoria, British Columbia

San Francisco Airport Museum and Archives, San Francisco, California

San Francisco Public Library, San Francisco, California

Stanford University Green Library, Stanford, California

UC Davis Shields Library, Davis, California

Vancouver Public Library, Vancouver, British Columbia

Endnotes

Prelude

1. S. Knapp
2. Ibid

PART ONE

Chapter 1

1. 'Joy of Being Above the Clouds' *Western Daily Press and Bristol Mirror* (Bristol, 18 September 1936)
2. W.A. Magill, 'From Hairdresser to Crack Aviatrix' *Richmond Times-Dispatch* (Richmond, 18 June 1939)
3. 1911 Vancouver Directory.
4. 'Stevenston – BC's Most Picturesque Cannery Town' *The Province* (Vancouver, 27 August 1917)
5. J. Spring
6. T. Gwynn-Jones
7. 'Mainly About Malayans' *The Straits Times* (Singapore, 23 June 1940)
8. '3,000 Hours Flying Planes Helen Now a Test Pilot' *Toronto Star* (Toronto, 15 December 1945)
9. W.A. Magill

Chapter 2

1. 'Joys of Flying' *Gloucestershire Echo* (Cheltenham, 20 February 1936)
2. Y. Gordon, 'Women are Good Pilots' *Evening Despatch* (London, 26 May 1933)
3. 'Flying Notes' *Saffron Walden Weekly News* (Saffron Walden, 1 November 1935)
4. Y. Gordon, 'Women are Good Pilots' *Evening Despatch* (London, 26 May 1933)
5. Ibid
6. W.A. Magill
7. '3,000 Hours Flying Planes Helen Now a Test Pilot' *Toronto Star* (Toronto, 15 December 1945)
8. S. Render
9. W.A. Magill
10. L. Mlllward
11. Ibid
12. Ibid
13. 'Flying for Women' *The Guardian* (Manchester, 22 October 1922)
14. L. Mlllward
15. Ibid
16. E. Watson, 'Amelia Earhart: The Flying Feminist' *Flight Paths: Purdue University's Aerospace Pioneers* (West Lafayette, 13 September 2016)
17. W.A. Magill
18. Cecil Lawrence Pashley was conferred an honorary companionship in the Royal Aeronautical Society in 1963
19. 'Canadian Girl Pilot Trains Royal Air Force Fliers' *Star Weekly* (Toronto, 29 July 1939)
20. L. Mlllward
21. 'Cardiff Aeroplane Club's Progress: Thrilling Spectacle at Today's Air Display' *Western Mail* (Cardiff, 6 October 1934)

Chapter 3

1. 'Aviation in Malaya' *Sunday Tribune* (Singapore, 18 August 1935)
2. 'Canadian Girl Pilot Trains Royal Air Force Fliers' *Star Weekly* (Toronto, 29 July 1939)

3. W.A. Magill, 'From Hairdresser to Crack Aviatrix' *Richmond Times-Dispatch* (Richmond, 18 June 1939)
4. 'Training Policy at Flying Club' *The Straits Times* (Singapore, 18 January 1935)
5. 'Mainly About Malayans' *The Straits Times* (Singapore, 23 June 1940)
6. 'Miles Hawk for Flying Club' *The Straits Budget* (Singapore, 2 May 1935)
7. T.S. Sprigg, 'The Light Aeroplane Boom' *Singapore Free Press* (Singapore, 21 October 1930)
8. 'Record Number of Flying Hours by RSFC' *Singapore Free Press* (Singapore, 4 April 1935)
9. W.A. Magill, 'From Hairdresser to Crack Aviatrix' *Richmond Times-Dispatch* (Richmond, 18 June 1939)
10. Aviation in Malaya' *Sunday Tribune* (Singapore, 18 August 1935)
11. The SS *Kedah* was a passenger and cargo turbo steamer built for the express service between Singapore and Penang
12. 'Aviation in Malaya' *Sunday Tribune* (Singapore, 11 August 1935)
13. 'Seaplane Channel Works' *Malaya Tribune* (Singapore, 3 December 1935)
14. 'Mile-Long Seaplane at Kallang' *Singapore Free Press* (Singapore, 27 July 1936)
15. R. Welch
16. 'Flying Club Plane Capsizes' *Malaya Tribune* (Singapore, 16 April 1935)
17. 'Singapore Plane Blown Over' *Pinang Gazette and Straits Chronicle* (Singapore, 13 May 1935)
18. S. Render

Chapter 4

1. 'Aviation in Malaya' *Sunday Tribune* (Singapore, 18 August 1935)
2. William Courtenay, 'Women Who Fly High' *Evening Standard* (London, 15 August 1935)
3. Ibid
4. W.A. Magill, 'From Hairdresser to Crack Aviatrix' *Richmond Times-Dispatch* (Richmond, 18 June 1939)
5. J. Spring
6. W.A. Magill
7. W. Makin
8. W.A. Magill
9. Ibid
10. R. McCormack

11. G. Pirie
12. Ibid
13. H. Klein
14. 'Woman Halts Long Plane Trip to View Wonders of Miami' *Miami News* (Miami, 3 March 1935)
15. W. Makin
16. Ibid
17. G. Crile
18. G. Pirie
19. G. Crile
20. W. Makin
21. G. Crile
22. Ibid
23. G. Pirie
24. Y. Gordon, 'Women Are Good Pilots' *Evening Despatch* (London, 26 May 1933)
25. 'Blind Flying' *Sydney Morning Herald* (Sydney, 6 February 1936)
26. Flying Notes' *Saffron Walden Weekly News* (Cambridge, 24 April 1936)
27. Ibid
28. S. Render
29. B. Markham
30. 'Flying Notes' *Saffron Walden Weekly News* (Saffron Walden, 6 March 1936)
31. J. Spring
32. W.A. Magill, 'From Hairdresser to Crack Aviatrix' *Richmond Times-Dispatch* (Richmond, 18 June 1939)
33. 'Midland Woman's Day' *Evening Despatch* (London, 3 September 1936)
34. 'Her Imperial Airway' *Huddersfield Daily Examiner* (Huddersfield, 13 January 1937)

PART TWO

Chapter 5

1. K. van der Spuy
2. Ibid
3. Ibid
4. Ibid
5. J. Illsley

6. 'Appeal to Universities for Air Force Pilots' *Rand Daily Mail* (Johannesburg, 4 December 1936)
7. J. Illsley
8. S. Render
9. Ibid
10. Ibid
11. W.A. Magill
12. S. Render
13. Ibid
14. 'Her Imperial Airway' *Huddersfield Daily Examiner* (Huddersfield, 13 January 1937)
15. Ibid
16. S. Knapp
17. H. Klein
18. Ibid
19. Her journal, *A Bird-Watcher's Diary*, was published posthumously in 1938.
20. 'Pilot-Instructor' *Rand Daily Mail* (Johannesburg, 14 September 1937)
21. The HG Hawker Demon was a two-seater fighter plane which was derived from the Hawker Hart day bombers
22. 'First Woman Instructor' *Rand Daily Mail* (Johannesburg, 20 October 1937)
23. *Rand Daily Mail* (Johannesburg, 11 December 1937)
24. 'English Visitors' *Rand Daily Mail* (Johannesburg, 16 February 1938)
25. 'Large Attendance at Funeral' *Rand Daily Mail* (Johannesburg, 22 February 1938)
26. 'Canadian Aero Clubs Train 200 Pilots' *Rand Daily Mail* (Johannesburg, 19 April 1938)
27. 'Visiting Aviatrix Helped to Train Military Pilots' *Hamilton Spectator* (Hamilton, 8 July 1939)
28. T.G.E. Cockbain
29. K. van der Spuy
30. 'Lost in the Air' *Rand Daily Mail* (Johannesburg, 5 August 1938)
31. M. Egerton Bird and M. Botes
32. 'Women Want to be Pilots in Air Guard' *Rand Daily Mail* (Johannesburg, 28 October 1938
33. Ibid
34. Ibid
35. Ibid
36. Ibid

37. M. Egerton Bird and M. Botes
38. F. Hatfield, 'South African Women of the Air Guard' (31 March 1939)
39. 'South African Women Want Civil Air Guard' *Rand Daily Mail* (Johannesburg, 29 November 1938)
40. M. Egerton Bird and M. Botes
41. '200 Women at Civil Air Guard Meeting' *Rand Daily Mail* (Johannesburg, 6 December 1938)
42. Ibid
43. 'Women Pilots Must do Steady Work in Aviation' *Rand Daily Mail* (Johannesburg, 25 January 1939)
44. J. Vibart, 'Airwomen of the Union' *Rand Daily Mail* (Johannesburg, 13 April 1939)
45. Ibid
46. 'Flying for Women' *Rand Daily Mail* (Johannesburg, 7 January 1939)
47. J. Illsley
48. 'Flying for Women' *Rand Daily Mail* (Johannesburg, 7 January 1939)
49. S. Render

Chapter 6

1. 'Learns Appeal of Royal Canadian Air Force' *Waterloo Region Record* (Waterloo, 25 November 1939)
2. S. Render
3. J. Spring
4. 'Women Pilots' Duties in War' *Daily Mirror* (London, 11 January 1939)
5. 'Women as Pilots' *Birmingham Evening Mail* (Birmingham, 17 January 1939)
6. 'Women Pilots in Wartime' *Liverpool Daily Press* (Liverpool, 18 May 1939)
7. 'Tragedy of Famous Airwoman' *Birmingham Gazette* (Birmingham, 10 May 1939)
8. 'Visiting Aviatrix Helped to Train Military Pilots' *Hamilton Spectator* (Hamilton, 8 July 1939)
9. 'Former BC Girl is Now Expert Pilot.' *Times Colonist* (Victoria, 27 June 1939)
10. 'BC Girl Instructor Shows Aviation Not only for Male Sex' *Ottawa Citizen* (Ottawa, 27 June 1939)
11. 'Visiting Aviatrix Helped to Train Military Flyers' *Hamilton Spectator* (Hamilton, 8 July 1939)

12. 'Canadian Girl Pilot Trains Royal Air Force Fliers' *Star Weekly* (Toronto, 29 July 1939)
13. S. Render
14. 'Visiting Aviatrix Helped to Train Military Flyers' *Hamilton Spectator* (Hamilton, 8 July 1939)
15. S. Render
16. 'Canadian Girl Pilot Trains Royal Air Force Fliers' *Star Weekly* (Toronto, 29 July 1939)
17. 'Air Official Sees Little Need for Women Pilots in Canada' *The Province* (Vancouver, 26 July 1939)
18. 'Woman Flier Does Stunts' *Toronto Star* (Toronto, 5 September 1939)
19. 'Noted Aviatrix Offers to Train War Pilots' *The Gazette* (Montreal, 6 September 1939)
20. J. Spring
21. J. From
22. S. Serup
23. 'Women Fliers' *Ottawa Journal* (Ottawa, 1 September 1939)
24. 'Women Pilots for French Red Cross' *Evening News* (Manchester, 27 November 1939)
25. 'Women Pilots Not Needed in RAF' *Birmingham Gazette* (Birmingham, 6 October 1939)
26. 'RAF Will Have No Women Pilots' *Daily Mirror* (London, 4 October 1939)
27. 'Ferrying Our New War Planes' *The Herts and Essex Observer* (Bishop's Stortford, 14 December 1940)
28. 'RAF Pilots in Role of Ferrymen' *Evening Post* (London, 1 December 1939)
29. A. King
30. 'Miss Pauline Gower's Appointment' *Medway News* (Chatham, 8 December 1939)
31. Ibid
32. K. Grint
33. K. Grint
34. R. Du Cros
35. K. Grint
36. L. Curtis
37. R. Rees
38. Ibid
39. Ibid
40. Ibid

41. 'Trains Future War Birds' *Times Colonist* (Victoria, 26 December 1939)
42. 'Military Pilots in Kitchener Being Trained by Woman' *Calgary Herald* (Calgary, 30 December 1939)
43. S. Knapp
44. Ibid
45. 'Aviation Opens Many Doors to Women' *Pinang Gazette and Straits Chronicle* (Singapore, 29 March 1940)
46. 'Helen Harrison Got Her Licence Here' *Ottawa Citizen* (Ottawa, 21 December 1939)
47. 'Woman Military Instructor' *Rand Daily Mail* (Johannesburg, 30 April 1940)

Chapter 7

1. M. Ecker Francis, 'Vancouver Women are Trail Blazers for those who seek wings in the sky' *The Province* (Vancouver, 6 July 1940)
2. 'Three Pilot Officers Pass Their Tests' *Waterloo Region Record* (Waterloo, 5 January 1940)
3. J.C. Kirkwood, 'Keeping Posted' *National Post* (Toronto, 24 February 1940)
4. M. Ecker Francis, 'Vancouver Women are Trail Blazers' *The Province* (Vancouver, 6 July 1940)
5. 'The Home Front Depicts War Activities of Women' *The Sun Times* (Toronto, 22 June 1940)
6. 'Expect a Big Jump in Air Recruiting' *The Calgary Herald* (Calgary, 20 June 1940)
7. 'Will Turn Out 24 Pilots Monthly at New School' *The Toronto Star* (Toronto, 25 June 1940)
8. 'Role of Women in Aerial War is Considered' *Chattanooga Daily Times* (Chattanooga, 4 August 1940)
9. 'British Use of Women as Ferry Pilots Seen' *Windsor Star* (Windsor, 13 August 1940)
10. 'Hundreds of Pilots Applying in States to Aid Allied Cause' *Star Weekly* (Toronto, 31 August 1940)
11. Paine, Ernest G. 'Join up in Manhattan, Aid Case' *Star Weekly* (Toronto, 17 August 1940)
12. Ibid
13. Ibid
14. 'Air Path to War' *Kansas City Star* (Kansas City, 27 August 1940)

15. 'Sea Ferry Fliers Sought by Britain' *Daily News* (New York, 8 August 1940)
16. S. Knapp
17. 'Girls Sacrifice New Hats to Afford Flying Lessons' *The Toronto Star* (Toronto, 21 October 1940)
18. S. Knapp
19. S. Render
20. 'Girls Sacrifice New Hats to Afford Flying Lessons' *The Toronto Star* (Toronto, 21 October 1940)
21. 'Aeronautical School for Women Now Operating in Eastern City' *The Province* (Vancouver, 23 October 1940)
22. 'Plane Supply Situation is Improving' *The Ottawa Journal* (Ottawa, 31 October 1940)
23. 'War Flying for Women' *Newsday* (New York, 19 September 1940)
24. 'Flying Schoolmarm Passes Pilot Tests' *The Toronto Star* (Toronto, 3 January 1941)
25. A. King
26. Ibid
27. Ibid
28. R. Du Cros
29. A. King
30. 'No Passenger in Miss Amy Johnson's Plane' *The Guardian* (London, 9 January 1941)
31. A. King
32. 'Amy Johnson died doing her bit for Britain' *South Wales Evening Post* (Swansea, 7 January 1941)
33. G. Whittell
34. 'Around the Airports' *The Toronto Star* (Toronto, 18 February 1941)
35. 'Women in the War' *North Bay Nugget* (North Bay, 24 February 1941)
36. 'Former Hamiltonian Flying Instructor' *The Hamilton Spectator* (Hamilton, 12 February 1941)
37. 'Around the Airports' *The Toronto Star* (Toronto, 18 March 1941)
38. 'Youngest fighting pilot in RCAF Dies in Crash' *Toronto Star* (Toronto, 26 March 1941)
39. South Africa War Graves Project
40. L. Wise
41. Ibid
42. 'Ready to Tackle Any Flying Job, Girl Pilots Say' *Toronto Daily Star* (Toronto, 26 July 1941)

43. Ibid
44. Ibid
45. Ibid
46. Ibid
47. 'British Air Chief Arrives in Toronto' *Toronto Daily Star* (Toronto, 16 July 1941)
48. Ibid
49. 'Girls Taking Air Training' *Windsor Star* (Windsor, 22 October 1940)
50. 'Around the Airports' *Toronto Star* (Toronto, 9 September 1941)
51. Ibid
52. 'Says Women Capable Fliers' *Edmonton Journal* (Edmonton, 20 September 1941)
53. S. Render
54. D. Metcalfe-Chenail, 'The Job for Me: Women in Canadian Military Aviation' *Legion* (Kanata, 6 March 2017)
55. S. Render

Chapter 8

1. Hargrove, R., 'Women Fliers Doing Big Job in England Relieving Pilots' *Kingston Whig-Standard* (Kingston, 9 July 1941)
2. Oestreichen, J.C., 'Jacqueline was Right' *Humbold Times* (Eureka, 20 July 1941)
3. 'Evening Dresses a "Must" for Atlantic Bomber Run' *Toronto Star* (Toronto, 5 July 1941)
4. National Air and Space Museum, Smithsonian Institution, Summer 1981
5. Darvell, J., 'J. Cochran: A Lifetime of Firsts' *Disciples of Flight* (https://disciplesofflight.com/jacqueline-cochran-a-lifetime-of-firsts/)
6. 'Evening Dresses a "Must" for Atlantic Bomber Run' *Toronto Star* (Toronto, 5 July 1941)
7. J. Cochran
8. Ibid
9. Ibid
10. Ibid
11. Ibid
12. J. Cochran
13. I. Wolfert, 'Examination in Canada was Worry of Woman War Flyer' *The Province* (Vancouver, 11 July 1941)

14. J. Cochran
15. Ibid
16. Ibid
17. Ibid
18. J. Cochran
19. 'Women Pilots US Bomber Over Atlantic' *Leicester Mercury* (Leicester, 20 June 1941)
20. W.M. White, 'Ferry Pilot Glamor Girl Upsets London Censors' *Calgary Albertan* (Calgary, 21 June 1941)
21. L. Yount
22. 'US Aviatrix Back from Ocean Flight' *The Gazette* (Montreal, 2 July 1941)
23. 'Jacqueline Cochran Seeks Women to Ferry Bombers' *Portland Press* (Portland, 24 June 2025)
24. Ibid
25. Ibid
26. H. Harrison, *Letter to J. Cochran*, (29 January 1942)
27. J. Cochran, *Letter to H. Harrison*, (16 February 1942)
28. J. Williamson Letter, Jacqueline Cochran Series Air Transport Auxiliary Series
29. W.C. Kennedy Letter, Jacqueline Cochran Series Air Transport Auxiliary Series
30. P.E. Smith Letter, Jacqueline Cochran Series Air Transport Auxiliary Series
31. G.R. Haller Letter, Jacqueline Cochran Series Air Transport Auxiliary Series
32. J. Cochran
33. A. Kerr, 'Jacqueline Cochran Will Lead Women Flying Behind the War Front' *Cumberland Evening Times* (Cumberland, 26 February 1942)
34. H. Harrison, *Letter to J. Cochran* (6 March 1942)
35. A. Gibb, 'Test Girls in Canada for Ferry Pilot Job Overseas' *Toronto Star* (Toronto, 6 May 1942)
36. 'Miss Mary Nicholson' *News and Record* (Greensboro, 25 May 1943)
37. *NASA Oral History Project*
38. G. Whittell
39. 'Helen Richey Arrives in England as Pilot in Transport Services' *Pittsburgh Sun-Telegraph* (Pittsburgh, 25 March 1942)
40. G. Whittell

41. Ibid
42. J. Spring
43. R. Sandoz Leveaux, *NASA Oral History Project*
44. K. Harriman, 'American Girls Ferry Bombers to England for those RAF Raids' *Tampa Bay Times* (St Petersburg, 19 June 1942)
45. 'Women Killed in Air Crash' *Hull Daily Mail* (Hull, 17 March 1942)
46. '5 American Women Now with ATA' *Evening Standard* (London, 30 March 1942)
47. A. King

Chapter 9

1. G. Whittell
2. Form Letter Regarding British ATA, Jacqueline Cochran Series Air Transport Auxiliary Series. (undated)
3. S. Render
4. J. Cochran
5. A. King
6. Ibid
7. 'Second Group of Experienced Flyers to Join RAF's Air Transport Auxiliary' *St Louis Star* (St Louis, 5 June 1942)
8. 'Ferries Planes in Britain Toronto Girl Enjoys Work' *Toronto Star* (Toronto, 27 February 1942)
9. J. Spring
10. 'Women's War Work: Ferries Planes in Britain Toronto Girl Enjoys Work' *Toronto Star* (Toronto, 27 February 1943)
11. A. King
12. A. Welch
13. A. Welch
14. S. Render
15. K. Grint
16. A. Welch
17. Ibid
18. Ibid
19. Ibid
20. Ibid
21. R. Du Cros

22. V. Warren
23. Ibid
24. 'A Day's Work' ATA Museum and Archives (Maidenhead)
25. J. Spring
26. 'Jacqueline Cochran Named Director of Women's Flying Training in Army' *US War Bureau of Public Relations* (14 September 1942) Jacqueline Cochran Series Air Transport Auxiliary Series
27. Ibid
28. Ibid
29. L. Curtis
30. Ferry Pilots of the ATA
31. Ferry Pilots of the ATA, *Accidents & Incidents*
32. S. Render
33. Ferry Pilots of the ATA, *Accidents & Incidents*
34. 'Only Canadian in BATA Learns to be Ferry Pilot' *Toronto Star* (Toronto, 11 July 1942)
35. J. Cochran, *Letter to Gertrude Testemale* (Washington DC, 5 October 1942)
36. G. Testemale, *Letter to Jackie Cochran* (Toronto, 8 October 1942)
37. 'Mrs Roosevelt Praises Women Ferry Pilots' *Wolverhampton Express* (Wolverhampton, 26 October 1942)
38. 'Women's War Work: Ferries Planes in Britain Toronto Girl Enjoys Work' *Toronto Star* (Toronto, 27 February 1943)
39. A.R. Coupar, 'God in the City' *Huddersfield Daily Examiner* (Huddersfield, 28 October 1942)
40. 'Women's Part in War' *Evening Express* (Liverpool, 24 October 1942)
41. A.R. Coupar, 'God in the City' *Huddersfield Daily Examiner* (Huddersfield, 28 October 1942)
42. 'Ferry Pilot Now A Taxi Driver' *Nanaimo Daily News* (Nanaimo, 29 May 1944)
43. L. Curtis
44. G. Whittell
45. Ibid
46. Ibid
47. A. Welch
48. Ibid
49. '3,000 Hours Flying Planes Helen Now a Test Pilot' *Toronto Star* (Toronto, 15 December 1945)

Chapter 10

1. A. Welch
2. 'Toronto Girls ATA Pilots' *Toronto Star* (Toronto, 20 July 1943)
3. 'Women Pilots' *Evening Express* (Liverpool, 18 May 1943)
4. 'Women Pilots' Equal Pay' *Liverpool Echo* (Liverpool, 3 June 1943)
5. 'Pay of Women Pilots.' *The Citizen* (Gloucester, 19 May 1943)
6. Oliver, Gill, 'Remembering the Attagirls' *Oxfordshire Times* (Oxfordshire, February 2011)
7. R. Du Cros
8. 'Mary W. Nicholson' *Winston-Salem Journal* (Winston-Salem, 26 May 1943)
9. H. Harrison, *Letter to Jackie Cochran* (8 June 1943)
10. J. Cochran, *Letter to H. Harrison* (23 June 1943)
11. '3,000 Hours Flying Planes Helen Now a Test Pilot' *Toronto Star* (Toronto, 15 December 1945)
12. Original Accident Reports, Ferry Pilots of the ATA (April 1943)
13. '3,000 hours Flying Planes Helen Now a Test Pilot' *Toronto Star* (Toronto, 15 December 1945)
14. D. Hadfield, 'Flying the Westland Lysander' *Vintage Wings of Canada* (Ottawa)
15. S. Render
16. '3,000 hours Flying Planes Helen Now a Test Pilot' *Toronto Star* (Toronto, 15 December 1945)
17. S. Render
18. S. Knapp
19. S. Render
20. S. Knapp
21. S. Render
22. '3,000 hours Flying Planes Helen Now a Test Pilot' *Toronto Star* (Toronto, 15 December 1945)
23. A. Freedman, 'Vancouverite Helen Harrison Ace Flyer' *The Province* (Vancouver, 10 June 1944)
24. J. Spring
25. Ferry Pilots of the ATA, *Accidents & Incidents*
26. Ibid
27. 'Women's War Work: Ferries War Planes to Job Girl Would Like to Fight' *Toronto Star* (Toronto, 19 August 1943)

28. Ibid
29. Ibid
30. 'Man's Superiority Fades When Woman Pilot Talks' *Globe and Mail* (Toronto, 19 August 1943)
31. Ibid
32. Ibid
33. 'Women's War Work: Ferries Planes in Britain Toronto Girl Enjoys Work' *Toronto Star* (Toronto, 27 February 1943)
34. S. Knapp
35. H. Harrison, *Letter to Jackie Cochran* (8 June 1943)
36. Ibid
37. 'Six Women Fly Bombers Overseas This Week' *Sun Times* (Owen Sound, 17 September 1943)
38. S. Render
39. 'Six Women Fly Bombers Overseas This Week' *Sun Times* (Owen Sound, 17 September 1943)
40. Helen Harrison-Bristol Interview
41. 'Toronto Woman to be Co-Pilot Ferrying Plane Across Atlantic' *Toronto Star* (Toronto, 15 September 1943)
42. J. Spring
43. Ibid
44. Ferry Pilots of the ATA
45. S. Render
46. 'Toronto Woman to be Co-Pilot Ferrying Plane Across Atlantic' *Toronto Star* (Toronto, 15 September 1943)
47. G. Whittell
48. S. Render
49. J. Spring
50. S. Render
51. Helen Harrison-Bristol Interview
52. 'Woman Flier Home' *The Gazette* (Montreal, 26 May 1944)
53. S. Render
54. A. Freedman, 'Vancouverite Helen Harrison Ace Flyer' *The Province* (Vancouver, 10 June 1944)
55. S. Render
56. '3,000 Hours Flying Planes Helen Now a Test Pilot' *Toronto Star* (Toronto, 15 December 1945)

57. G. Whittell
58. Ibid
59. Ibid
60. Ibid
61. Ibid
62. Ibid
63. R. Du Cros
64. Ibid
65. 'The Air Transport Auxiliary' The Hangar Museum (Calgary)
66. R. Du Cros
67. A. King
68. 'Miss Mary Nicholson' *News and Record* (Greensboro, 25 May 1943)

PART THREE

Chapter 11

1. J.A. Foster
2. '3,000 Hours Flying Planes Helen Now a Test Pilot' *Toronto Star* (Toronto, 15 December 1945)
3. A. Freedman, 'Ferry Pilot Now a Taxi Driver' *Nanaimo Daily News* (Nanaimo, 29 May 1944)
4. S. Knapp
5. 'Pilot Tells Story of Air Fight' *Clovis News-Journal* (Clovis, 26 October 1941.
6. George Raisbeck Haller. WWII Liberated POW Questionnaire 1945–1946
7. J. Cochran, *Letter to Helen Harrison* (23 June 1943)
8. J. Cochran, *Deactivation of WASP* (1 October 1944)
9. J. Cochran, *Letter to WASPs* (12 October 1944)
10. J. Cochran
11. C. Russo
12. 'Vancouverite Helen Harrison Ace Flyer' *The Province* (10 June 1944)
13. S. Knapp
14. J. Adams, 'Egalitarian status is gone' *Edmonton Journal* (Edmonton, 4 January 1986)
15. Ibid
16. 'Women in the Royal Canadian Air Force' *The Hangar Museum* (Calgary)

17. '4-Day Aviation Clinic Ends with Talk by Noted Aviatrix' *Capitol Hill Beacon* (Oklahoma City, 21 November 1944)
18. 'Deactivation of WASPs Doesn't Discourage her' *St Louis Globe-Democrat* (St Louis, 6 November 1944).
19. 'Woman Flier Home' *The Gazette* (Montreal, 26 May 1944)
20. J. Spring
21. S. Knapp
22. Ibid
23. 'Forced Landing Ends Girl's 1,200 mile Flight' *Winnipeg Tribune* (Winnipeg, 29 January 1946)
24. Ibid
25. 'Forced Landing Ends Girl's 1,200 mile Flight' *Winnipeg Tribune* (Winnipeg, 29 January 1946)
26. 'Military Aviatrix Tests British Plane' *Edmonton Journal* (Edmonton, 22 February 1946)
27. Helen Richey and her fellow WASPs were awarded, posthumously, the Congressional Gold Medal in 2010
28. 'Green Pilot Flouts Warning, Dies with Brother in Crash' *Vancouver Sun* (Vancouver, 29 May 1947)
29. S. Render
30. T. Schrader, 'Planes No Problem for Duncan Woman' *Vancouver Sun* (Vancouver, 11 May 1948)
31. L. d'Easum, 'Girls Flock to Flying Schools' *Vancouver Sun* (Vancouver, 16 May 1948)
32. K. Hassard, 'Women with Wings' *Vancouver Sun* (Vancouver, 29 November 1958)
33. *The Straits Times* (Singapore, 31 December 1947)
34. 'Aviation Council to Meet Here: Licensing Regulations Attacked' *Times Colonist* (Victoria, 18 May 1949)
35. Ibid
36. S. Render
37. Ibid
38. Ibid
39. H. Hodgson, 'Flying Clubs to Map Details (of) Training Plan' *The Sault Star* (Sault St Marie, 21 January 1949)
40. 'Wings for Canada' *Nanaimo Daily News* (Nanaimo, 13 June 1949)
41. 'PNE Crowd Thrilled by Aerial Pageant' *Vancouver News-Herald* (Vancouver, 30 August 1949)

Chapter 12

1. J. Thormahlen, 'Air Space for Women, please' *The Province* (Vancouver, 2 July 1955)
2. 'Victoria Women Pilots Charter Members of BC Ninety-Niners' *Times Colonist* (Victoria, 2 January 1953)
3. B. Lawrence
4. 'Veteran Pilot is New Instructor Here' *The Citizen* (Prince George, 9 August 1954)
5. *Prince George Citizen* (Prince George, 28 October 1958)
6. Ibid
7. Helen Harrison-Bristol Interview
8. 'Urges More Women Train as Pilots' *Windsor Star* (Windsor, 14 July 1955)
9. 'Opportunity on Wings' *Vancouver News-Herald* (Vancouver, 31 May 1955)
10. Ibid
11. M. Francis, 'Sky Isn't the Limit for Women Pilots' *Vancouver News-Herald* (Vancouver, 26 June 1956)
12. K. Hassard, 'Women With Wings' *Vancouver Sun* (Vancouver, 29 November 1959)
13. M. Francis, 'Sky Isn't the Limit for Women Pilots' *Vancouver News-Herald* (Vancouver, 26 June 1956)
14. 'Flying is More than a Job to Canadian Aero Expert' *The Gazette* (Montreal, 20 May 1957)
15. Ibid
16. Ibid
17. British Columbia Archives
18. 'Testemale' The Province (Vancouver, 29 January 1958)
19. 'Quesnel Pilots Get Advance Check-out' *Quesnel Cariboo Observer* (Quesnel, 27 August 1964)
20. 'Women Earn Wings Hard Way' *Calgary Albertan* (Calgary, 9 January 1965)
21. Ibid
22. 'Flying Grandmother Heads Sales for Helicopter Firm' *Calgary Herald* (Calgary, 14 October 1966)
23. Ibid
24. Ibid
25. 'First Woman Instructor' *Chilliwack Progress* (Chilliwack, 14 December 1966)

26. 'Helen Flies Million Miles – From Vancouver to Chilliwack' *Chilliwack Progress* (Chilliwack, 4 January 1967)
27. Ibid
28. 'Helen Flies Million Miles – From Vancouver to Chilliwack' *Chilliwack Progress* (Chilliwack, 4 January 1967)
29. 'Flying instructress Guest Speaker' *Chilliwack Progress* (Chilliwack, 1 February 1967)
30. 'Airport Home Again for Flyers' *Chilliwack Progress* (Chilliwack, 5 July 1967)
31. Ibid
32. S. Render
33. Ibid
34. 'Boundary' *The Province* (Vancouver, 18 September 1968)
35. S. Render
36. Helen Harrison-Bristol Interview, Canadian Museum of Flight and Transportation, BC Archives (Victoria, 1985)
37. Ibid

Postscript

1. 'Helen Marcelle Harrison (nee Testemale)' Air Transport Auxiliary Ferry Pilots
2. D. Bly, 'Pioneer Pilot's Dreams Take Flight' *Calgary Herald* (Calgary, 5 December 2004)
3. L. Brown, 'Canada's Airlines Have 2,800 Pilots – 1 Is a Woman.' *Toronto Star* (Toronto, 25 April 1978)
4. A. Hillerman, '*WWII Women Pilots: Mavericks of the Sky*' *Sante Fe New Mexican* (Sante Fe, 26 August 1979)
5. D. Seymour, *NASA Oral History Project*
6. R. Sandoz Leveaux, *NASA Oral History Project*
7. M. Atwood 'Modern Military Women Aviators' *Air Force District of Washington* (Washington DC, 13 March 2002)

Bibliography

Archival Collections

'Helen Bristol Interview' Canadian Museum of Flight and Transportation. Royal BC Museum and Archives (Victoria, BC), 1985

'Jacqueline Cochran Series Air Transport Auxiliary Series' Dwight D. Eisenhower Presidential Library, Museum and Boyhood Home (Abilene, KS), 1941

Secondary Sources

Books

Bader, Douglas, *Fight for the Sky: The Story of the Spitfire and Hurricane* (Pen & Sword, 2003)

Cheesman, E.C., *Brief Glory: The Story of the ATA* (Harborough, 1946)

Cochran, J., *Jackie Cochran: The Autobiography of the Greatest Woman Pilot in Aviation History* (Bantam, 1987)

Cochran, J., *The Stars at Noon* (Little, Brown & Co., 1954)

Cockbain, Tom, *Sweeping Circles in the Sky* (Freeworld, 2003)

Curtis, Lettice, *The Forgotten Pilots* (Nelson & Saunders, 1971)

Crile, Grace, *Skyways to a Jungle Laboratory* (Norton & Co., 1936)

Du Cros, Rosemary, *ATA Girl: Memoirs of a Wartime Ferry Pilot* (Frederick Muller, 1983)

Earhart, Amelia, *Last Flight* (Crown, 1964)

Forster, Merna, *100 Canadian Heroines* (Dundurn, 2004)

Foster, J.A., *The Bush Pilots* (McClelland & Stewart, 1990)
From, Joel, *In Plain Sight: A Biography of the RAF Airbase at Caron, Saskatchewan* (Friesen, 2019)
Gibbs-Smith, Charles, *The Rebirth of European Aviation 1902–1908* (The Stationery Office, 1974)
Grint, Keith, *A Cartography of Resistance* (OUP, 2024)
Gwynne-Jones, T., *Further and Faster* (Smithsonian, 1991)
Hymans, Jackie, *The Female Few* (The History Press, 2012)
Klein, Harry, *Winged Courier* (Howard B. Timmins, 1955)
King, Alison, *Golden Wings: The Story of Some of the Women Ferry Pilots of the Air Transport Auxiliary* (White Lion, 1975)
Knapp, Sally, *New Wings for Women* (Thomas Y. Crowell, 1946)
Lawrence, Barb and Robb, Judy, *Where Eagles Flew* (Fraser Valley, 1987)
Lomax, Judy, *Women of the Air* (John Murray, 1986)
Makin, William James, *Swinging the Equator* (Dutton & Co., 1936)
Markham, Beryl, *West With the Night* (North Point, 1942)
Milward, Liz, *Women in British Imperial Airspace 1922–1937* (McGill-Queen's, 2008)
Moggridge, Jackie, *Spitfire Girl* (Head of Zeus, 2014)
Moolman, Valerie, *Women Aloft* (Time-Life, 1981)
Muir, Elizabeth Gillian, *Canadian Women in the Sky* (Dundurn, 2015)
Render, Shirley, *No Place for a Lady* (Portage & Main, 1992)
Rickman, Sarah Bryn, *WASP of the Ferry Command* (UNT, 2016)
Russo, Carolyn, *Women and Flight* (Little, Brown & Co., 1997)
Schrader, Helena Page, *Sisters in Arms* (Pen & Sword, 2006)
Serup, S., *Found Fragments* (First Choice, 2023)
Sharp, Landdeck Katherine, *The Women With Silver Wings* (Crown, 2020)
Spring, Joyce, *Daring Lady Flyers: Canadian Women in the Early Years of Aviation* (Pottersfield, 1994)
Van der Spuy, Kenneth R., *Chasing the Wind* (Books of Africa, 1966)
Walker, Diana Barnato, *Spreading My Wings* (Patrick Stephens, 1994)
Welch, Ann, *Happy To Fly* (John Murray, 1983)
Welch, Rosanne, *Encyclopedia of Women in Aviation and Space* (ABC-CLIO, 1998)
Wheeler, Jo, *The Hurricane Girls* (Michael Joseph, 2018)
Whittell, Giles, *Spitfire Girls* (William Collins, 2021)
Winters, Kathleen C., *Amelia Earhart* (Palgrave MacMillan, 2010)
Wynn, Stephen, *Air Transport Auxiliary at War* (Pen & Sword, 2021)
Yount, Lisa, *Women Aviators* (Facts on File, 1995)

Journal Articles

Cockbain, T.G.E., 'Early History of Aviation in the Eastern Province' (1994) 24 *Scientia Militaria*

Egerton, Bird M. and Botes M, 'Flying High: The Story of the Women's Auxiliary Air Force 1939–1945' (1982) S. Afr. MHJ

McCormack, R.L., 'Imperial Mission: The Air Route to Cape Town 1918–32' (1974) 9 *J. Contemp. Hist.* 77–97

Pirie, G., 'Incidental Tourism: British Imperial Air Travel in the 1930s' (2009) 1 *J. Tour. Hist.* 49–66

Scott, Shaw C., 'Was Captain Rosamund Everard Steenkamp the First Woman to Fly a Jet?' (1976) 3 *S. Afr.* MHJ

Wise, L., 'I Remember Helen' (2002) 40 *CAHS Journal* 52–55

Unpublished Sources

Illsley, J.W., 'Aerial Symbiosis: The Interrelationship between Military and Civil Aviation in the Union of South Africa 1912–1940' (2018) Historical and Heritage Studies, Humanities, University of Pretoria, South Africa

Electronic Sources

Ferry Pilots of the ATA, https://www.ata-ferry-pilots.org/index.php

Roberta Boyd Sandoz Leveaux Interview by Rebecca Wright, NASA Headquarters Oral History Project. Tucson, Arizona. 25 March 2000. https://www.nasa.gov/history/history-publications-and-resources/oral-histories/

Index

Africa 19, 43–7, 49, 54, 61, 74, 89
African Flying Services 76, 82, 145
Air Cadet League of Canada 217
Air Ministry 9, 15–16, 18, 34, 54, 56, 99, 102–104
Air Services Training Ltd, Hamble 30, 55
Air Taxi Co. Ltd 69, 71, 144
Air Transport Auxiliary (ATA) 102–110, 121, 124–5, 127–8, 135, 137–8, 142–3, 146–52, 154–6, 159–60, 162, 164–73, 176–7, 179, 182, 184–5, 187, 189, 191–5, 199–202, 204, 206–207, 209–10, 217, 222, 234–5
Air Transport and Training Company 129–30
Armstrong Whitworth,
  Atalanta 46–7
  Ensign 30
Australia 21, 44, 65, 74, 103, 123, 127, 189
Aviation Hall of Fame 232, 236
Avro 30
  504 10, 13
  540K 3, 11
Anson 157, 166, 168, 192
Avian 19–20

Bailey, Lady Mary 16, 18–20
Barnes, Brian Robert 8, 25, 40, 86, 208, 236
Barnes, David Brinson Albert 8, 25, 40, 86, 208, 236
Barnes, Peter John Ratford 16, 25, 40, 86, 208, 236
Barnes, Robert Walter 8, 25
BC Aero Club/Aero Club of BC 210, 213, 215, 217, 220, 222, 224
Beurling, Flight Lieutenant George Frederick 'Buzz' 203–204, 211
Bird, Marjorie Egerton 80–2, 85
Blake, Joan 81–2
Bournemouth 8
Boyd, Captain J. Errol 118–20
Bristol, Donald McGlasson 231, 233, 236
British Airways 102, 106, 193
British Columbia (BC) 3–6, 25, 93–4, 115, 208–210, 215–18, 221, 224, 228, 230

British Commonwealth Air Training Program 117
British Overseas Airways Corporation 102, 149
Brooklands 9, 19, 162, 166

Cairo 43–5, 47, 50, 53
Canada 4, 7, 37–8, 65, 75, 78, 89, 93–101, 103, 110–13, 115–17, 119–23, 132–5, 138, 140, 143–4, 147, 153, 186, 191, 199–200, 202, 209–10, 212, 216–18, 220, 222–5, 227, 229–36
Canadian Pacific Railway 7
Cape Town 3, 19, 21, 40–7, 61, 66, 68–9, 71–2, 75, 127, 144–5
Cape Town Flying Club 69, 144
Carlisle, Captain 136–7, 140–2
Cessna 213, 216, 231
  120-140 95
  140 218–20
  150 225
  152 227
  170 212, 227
  172 225, 227
  182 225
  195 95
Chilliwack 217–18, 222, 226–8
Civil Air Guard 81–3, 89–91, 106, 121
Civil Aeronautics Authority 93, 123, 143
Cochran, Captain Jacqueline 'Jackie' 137–8, 140–4, 146–7, 149–50, 152, 155–6, 159–60, 167, 170, 179, 186, 200–201, 203, 207, 221
Cockbain, Major General Tom G.E. 78–9
Cranbrook Flying Services 216–17
Croydon 16, 19, 21, 26, 44, 73

de Havilland 37, 54–5, 156, 216
  Beaver 213
  Cirrus Miles Hawk 22–3, 25–6
  Cirrus Moth 27
  Dominies 157, 189
  Dragonfly 96
  Gipsy Moth 8, 13, 15, 19, 21–3, 34, 59, 65, 105
  Hercules 45–6, 66
  Hermes II Moth 34
  Hermes Miles Hawk 34
  Hornet Moth 26
  Leopard Moth 55
  Mosquito 156–7, 161, 164–6, 184–5, 190, 192–3, 204, 219
  Puss Moth 21, 55, 72, 157
  Tiger Moth 11, 55–6, 82, 98, 107–108, 163, 180, 192, 213, 219
de Waal, Colonel Louis Botha 76–8, 85–6
de Waal, Danie 76
de Waal, The Honourable Mr Justice Daniel 77
Demon Hart 75
Dixon, John Taylor 217, 224
Dorval airport 141, 158, 176, 186–8
Duncan Flying Club 210–12

Earhart, Amelia 20, 74, 217, 221
Eastbourne 3, 10–11, 16
England 3, 7–8, 10, 18, 21, 26, 30, 40–3, 49, 55, 58, 60–1, 71, 73, 75, 81, 84, 89–90, 92–3, 96, 99–100, 102, 105, 107, 112, 115, 119–21, 123–4, 128–9, 133, 135, 138, 142–4, 146–8, 151–2, 155, 158–9, 164, 167, 170, 174, 176–7, 185–9, 193, 203–204, 211, 222, 224, 227
Everard-Steenkamp, Captain Rosamund King 83, 206–207

Fairchild 157, 159, 216
  24 Argus 95, 166
  Bolingbroke 192
  Cornell 208

Fairey,
Battle 98, 158, 192, 219
First World War 9–10, 13, 16–17, 25, 44, 65–6, 73, 119, 133, 232–3
Flying Seven 98, 101, 115, 134, 210, 223
Fraser River 3–7, 206, 221

Gower, Commander Pauline Mary de Peauly 40, 84, 90, 105–108, 110, 126, 183, 195, 207
Grahamstown 69, 71, 78, 80, 84–5, 112, 145
Grahamstown Flying Club 78
Guild of Air Pilots and Air Navigators 40

Halifax, Nova Scotia 4, 148–9, 151
Haller Aviation 77–8, 129, 145, 190, 199–200
Hamilton Flying Club 94–6, 115
Harrison Testemale, Gertrude Helen Marie 4–8, 25, 40–1, 86, 170, 208, 224, 228, 236
Harrison, Margaret Helen (née Ayre) 4
Harrison, Thomas Hudson 4, 7
Hatfield airport 22, 54–6, 71, 126–7, 150, 156
Hawker,
Fury 66, 71, 106
Hart 70
Hurricane 98, 157–9, 162–4, 167–9, 172, 180, 192, 194, 219
Heath, Lady Sophie 16–20, 92
Henderson, Flying Officer Charles Paul 111, 114, 125, 129
Hooper, Doreen 75, 82–4

Imperial Airways 43–4, 46, 55, 60, 120
India 21, 44, 73–4, 151, 199
International Commission on Air Navigation (ICAN) 17–18
Ireland 20, 58, 74, 118, 121, 136, 142, 148, 151

Johannesburg 42–3, 47, 71–2, 75–6, 82, 99, 112, 145
Johnson, Amy 21–2, 40, 90, 105, 125–8

Kabwe 'Broken Hill' 19, 47–8
Kallang Airport 26
Kallang River 34
Khartoum 47, 51–2
King, Flight Captain Alison 125–7, 153, 156–7, 160, 195, 207
Kitchener-Waterloo Flying Club 88, 99–100, 110–11, 114–15, 122, 128, 220
Knight, Clayton 119, 138
Kroonstad 76, 145

Lake Ontario 98, 124, 129, 130
Liverpool 4, 92, 147, 149, 150–1, 163
Lockheed 231
Electra 74
Hudson 100, 141, 157
Lodestar 145
Ventura 187
London 3, 10–11, 13, 16–22, 36, 44, 53, 55, 73–4, 78, 86, 90, 92, 102, 107, 125, 127, 137, 142, 149–50, 156, 164, 167, 179, 190, 211
London Aeroplane Club 55, 127

MacGill, Dr Elizabeth 'Elsie' Gregory 113, 115–16
Markham, Beryl 58–60
Maxwell, Mabel 122, 124, 133
McColl's Air Transport Limited 225
Miles, Frederick George 9–10, 13
Miles Hawk 21–3, 25–6, 34

Montreal 119, 136, 141, 144, 146–7, 149–51, 158, 176, 184, 186–8
Moore, Rosalie 'Rolie' 98, 115, 210

New York 58, 60, 86, 92, 119–21, 142, 145, 149, 184, 225
Newfoundland 20, 74, 118, 121, 141
Nicholson, Mary Webb 147, 151, 178–9, 194–5
Noonan, Fred 73–4
North America 58, 60, 94, 138, 140, 148, 151–2, 176, 206–207, 233, 235
North American 118, 157, 187
  Harvard 192
  Mitchell 157, 187
  P-51 Mustang 190, 192
No. 1 Elementary Flying Training School 56

Ontario 94, 96, 114, 132–3, 205
Ottawa 94, 96, 101, 111, 122, 132, 134, 144

Pashley, Cecil L. 9, 11, 21
Pangborn, Clyde 119, 121
Patterson, Gabrielle 60–1, 106
Percival Aircraft Ltd 204–206, 222
  Proctor 95, 204–205
Pope Sintes, Yvonne 225, 229, 233
Port Elizabeth 40, 69, 78, 145
Port Hardy 228
Pretoria 47, 66, 68, 75–7, 80, 85, 145
Pretoria Flying Club 69–71, 75–6, 94, 145

Quebec 4–5, 119, 149–50
Quesnel 225–6, 229

Rees Du Cross, Rosemary 106–110, 164, 195
Reitz, Leila Deneys 82–3
Robert Heights 66, 70, 75
Royal Air Force 10–11, 58, 70, 78, 89–91, 102–109, 118, 120, 133, 137, 144, 148, 154, 158, 164, 179–82, 187, 189, 192, 194–5, 204, 211
Royal Aero Club 15, 36, 127, 168
Royal Canadian Air Force 88–9, 96, 98–100, 110–12, 114–19, 121–2, 125, 128, 130, 132–5, 187–8, 202–203, 206, 212, 217
Royal Singapore Flying Club 26–7, 36
Rutledge, Margaret Fane 223

Sale, Flight Lieutenant John Alexander 'Jack' 10–11, 21–3, 26, 28, 30, 211
Saro,
  A17 Cutty Sark 28
Seabrook, Mabel Daisy 25, 40, 85–6, 89
Second World War 21, 100, 118, 124, 129, 131, 180, 190, 194, 199, 202–204, 211, 220, 223, 226, 233
Sheffield Flying Club 92, 145
Shelfoon, Daphne 101, 117, 133
Shoreham Airport 9–10, 13, 22
Singapore 26–31, 34, 36–8, 40, 42, 44, 74, 210–11
Singapore Flying Club 26–8, 36
Somerset West 41
South Africa 3, 9, 19, 40–3, 47, 55, 61, 64–7, 69–73, 75, 78, 81, 83–87, 89, 92–97, 99, 111, 115, 123, 129, 135, 145, 190, 199–200, 206–207, 209–10, 224, 227, 233
South African Air Force 64–70, 77–9, 83, 86, 92, 99, 129, 144, 190, 199
South African Airways 64
South African Women's Auxiliary Air Force 206
South African Women's Aviation Association 83–4, 86
Southern Aero Club 9–10

Spicer Pearse, Dorothy 40, 84, 90, 105–106, 207
Steveston 3–7, 206
Supermarine,
Spitfire 158, 172, 179, 190, 192
Stranraer 213
Sussex Aero Club 9–10, 15, 22

Testemale, Albert Jules 4–8, 25, 40, 124, 151, 208, 224, 228, 236
Testemale, Captain James 'Jim' Albert 6–7, 191, 199, 224, 228
Testemale, Percy 3–5, 224, 236
Trans-Canada Air Lines 97, 99–100, 115, 128, 134, 146, 202, 230
Toronto 96, 98, 101, 114, 117, 120, 122, 124, 127–30, 132–4, 144–5, 184, 204–205, 211
Toronto Flying Club 117, 185
Tribe, Mary du Caurroy, Duchess of Bedford 73

United States 10, 86, 92, 95, 115, 143–4, 148, 227, 229, 231, 235

Vancouver 4–7, 93, 98, 101, 113, 115, 199, 206, 208, 210, 212–13, 217, 220–1, 223, 228
Vickers-Armstrong 166
Wellington 187, 192

Wales 4, 20, 170, 179
Westland,
Lysander 98, 180–3, 192, 219
Wapiti 66
White Waltham 103, 151, 158, 166, 169, 171–2, 176, 194
Wilburne, Harriet Grace 7
Wise, Lou 129–31
Women's Civil Air Guard 83
Women's Federation League 90–1
Wood, Ann Watson 146–7, 150, 159, 167, 184, 190, 193–4